SCC Faculty Institute

# Community College Faculty

# Community College Faculty

## At Work in the New Economy

*John S. Levin,*

*Susan Kater,*

*and*

*Richard L. Wagoner*

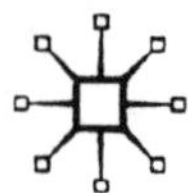

COMMUNITY COLLEGE FACULTY


First published in 2006 by
PALGRAVE MACMILLAN™
175 Fifth Avenue, New York, N.Y. 10010 and
Houndmills, Basingstoke, Hampshire, England RG21 6XS
Companies and representatives throughout the world.

PALGRAVE MACMILLAN is the global academic imprint of the Palgrave Macmillan division of St. Martin's Press, LLC and of Palgrave Macmillan Ltd. Macmillan® is a registered trademark in the United States, United Kingdom and other countries. Palgrave is a registered trademark in the European Union and other countries.

ISBN 1–4039–6667–2

Library of Congress Cataloging-in-Publication Data

Levin, John S.
Community college faculty : at work in the new economy / John S. Levin, Susan Kater, and Richard L. Wagoner.
p. cm.
Includes bibliographical references and index.
ISBN 1–4039–6667–2
1. Community colleges—Faculty—United States. 2. Community college teachers—Professional relationships—United States. 3. Community colleges—Economic aspects—United States. I. Kater, Susan. II. Wagoner, Richard. III. Title.

LB2331.L475 2005
378.1′2—dc22 2005051258

A catalogue record for this book is available from the British Library.

Design by Newgen Imaging Systems (P) Ltd., Chennai, India.

First edition: February 2006

10 9 8 7 6 5 4 3 2 1

Printed in the United States of America.

# Table of Contents

# List of Tables

# Preface

At a scholarly conference in 2004, Australian scholar Simon Marginson responded to Burton Clark's remark that teaching in higher education is an action that cannot be judged because there are no adequate measures and is thus not viewed as significant; and that, therefore, it is difficult to legitimate teaching. Marginson noted that institutional survival and preeminence are based on status and status comes from research, which includes the productivity of publication and grants.[1] No doubt both Marginson and Clark, two eminent scholars, are correct in how higher education institutions are judged and valued. Where does this leave the community college and its faculty? Both seem to be tethered to the same post: low status and questionably legitimate.

In addressing the work of community college faculty, we come face to face with issues of institutional characteristics and qualities: what are the purposes and outcomes of community colleges and to what extent are these valued? Our goal in this book is to explain the work of community college faculty in the context of what is referred to as the New Economy. We see faculty work entwined with social, political, and economic forces beyond the institution. While organizational history and culture—the context of individual community colleges—are influential in faculty work, forces beyond the college itself, particularly the political economy, are shaping faculty and faculty work. These same forces are acting upon the institution and the institution in turn responds to these forces. Thus, both faculty and the institution are interdependent in that faculty are the major work force of the institution, what Henry Mintzberg calls the core operators.[2] Their work is an extension of institutional goals, institutional power, and institutional identity. Faculty and the community college have a shared identity: we cannot treat one without implicating the other. Thus, if teaching is a low prestige activity, then the community college is a low prestige institution in that the majority of the work at community colleges is teaching. If the community college is enmeshed in a state's economic development and this work is central to the college, or the college is economically dependent upon this work, then faculty are a party to resource acquisition or capitalistic behaviors and their role is in part defined by these behaviors. This may have been the condition for community colleges and their faculty for decades, but only in the past twenty years—since the 1980s—has this pattern become evident to scholars and is seemingly on the increase. With this trajectory, we might assume that community college faculty are not only New Economy workers—instruments so to speak of the interests of business, industry, and government—but also function without a professional role and identity, given their lack of autonomy and the managerial control that qualifies their actions.[3]

For us as practitioners and scholars of the community college, these are significant matters as we value the institution both professionally and personally. As former community college faculty, we share a personal history with those whom we are investigating. We have taught similar students and worked with similar colleagues. As former and present college administrators, we share the experience of managing a college with multiple pressures, both internally and externally, on our work and our actions. As scholars who study the community college, we understand the points of view of other scholars who pass judgment on the institution, using measures and constructs that are appropriate generally for higher education institutions, although not always so for community colleges.

While our audience may be a disparate group, we intended on the one hand to change the way observers view the community college and on the other hand to verify the perceptions of faculty and administrators who work in the community college and who experience what we describe on a daily basis. Although one of the themes that propelled this project was an observation by a business instructor—"We are volume-oriented worker-bees"—we turned this into a question: are community college faculty simply "worker-bees," and if so, why and if not, what is the professional identity of community college faculty? This we suggest is both an empirical question and an imaginative one. In answering these questions, we intend to settle a number of problems in how observers, including scholars, view and discuss both the community college and the faculty. Our discussions and explanations may also solve a number of personal and institutional dilemmas about the work and experiences of faculty at community colleges.

# Acknowledgments

Our book is the culmination not only of our collective efforts and backgrounds but also of the assistance and support we received from others. Each of us wants to acknowledge this help.

Rick Wagoner recognizes and thanks the Marshall Foundation whose dissertation fellowship allowed him to conduct much of the quantitative research for chapter 6. Rick is also deeply indebted to and grateful for the guidance and support of John Cheslock, his doctoral advisor and dissertation chair, who provided perceptive insight into the problems of effectively analyzing the National Study of Postsecondary Faculty data sets and accurately interpreting those findings. He would also like to thank his coauthors for their intellectual stimulation and unflagging support throughout the process. Finally, Rick would like to thank his wife, Sherrie, and daughters, Megan and Lydia, for their love and support during the course of this project.

Sue Kater acknowledges and thanks the many community college faculty and administrators in the United States and Canada who enthusiastically shared their community college experiences and views—good and bad—in the name of research. To John Levin, who continues to raise community college scholarship to new levels; to Rick Wagoner, a colleague and friend, who has the ability to think beyond the boundaries, and ask the right questions unfettered by community college biases; and to John Cheslock and Veronica Diaz, Sue expresses her gratitude.

She owes much to the Maricopa County Community College District for putting students first (ahead of other issues), for the work it does in the community, and for supporting the professional development of its staff. A special thanks goes to her colleagues and friends at GateWay Community College, who not only supported her endless questions about faculty work, but who continue to inspire her with their dedication to their work as professionals. Finally, she dedicates this work to her family, husband Dale, son Dee, and daughter Lauren, and thanks them for their love and support.

John Levin acknowledges the assistance and support from several sources for his contribution to this book. First, the Social Sciences and Humanities Research Council of Canada provided financial assistance for much of the research for chapter 7. Second, the Joseph D. Moore Distinguished Professorship at North Carolina State University supported parts of our efforts through assistance with travel and financing some of the work of graduate student assistants. Third, several individuals have contributed to the ideas that we have worked out in this book. Principal among these is Gary Rhoades, who as a colleague of John Levin's and as a professor of Sue Kater and Rick Wagoner provided considerable stimulation and challenge in our examination and explanation of faculty at the community college. Cristie Roe, who was one of our partners in the project, left us before we began the book, but her contributions to our understanding of faculty work and the use of technology were considerable. When Cristie departed we turned to John Cheslock and Veronica Diaz who agreed to provide us with a chapter on distributed learning and the use of technology.

For the content of the book, we are also grateful to Jennifer Hildreth, a graduate student at North Carolina State University who worked with John Levin during the 2003–04 academic year and provided not only an analysis of literature but also assistance with the theoretical and conceptual underpinnings of this book. Chapter 3 owes a great debt to Jennifer who wrote this with John Levin and deserves special acknowledgement. Other chapters owe a great deal to the community colleges in both the United States and Canada and the many faculty and administrators at these institutions who worked with us. These college members gave considerable time to us and they provided substantial data for our analysis.

Several specialists—scholars and practitioners—gave their thoughts to our project and read our manuscript: Marilyn Amey of Michigan State University, John Dennison of the University of British Columbia, and Rufus Glasper of the Maricopa Community Colleges. Brian Pusser of the University of Virginia gave us stimulation and advice for chapter 8. Carol Burton of Western Carolina University, who is completing her dissertation on faculty cultures, offered editing advice on several chapters of the manuscript. Chapter 7 which draws upon John Levin's article in *The Journal of Higher Education* owes a debt to the reviewers and especially to its editor Leonard Baird for his patience and thoughtful suggestions.

Every project needs an instigator, and ours was Lee Levin, who after attending one of our presentations at a scholarly conference, and before we had any long-term goals for our work, suggested that we spend less time on presentations and more time on writing, especially writing a book. The thought prompted us to ask our publisher, Palgrave, and specifically Amanda Johnson, if they were interested. Amanda's enthusiasm for our topic and eventual proposal was motivational and no doubt with Lee's initial nudge served as the salve that nourished us in our early efforts to work this project through.

# 1

# Themes and Overview

In this chapter, we introduce readers to a complex topic that involves both an academic labor force—community college faculty—and their occupational and institutional context. This context includes a political and economic environment that has been variously termed "the new economy," "neoliberalism," "new capitalism," and "fast capitalism."[1] Although we pose an argument in this chapter, it is not until chapter 3 that we offer an extended discussion of the concepts and theories that form the basis of this argument. The reader may find that there is greater clarity in our argument if chapter 3 is read first, and we offer this as an alternative to following our numerical ordering of chapters. We aver to those who move with us chapter by chapter that what is not explained satisfactorily in one chapter will be clarified in a later chapter. We begin, then, with what we view as the enunciation of our major theme and the issues that both frame and characterize our treatment of community college faculty.

Community colleges as work sites and organizations are congruent with the new economy.[2] They have adapted to a changing labor force through workforce preparation programs and contract training (involving partnerships with private organizations to provide specialized training) and by modifying the traditional curriculum to emphasize employability skills. They have been the victims of contraction and withdrawal of state funding, particularly in the 1990s and recently in the 2000s, and thus they have had to seek alternate funding sources and fulfill the expectations of these new resource providers. As a result, community colleges have developed a more overt entrepreneurial culture, with a "managed" organization that can provide efficient and flexible programs tied to market demands. And this entrepreneurial culture has required a faculty who work predominantly part-time.

The employment status of the workforce is not the only employee characteristic that community colleges share with the business and industrial corporate workplace. Catherine Casey refers to the "corporate colonialization of the self,"[3] a condition whereby corporate workers are socialized, indoctrinated, coerced, and rewarded to fit the requirements of the corporation and become identified with it. "The person's values, attitudes, and general orientation must correspond with those promoted by the organizational culture."[4] In this organizational culture, employees are largely self-managing; there is self-imposed censorship, so that the undesirable features of the organization and work are either eliminated or ignored. Values and views are homogeneous in that there is valorization of the characteristics and qualities of the company and its goals, with emphasis on high productivity, global competitiveness, and dynamic change. As a consequence of this form of corporate identity, employees derive personal satisfaction, relatedness, and meaningfulness from participating in the corporate culture. Indeed, employees personalize this culture and thus there is little separation of working lives from domestic or personal lives. Work is "24/7," if not in practice at least with respect to personal values, attitudes, and identity. The company is family. One significant outcome of this culture is that worker identification with occupation is replaced by identification with corporate norms and values.

This type of identification can be problematical for part-time employees if they are not allowed to access or participate in the cultural norms and values of the organization.[5] Without access, temporary employees become not only marginal but also alienated from the organization, which, in turn, deprives part-timers from the personal satisfaction, relatedness, and meaningfulness of participating in a college's culture. This is particularly important for those part-time faculty who do not have full-time employment elsewhere, and it is especially salient in the community college as part-time faculty comprise the majority of faculty: 64 percent nationally.[6]

Community college faculty, committed to institutional mission, have become captive to the corporate culture that relies upon neo-liberal practices. What was once in the foreground—mission—is relegated to the background, and the practices of a corporate ethos, including behaviors aligned with economic competition, dominate organizational behaviors. George Vaughan, Norton Grubb, and others[7] have argued that the expanding mission that leads to the accommodation of increasing numbers of students without appropriate state funding reduces the quality of instruction. In order to accommodate students, colleges resort to the hiring of part-time faculty while maintaining full-time faculty salaries at low levels to contain costs. Governments, too, are a party to these actions and outcomes as they restrict funding and implement policies and practices that encourage greater student enrollments in colleges: in most jurisdictions, colleges receive their funding from governments based upon a formula or allocation mechanism contingent upon student enrollments.

Both the ideology of neo-liberalism and the process of economic globalization are key contributors to the work and identity of community college faculty. Over the past two decades, the community college has prized and pursued entrepreneurial activities.[8] In numerous cases, community colleges developed an entrepreneurial culture where economic goals, such as productivity, efficiency, and revenue generation, have moved to occupy a central place in the institutional mission. Accompanying and perhaps abetting this shift to an orientation of economic competition are structural and labor alterations, which include substantial increases in the use of instructional technology, the reconceptualizing and reshaping of institutional governance, and the formation of a new major permanent workforce—part-time and other temporary faculty. Community college faculty—particularly full-time faculty—are both recipients and promulgators of these actions.[9]

As recipients, faculty are affected in both work and workload. They participate in managerial work; yet they are peripheral to substantial decision making. They are beneficiaries of technology, both hardware and software, as state funding favors new technologies and managers allocate these resources to faculty. Moreover, they are objects of managerial expectation for increased usage of new technologies and increased workloads; and they are models for students' expectations as the users and demonstrators of new technologies. With the institutionalization of a part-time labor force, a class of faculty with limited pay, roles, and responsibilities as well as second class status, full-time faculty workload increases.

As promulgators, faculty advance the neo-liberal project of an economic and utilitarian orientation to college operations. They are eager adopters of instructional technologies and integrators of these technologies into the curriculum.[10] They are participants in the policy development and implementation strategies of information and instructional technologies. Through collective bargaining, they are party to productivity and efficiency policies and regulations of their college; they are compliant with the management. Faculty take on more students when the institution lacks resources, thereby increasing their workload. Full-time faculty also take on an overload of teaching as part-time faculty and perpetuate the part-time role. In the context of the new economy, faculty work and faculty identity can be viewed as not only highly managed[11] but also corporatized.

Community college faculty are a major labor force in the United States and constitute one-third of all postsecondary education faculty. As a labor force, they epitomize professional work in the new economy and the post-bureaucratic organization: they are predominantly temporary or part-time; the majority bargain collectively for a restricted compensation package; they are not only influenced but also structured in their work by new technologies; and, they are agents of a corporate ideology that arguably makes them instruments and not autonomous professionals.

Our objective in *Community College Faculty: At Work in the New Economy* is to shape an understanding of community college faculty behaviors in the areas they work: in instruction, in governance, and in their administrative or noninstructional duties. We also seek to explain the identity of faculty: whether as professionals, as a transient yet paradoxically permanent workforce, or as agents of the state. We bring together four separate strands of research: one addresses faculty's roles and responsibilities in governance; a second focuses upon faculty's use of electronic technologies in instruction; a third addresses the increasingly crucial yet conflicted role of part-time faculty; and the fourth examines the values and meanings of faculty work.

With approximately 1,000 public community colleges in the United States and a total number of faculty in excess of 270,000, with 172, 800 or 64 percent of these as part-time, out of a postsecondary total of 976,000 full and part-time faculty nation-wide,[12] one might assume that we would know more about present day community college faculty than just their hours of teaching, salaries, or educational backgrounds. Although Seidman[13] endeavored to portray the plight of community college faculty, his research is both dated and limited in that it reveals little about faculty work. Even Grubb's in-depth examination of instruction at community colleges,[14] while a major contribution to our understanding of teaching, is confined largely to classroom behaviors, categorizing faculty instructional work as teaching well or poorly, or using didactic or constructivist teaching methods. We do not know if and why, for example, faculty participate in the hiring of new colleagues, why faculty adopt or reject new technologies or why they participate in distance delivery of the curriculum. We do not know the extent to which they shape or resist the changes undertaken at their institutions. Nor do we know if faculty labor in community colleges is stratified according to employment status or disciplinary affiliation. And, we do not know much about how college administrators perceive and conceive faculty. Greater knowledge about the faculty should enhance our understanding of the community college, both its goals and its operations. This understanding will permit a wider perspective of the institution that serves 38 percent of postsecondary education students.

Increasingly, professional work in higher education institutions has been described as controlled by managerialism or new managerialism.[15] Cynthia Hardy defines managerialism as "a concept that encompasses an increased emphasis on professional management, formal planning, systematic performance evaluation, centralized resource allocation, and directive leadership . . . This concept advocates greater accountability, centralized authority, and objective resource allocation to improve performance."[16] And, similar to other scholars' views on corporatism,[17] Hardy declares that managerialism "is predicated on a unitary perspective in which all interested parties are assumed to be bound together by a common goal."[18] Rosemary Deem[19] uses the term "new managerialism" for higher education to refer to management practices and values commonly associated with the private sector. Casey indicates that the effects of managerialism and corporatism include the homogenization of views and values among workers and the alignment of these views and values with those promoted by the organization.[20] In contrast to earlier discourses and behaviors within higher education institutions, the views and values of the past two decades are oriented toward the marketplace and to entrepreneurial behaviors.[21] Institutions are focused upon generating revenue and reducing labor costs. High productivity, global competition, and rapid change[22] are the new norms for higher education,[23] and both university and four-year college faculty are designated "managed professionals."[24]

Productivity and efficiency behaviors in the context of institutional orientation to the marketplace impact both faculty work and faculty values. One of the characteristics of professionals is their exercise of control over their conditions of work and indeed over definitions of work itself.[25] That is, autonomy in how work is to be accomplished is a hallmark of professionals.[26]

The behaviors associated with managerialism and corporatism, including organizational emphasis on productivity and efficiency, are bound to circumvent faculty autonomy. There is evidence that in universities faculty professional values are circumvented by managerialism and corporatism;[27] yet, there is little evidence to corroborate this condition in community colleges. Although community college faculty may not be aligned with specific disciplinary values,[28] traditionally they have been identified with values associated with teaching and with the educational development of students,[29] suggesting an occupation if not a profession of teaching adults. Notwithstanding Arthur Cohen and Charles Outcalt's rejection of community college faculty as professionals,[30] community college faculty do share occupational traits with their university counterparts, including considerable autonomy in their teaching roles. Community college faculty, however, may be affected more by managerial and political-economic forces than their university counterparts.

"Neo-liberalism" is a term that is rarely, if at all, used by those designated neo-liberals; instead, it is a label applied by those with considerable animosity toward its actors and their behaviors. It carries the connotation of a social disease, eroding the benevolence of the state, upsetting the social order, and undermining community. Nelly Stromquist offers a relatively neutral definition: "Neoliberalism . . . is an economic doctrine that sees the market as the most effective way of determining production and satisfying people's needs."[31]

Guiding principles of neo-liberalism begin with the valorization of individualism and the claim of unfettered economic growth as the key to human progress. These principles include goals that will maximize profits and increase economic performance through the elimination or reduction of regulations and restrictions, such as government standards and legislation and impediments to the free flow of capital and investment. Behaviors are thus directed toward the diminution of the state in the social lives of citizens with a corresponding reduction of public expenditures on social services, privatization of public enterprises, free mobility of capital, de-unionization of labor, while placing an emphasis on individual responsibility.[32] Campbell and Pedersen argue that neo-liberalism is a political project concerned with institutional change.[33]

The neo-liberal project applied to higher education has resulted in a stretching of institutional purposes to fashion colleges and universities as businesses serving private and individual interests. These are responses to growing concerns about the shift of higher education institutions internationally to behaviors that suggest a prevailing orientation to economic matters as opposed to more social or cultural endeavors. For higher education scholar Simon Marginson and political scientist Mark Considine, students from the perspective of universities have become economic entities and no longer citizens. For higher education scholars Sheila Slaughter and Larry Leslie, faculty in research universities have become independent entrepreneurs, seeking funds to support research but directed by those resources to provide research for the private sector's economic returns. For former

Harvard president Derek Bok, higher education institutions have turned to commercialization, selling the work of employees and students, whether that work is created in university laboratories or on the gridiron. In spite of the differences of higher education institutions—differences of institutional type and of national location—behaviors have become isomorphic and the outcomes similar.[34] More recently, Sheila Slaughter and Gary Rhoades have referred to the "neo-liberal university" as well as to the "academic capitalist knowledge/learning regime" in universities and colleges that supports and furthers the neo-liberal project.[35] These attributions are not dissimilar to the manifestation of the "globalized community college" whose missions and purposes have been refashioned to serve as instruments of a neo-liberal ideology.[36]

*Community College Faculty: At Work in the New Economy* is an intellectual extension of John Levin's *Globalizing the Community College*,[37] adding a focus not only upon community college faculty but also upon the implications of a workforce in higher education that is structured by global economic competition. As community colleges organize themselves to respond to local economic needs and employer demands, and as they rely more heavily upon workplace efficiencies such as the use of technology and part-time labor, they have the potential to turn themselves into businesses or corporations, which threatens their social and educational mission. This new environment of high productivity, dynamic change, and competition has become the norm for numerous colleges. Casey suggests that this condition is "an elaborate adaptive strategy for both the corporation and its employees in the condition of post-industrial production."[38] To consider education at community colleges as post-industrial production is to join this branch of higher education with the new economy and economic globalization.

Alongside a mixed-methods approach in researching community college faculty we employ a collaborative model in the writing of this book. Although the three of us have separate research strands using differing research methodologies and data collective methods, we bring these strands together to present a unified view of community college faculty. We also include the research of Veronica Diaz, a higher education technology scholar, and John Cheslock, a higher education economist. We collect data from large data sets (for example, the 1999 National Study of Postsecondary Faculty and from a national sample of collective bargaining agreements), and we conduct quantitative analyses. We also use multiple case study methods, collecting data from interviews and observations and analyzing data qualitatively. By employing this mixed-methods approach we hope to create a synergy where our various data sources, analytical approaches, and personal perspectives inform and challenge one another, creating a deeper and richer analysis than any single approach.

Our theoretical orientations are broad, including political, economic, sociological, and cultural perspectives. We rely upon globalization theory, following from the theoretical work of Robertson, Held, McGrew, Goldblatt, and Perraton, and Waters and the application of this work by

Levin to higher education organizations.[39] We view community colleges as inextricably tied to economic globalization through their emphasis on local markets and dependency upon the government for resources and authority. Furthermore, we see in the community college an exemplary site where new technologies are instruments of fulfilling institutional mission, particularly the access mission, and where these same technologies are structuring faculty work. Finally, we view the community college as progressively adopting the ideology of a corporation, assuming the identity of a business, and defining its core workforce—the faculty—as industrial or business labor, in line with the ideology of neo-liberalism.[40]

It is the neo-liberal project applied to higher education institutions that we follow and illuminate in this book. In spite of the grim images of the neo-liberal perspective, we argue in the final chapter that both the community college and community college faculty can alter the trajectory of the role and work of faculty.

In keeping with the globalization theme, we also see the patterns of U.S. colleges repeated or duplicated in Canadian colleges through a comparative research investigation. Although the community college is traditionally a local institution, it is also a component of the global economy and particularly an instrument of neo-liberal ideology. While we do not undertake a major comparison between two nations' community colleges, we highlight examples from Canadian institutions to both elucidate and further our points. The large data sets on community college faculty are U.S. national data sets—Canada has no such available data. However, in our field research, we were able to collect large quantities of data from Canadian institutions, including interview data in the provinces of British Columbia and Alberta, and institutional and provincial document data in these provinces as well as in Ontario. The origins of community colleges in Canada are not unlike those in the United States and the legal and institutional framework of Canadian colleges bear resemblance to those in the United States. For example, the colleges of British Columbia and Alberta were modeled upon California community colleges—thus there is an historical connection.[41] Furthermore, the recent pressure in the United States for baccalaureate degree granting status for community colleges is preceded by the phenomena in Canadian colleges, particularly in British Columbia and Alberta, with Ontario a later addition to this trend.[42] Nonetheless, our major focus is upon community colleges in the United States and their faculty.

We organize *Community College Faculty: At Work in the New Economy* as a discussion of a major theme and its variations, a type of embedded case study,[43] where we enunciate the central issues and then focus upon related even nested issues. We use nine chapters to work through our discussion and reach not only conclusions but also suggestions for practitioners.

In chapter 2 (From Comprehensive Community College to *Nouveau* College), we explore the context of work for the faculty by addressing the characteristics of the community college. First we examine the problematic characteristics of the community college, including institutional purpose and goals as well as cultural and behavioral features. Second, we explain our conception of the community college by framing the discussion as two views of the institution—one that is the customary understanding in the literature and the other that is reflected in the perceptions of practitioners and in an emerging body of literature on the community college.

This later view suggests that the community college in the twenty-first century is a new institution—*nouveau* college—altered from previous decades along several dimensions. These alterations are explained in a large part as consequences of organizational responses to global forces. Today's community college is a globalized institution—an institution that reflects the globalizing processes in its organizational actions and perpetuates globalization through its actions. During the late 1980s and early 1990s the institution of the community college began to embark on a path of significant change, altering its identity and mission as an institution of higher education. The mission of the community college has shifted from student and community betterment to a workforce development model that seeks to serve the "global economy."[44] Those community colleges which will not only survive but also prosper in the current economy are resilient institutions: they have changed in response to economic, social, technological, and political forces. Their responsiveness, however, to new learners in the form of non-English speakers and displaced workers at one end of the adult education spectrum and to baccalaureate aspirants at the other end has stretched these institutions in both curriculum and instruction.[45] Their adaptation to both changing workplace and learner needs, including their embrace of electronic technologies and distributive learning, has altered work within the institution. And, their use as instruments of government and politicians without the fiscal largesse of these influencers has not only created labor and management pressures as well as severe economic pressures upon these institutions but also framed the identity of community colleges as economic institutions.[46]

Although access to education and training have been the cornerstone principles that define the traditional mission of the community college,[47] access has shaped both the institution as well as faculty culture through the admission of a wide range of students.[48] Access has led not only to enrollment of students with differing abilities and interests but also to greater numbers of student admissions, highlighting the institution's bias toward growth and quantitative measures of identity.[49] Although students can claim a central place in the goals of the community college, outcomes for students are viewed as contradictory or ambiguous.[50] In turn, this centrality of students and their needs may frame a particular faculty culture.[51]

The democratic and idealistic attributes of the community college—social mobility, open access, remediation—are the foundation for a corporate ethos that draws in and holds organizational members captive. Actions of community colleges are justified by a mission "to serve the underserved," and "strengthen communities," particularly in the past two decades through economic development, and to sustain a nation through workforce preparation. In order to fulfill the goals that will help realize this mission, community colleges have resorted to means that have neo-liberal features of economic competitiveness, including productivity and efficiency. A number of behaviors and actions have furthered the neo-liberal orientation. First, community colleges have expanded enrollments to generate additional revenues from state governments and consequently they have hired part-time faculty to reduce costs. Second, community colleges have instituted and participated in accountability programs directed, influenced, or shaped by governments or accrediting agencies in order to satisfy certain criteria and to compete with other colleges. Third, colleges have adopted and increased the use of electronic technologies for information processing and instruction to compete with other institutions, to meet the expectations of students, governments, the public, and the private sector, and to achieve efficiencies in work processes.

In chapter 3 (The Scholarly Literature, the Theoretical Bases, and Research Methods), we provide both the literature and the conceptual bases for our examination and explanation of community college faculty. We begin with theoretical frameworks and concepts pertinent to faculty work in the New Economy. Concepts and theoretical underpinnings of globalization, neo-liberalism, postindustrialism, new capitalism, and New Economy are identified and followed with related conceptual components that have implications for higher education. These include concepts such as resource dependence, entrepreneurialism, and managerialism among others. Once these concepts are identified and explained, we turn to the literature on community college faculty. We confine this discussion to the literature that illuminates our goal of explaining faculty work and issues pertinent to faculty work. We conclude this chapter with a succinct explanation of the research methodology and methods that guided our separate research strands in chapters 4, 5, 6, 7, and 8, and that inform the book as a whole including chapters 1 and 9.

In chapter 4 (Faculty and Institutional Management and Governance), we argue that, formally, community college faculty are expected to increase their participation in institutional governance largely to fit the institution to the requirements of a globally competitive economy. As resources decline in public institutions of higher education, an emerging commodity available to management in exchange for increased production by faculty may be participation in decision making.

We note the presence of new management and governance structures in community colleges that are grounded in a neo-liberal ideology. These structures are altering the formal roles of faculty. Where historically in the bargaining process, management and faculty have exchanged monetary rewards for productivity (teaching), we suggest the emergence of a new pattern of exchange in the current global economy—participation in governance for productivity. Here we conceptualize community colleges as professional bureaucracies whose decision-making processes function primarily as political processes of exchange.[52] By viewing shared governance not only as an academic tradition but also as an exchange of goods and services, we suggest a perspective indicative of the commodification of cooperation. In conjunction with globalizing pressures for economy and efficiency, management may be increasingly willing to share operational decision-making with faculty in return for faculty productivity. This reconceptualization of shared governance from a historical right to a commodity has significant implications for faculty and management not only in their bargaining relationships but also in their enactment of the mission of their institution.

The legal language in collective bargaining agreements stipulates faculty participation in governance in a number of areas implying that management and faculty have agreed to exchange participation in governance for an increase in faculty workload, or diminution in salary increases, or both. This would suggest the early stages of the commodification of cooperation in the bargaining process. We conduct a longitudinal comparison of collective agreements in selected states that were in effect in the early 1990s with updated agreements which are in effect in the early 2000s. We extend earlier work by Levin[53] and Kater[54] that examined the legal rights and roles of faculty in participation in governance as a snapshot in time.

We examine not only the alterations in faculty participation in management and governance but also the changing formal roles of faculty in the community college. We see these roles as furthering the economic competitiveness of community colleges and redefining the identity of faculty.

Chapter 5 (Faculty Use of Instructional Technology and Distributed Learning) examines two major issues on the increasing use of new technologies in the community college. The first issue concerns the effects that computer technology is having on both the work and the working conditions of faculty in community colleges. There is evidence that the use of advanced computer technology spread rapidly in public community colleges,[55] consistent with the mission shift to a workforce development model that seeks to serve the "global economy."[56] Since this global economy is also a technological economy, community colleges are naturally incorporating technology into their operations and instructional procedures. There is considerable debate among scholars concerning how this restructuring toward technology affects personnel. The implications of increasing emphasis on faculty use of electronic technology include alterations in faculty status, autonomy, or power due to increasing computer usage;[57] institutional pressure on faculty to adopt computer usage quickly, in the form of rewards for early adopters or penalties for resisters;[58] alterations in the work environment due to increasing computer usage;[59] and an interaction between the increasing use of computers and the rise in careerism in community college education.[60]

The second issue of increasing use of technology is faculty participation in what we refer to as distributed learning activities and how this participation expands the community college market. The role of faculty members as producers and consumers of instructional technology and software is central to instructional technology use in community colleges. While much of the literature on instructional technology has focused on innovation diffusion at the institutional level or the programmatic effects of using information technology for the purpose of faculty member development,[61] there has been very little research that has used national data to describe the characteristics of faculty members who have incorporated technology into instruction or are participating in other forms of emerging distributed learning structures.[62] We add to the literature by identifying which characteristics of faculty are associated with the adoption of instructional technology. In addition, we also examine the role of several institutional characteristics connected to the use of distributed learning.

The question of whether or not community colleges should continue to incorporate computer technology into instruction has become a moot issue in numerous community colleges. As Langdon Winner has predicted, once a technological system has been adopted and employed in an institution, it becomes virtually impossible to dislodge it because of the resources committed to it.[63] Furthermore, the inflexible nature of computer technology appears to have altered the community college environment to such an extent that the colleges are forced to allocate increasingly larger portions of their resources to maintaining and upgrading the computer systems that they have already purchased.[64]

Although there is strenuous debate about the usefulness of technology in instruction and whether or not faculty members will use technology in a way that will improve teaching and learning, instruction has altered in the community college.[65] Distributed learning has been used to address shrinking budgets, changing and growing student populations, corporate education demands, and learning outcomes. Meyer describes a changing marketplace, increasingly global in orientation, where technology enables the provision of adult education, executive training/retraining, competency-based programs, and education to remote geographical areas.[66] Furthermore, financing the community college is now impacted by faculty's use of technology. While the intent of distributed learning is to generate revenue and produce cost savings, technology actually increases instructional costs, for students as well as institutions, as it is expensive, and needs to be upgraded often, consequently straining educational budgets.[67]

In chapter 6 (Part-time Community College Faculty as New Economy Temporary Labor),[68] we illuminate the problematical role of part-time faculty. The deployment of part-time faculty in higher education institutions can be seen as an economic expedient and as a strategy of organizational adaptation,[69] an adaptation that causes community colleges increasingly to resemble corporations in the new global economy.

Scholarship on part-time faculty in higher education focuses on four broad areas or themes: quality of part-time faculty instruction; exploitation of part-time faculty; integration of part-time faculty; and, demographic studies of part-time faculty. Each of these themes tends to frame faculty labor from a traditional or functional perspective. As a result, they fail to acknowledge that the increased reliance on part-time faculty may be better understood using a lens other than the functional one traditionally employed. This is particularly the case for community colleges, the sector of higher education that relies most heavily on part-time faculty. Part-time faculty at community colleges no longer constitute a temporary or contingent workforce as they have been viewed traditionally, but they are now institutionalized as a highly managed[70] workforce as a result of the globalization of the community college.[71]

In this chapter, we focus on the use of part-time faculty in community colleges, seeking to reconceptualize adjuncts as globalized labor. Part-time faculty, we assert, are employed in a fashion that resembles the use of part-time or temporary employees in other sectors of the new economy.[72] We examine part-time faculty as comprising two distinct strata in community colleges: one possessing rare and highly valued skills and personal networks, the other possessing more common skills and limited personal networks. This schism holds implications both for the two strata of part-time faculty and for the community college as an institution connected to the new economy and "new managerialism."[73]

Managerial practices in community colleges are consistent with the philosophy and practices of the New Economy, and "new managerialism" is particularly evident in the usage of part-time faculty . Here a stratum of faculty, part-time labor in specific disciplines and programs, such as Humanities, Social Sciences, and Sciences, are used to achieve institutional productivity and efficiency,[74] and not to enhance student learning.

In chapter 7 (Corporatism and Neo-Liberal Ideology: The Values and Meanings of Faculty Work), we identify and explain the tensions between the educational values and the economic values of faculty work. Allegiances to students, to the curriculum, and to disciplinary discourse are examined and compared to the entrepreneurial culture of the institution. This furthers our view that community college faculty work is increasingly managed following the pattern of economic globalization.

We describe the views and judgments of administrators and faculty on faculty work, identifying perceptions of faculty use of technology, faculty subcultures, faculty instructional work, faculty values, and faculty allegiance to institutional goals and actions. Faculty are seen as managed according to the ideology of neo-liberalism and corporatism,[75] not unlike Rhoades' concept of "managed professionals." Administrators view faculty as extensions of management and as contributors to the corporate strategies and goals of the institution. College presidents articulate a corporate ideology that connects the community college to the "new global economy."[76] Faculty are assumed to be part of the corporate workforce that contributes to institutional productivity and efficiency as well as to local economic development.

From the perspective of faculty, the expression of their values is at odds with the economic behaviors of the institution. Although faculty are the agents of a preponderance of these behaviors—they develop and teach the curriculum that serves both government priorities and business interests, for example—they articulate their opposition to the serving of these interests by their college. As agents of the institution, faculty are compromised. Their work as educators—teaching, developing curriculum, counseling and advising students, and serving on committees—is configured or framed within an economic and competitive context, even though their values may be based upon other principles and other goals, such as personal and cognitive development of students or the social advancement of their society.

Faculty views frame this tension as a conflict between education and training, between traditional institutional goals, such as student-centeredness, and economic interests, such as business and industry centeredness, and between centralized, hierarchical decision making and decentralized, democratic or shared decision making. Yet, these tensions do not often or typically result in a condition of cultural conflict between faculty and faculty, faculty and administration, or faculty and external influencers including government and business. In this sense, faculty, with the exception of the faculty unions, could be considered to be situated at the periphery of both institutional decision making and institutional influence on matters of institutional action related to purpose, even though faculty work—curriculum and teaching—is the core of institutional action.

Although faculty claim that they are central to both institutional functioning and institutional purpose, and they certainly participate in the administration of work, including governance, at the community college, their goals for the institution are unrealized because economic goals, including training for a competitive global economy, and policies as well as accountability measures from governments are pursued as priorities. The press for greater productivity and efficiency by governments and other external influencers, such as business and industry, coupled with a managerial model of institutional decision making has called into question the professional identity of faculty and skewed their work as educators. Unless faculty can extricate themselves from these conditions and what we see as their corporatized identity or change institutional actions and the underlying corporate culture, this new environment of employee compliance with institutional purposes of a high productivity and market-oriented institution may constitute a more lasting norm for the community college.

Chapter 8 (In Their Own Words) offers recent extended narratives of three faculty members in two community colleges that we captured in 2004. We contextualize these narratives by posing the question of the accuracy of our analysis. Indeed, we are responding to practitioners and scholars alike who might challenge our view of the community college and its context and as one scholar reminded us

> My question would be to what extent the rhetoric diverges from reality . . . I have the impression that colleges are so busy avoiding deficits, accommodating more students than they have space, and addressing union issues that they would be perplexed with your description of the "new college." Much of what you say is true but it is done for pragmatic purposes rather than addressing the global corporate economy. I can hear college presidents saying "these professors are big on theory but too far from the day to day problems."[77]

The faculty in this chapter speak about themselves—about their work and their professional identity—as well as their institution. They reveal a complex set of behaviors and characteristics of community college faculty.

In the final chapter of the book, chapter 9 (The Professional Identity of Community College Faculty), we address the prospect of faculty as instruments of neo-liberal ideology and as corporate workers. We seek to generate a view of community college faculty as part professionals, as agents of knowledge dissemination and participants in a socially and personally transformative process, and as part workers, facilitators of postindustrial production. To do so, we must explain the products and outcomes of the community college over the past two decades, during which time managerial preferences that encompass technological advancement, neo-liberal values, and private sector business behaviors have played out in individual institutions and within the policy community. Here we explain the larger "real world context" of faculty at work in the new economy, using the framework of Roland Scholz and Olaf Tietje[78] for the embedded case study. In understanding, conceptualizing, and explaining community college faculty, we conceptualize their context and delve into the condition of the community college, a condition we begin to develop in chapter 2.

# 2

# From Comprehensive Community College to *Nouveau* College

Our purpose is to explore the multi-faceted work of community college faculty, including their occupational and professional identities and roles. The overarching observation we make and explore in this book is that community college faculty resemble, or indeed are, New Economy workers. That is, they have become aligned with a globalized economy that values flexible, specialized production, particularly knowledge production tied to new technologies, and "multifaceted, pan-occupational team players," who contribute to reduced costs, increased profits, or produce measurable outcomes, and expand markets.[1] Our perspective carries with it the assumption that community colleges are now different institutions from what they have been in the past. We use neo-liberalism, globalization, postindustrialism, new capitalism, and the New Economy as concepts that frame our understanding of the community college. These concepts suggest that advanced production relies upon new technologies, and the work ethic of a labor force that is shaped by both a managerial class and corporate elites, along with global competition, defines organizations that function in a contemporary political economy. In this chapter, we explore our conceptualization of the twenty-first century community college and how this conceptualization presents an alternative discourse about community colleges as institutions. As well, and of significance to this book as a whole, we suggest implications of this conceptualization for faculty.

A substantial body of scholarly literature as well as a considerable number of ruminations by practitioners has framed our understanding of the community college over the past three decades. Since 1981, with Patricia Cross' examination of the community college mission,[2] followed by the 1985 edited work from William Deegan and Dale Tillery, and particularly Cross' contribution within that edited work,[3] scholars began to mold the concept of a modern, comprehensive community college. While the community college discourse prior to the 1980s did reflect an institution with multipurposes and a variety of students, it nonetheless was conceived of as an alternative educational institution, framed by curriculum and instruction, as Arthur Cohen observed in 1969.

> It is viewed variously as democracy's college, as an inexpensive, close-to-home alternative to the lower division of a prestigious university; as a place to await marriage, a job, or the draft; and as a high school with ashtrays. For many of its enrollees, it is a stepping stone to the higher learning; for most, it is the last formal, graded, public education in which they will be involved. The community college is—or attempts to be—all things to all people, trying valiantly to serve simultaneously as custodian trainer, stimulant, behavior-shaper, counselor, advisor, and caretaker to both young and old.[4]

This "all things to all people" label was maintained through the following decades, even to the end of the twentieth century as Grubb notes in 1999 with respect to instruction, as do others when they argue about student access and outcomes.[5] But with advancing postindustrialism and competition, as well as leaders' efforts at institutional legitimacy, the smorgasbord approach and function began to abate.[6]

Through the 1980s, the work of scholars such as Arthur Cohen and Florence Brawer, Richard Richardson, Steven Brint and Jerome Karabel, and John Roueche and George Baker, as well as John Dennison in Canada, developed into a discourse that tied the institution to a more conceptually sound articulation of its purposes and identity.[7] This discourse became mainstream thinking about the comprehensive community college, even among national leaders and institutional practitioners such as Dale Parnell and George Vaughan. Indeed the comprehensive community college was an understood and accepted entity for critics and boosters alike. Historian John Frye speaks about the various perspectives of university professors, national leaders, and local practitioners; but they share a common discourse whether they are critics or boosters. The comprehensive community college—the center of the discourse about the institution—was an articulation based upon curriculum.[8] Several scholars categorized this curriculum (Patricia Cross, Arthur Cohen and Florence Brawer, John Dennison and Paul Gallagher, Dale Tillery and William Deegan); several critiqued its outcomes (Kevin Dougherty, Steven Brint and Jerome Karabel, Richard Richardson and Louis Bender, and Lois Weis);[9] and several argued to strengthen the resolve of those who championed its underlying values, such as access, and yet sought improvements in organizational performance (John Roueche and George Baker, John Roueche and Suanne Roueche).[10] Later works following along the lines of this discourse of the comprehensive community college include Robert Rhoads and James Valadez' *Democracy, Multiculturalism and the Community College* and W. Norton Grubb's *Honored but Invisible*.[11] Both extend the discourse through critical examination of curriculum and instruction, first of students and second of faculty as units of analysis. The so-called critics of the institution, such as Weis, for example, took the theoretical position that student opportunities and outcomes were the fundamental purposes of community colleges—either community colleges provided opportunities for social mobility or they reproduced structural social inequality.[12]

The comprehensive community college was not only conceptualized as curricula, programs, and instruction but also viewed as bounded by traditional notions of education and training, encapsulated in a closed and rational system. There was an absence of external connections, such as the political economy, in this system and in the face of postindustrialism and globalization, the conceptualization of a closed system became outmoded.[13] While the scholarly and practitioner literature was addressing the comprehensive community college, the institution and government policy makers were enamored with a political economy resembling if not identical with neo-liberal ideological tenets. The institution followed a different discourse than the comprehensive community college discourse, one reflected in the term "fast capitalism," applied by James Gee and his associates to educational change.[14] In fast capitalism, the goal is organizational transformation in the private sector, promoted by management consultants such as Peter Senge, Peter Drucker, and Tom Peters. Through organizational transformation, it was assumed that institutions could cope and thrive in a new economy. Alternate forms of operational thinking, such as Quality Management and Organizational Learning, along with ways of rethinking management and teaching in higher educational institutions, evident in the works of Margaret Wheatley and Parker Palmer, found their way into the mainstream of community colleges. One salient example of this new ethos is the "learning paradigm"[15] promoted to replace more traditional forms of curriculum and instruction with student centered teaching and learning strategies loosely based upon cognitive science.[16]

Almost overnight, the community college became known in national discussions as "the learning college."[17] A cursory examination of the vision, mission, and goals of several community colleges reflects "the learning college" focus or kinship. The 2004–2008 strategic plan of Lane Community College in Eugene, Oregon, articulates the college vision as "Transforming lives through learning." Their mission, "Lane is a learning-centered community college," furthers this emphasis upon learning. Palomar Community College in San Marcos, California, home of several of the proponents of the "learning paradigm," such as Robert Barr, John Tagg, and formerly George Boggs, now president of the American Association of Community Colleges, describes itself as "Palomar College . . . a learning community dedicated to achieving student success and cultivating a love of learning," as does a rural college—Cochise College—in Arizona. In Texas, the strategic plan of 2004–2009 for North Harris College in Houston sets out a vision statement ("North Harris College will be the center of learning and culture in our community by becoming the college of first choice for all learners") and a goal statement ("By responding to changing educational goals of learners, current programs will continue to facilitate learning; new program development will be continuous and systematic") suggestive of "the learning paradigm." Santa Fe Community College in Florida refers to itself as a "dynamic innovative learning community" in its college values. Colleges from Lansing Community College in Michigan to Edmonds Community College in

Washington State highlight the terms "learning" and "learning needs" of students in their descriptions and goals and define themselves either explicitly or implicitly as a "learning community." The implications for the status and role of faculty are significant as one characteristic of a professional—expert—is replaced by another—facilitator—in this paradigm.[18]

Out of this combination of "fast capitalism" (or organizational change behaviors to align the institution with the private sector) and new thinking about organizational and individual learning rises *nouveau* college—part University of Phoenix, part Motorola University and Hamburger University, and part Open University, comprehensive community college, four-year state college, and even research university. On-line instruction, corporate training, flexible scheduling (including fast-track programs and credentials) and the provision of baccalaureate degree programs (both with a university partner and stand-alone community college baccalaureate degree credentialing) are no longer aberrant practices but mainstream characteristics of the institution.[19] Indeed, some colleges highlight their research endeavors and others are accomplished in the acquisition of research and training grants, including grants from the National Science Foundation. These were not characteristics of the community college of the 1960s, nor in the mainstream of institutional focus in the 1980s.

Additionally, social services functions and community service continue to form components of the institution, and programs such as remedial education and English as a second language remain as substantial offerings at many colleges. These functions and activities along with the traditional curriculum of university transfer and occupational and vocational education clearly suggest that the comprehensive community college, in form at least, has accompanied this alteration. Possibly the maintenance of traditional curriculum and its structure justifies those scholarly examinations of the institution that assume traditional forms of curriculum—such as academic and vocational—are the defining characteristics of the community college. Although the many parts, including vestiges of the junior college of the 1930s and the comprehensive community college of the 1970s, suggest a complicated, perhaps fragmented, institution, to a large extent *nouveau* college is an integrated and coherent whole. It has altered not simply because it has added more components but because the ideology supporting, driving, and sustaining the institution—neo-liberalism—has incorporated the political economy in the mission, purposes, and behaviors of the institution.

How has this new college developed? In our view this can be explained in large part from the traditional narrative of the development of community colleges in the twentieth century. Yet the discourse on *nouveau* college is one that focuses on external constituencies, not local students and the communities from which they come. While access, and particularly access for new student populations, dominated scholarly discussions of the community college in the 1980s,[20] seeds of impending change emerged in the late 1980s and 1990s. In 1989, Fred Pincus recognized the progression of economic imperatives and revenue generation for community colleges,[21] and Kevin Dougherty and Marianne Bakia detailed the pull of contract training for community colleges in the 1990s.[22] In reviewing developments in Canadian community colleges since 1985, John Dennison noted that, by 1995, colleges were "forced . . . to become entrepreneurial in ways never anticipated at the time of their establishment [in the 1960s and 1970s]."[23] The shift away from a focus on access for all and comprehensiveness is probably a result of viewing the institution as part of a larger economic and social system, where interest groups are influenced by forces outside of education.[24] Indeed, the recognition of a postindustrial society by a handful of scholars began to alter the discourse to address " 'new learning paradigms,' the impact of information technology, and a shift in . . . rhetoric to a 'community economic development' model" for the community college.[25] Additionally and often ignored in the scholarly literature, the productivity-efficiency imperative—stemming from limited resources, especially from governments—increasingly took center stage in institutional organization and behaviors.[26] Thus, revised approaches to curriculum and instruction (for example, the learning paradigm, outcomes based-learning), electronic communications, economic development, and fiscal behaviors, such as efficiency measures as well as fundraising, began to preoccupy institutional members in the late 1990s and early 2000s.[27]

This stretching of functions and focus for the institution—from educational change to operational alteration—is euphemistically termed "innovation" and the community college has developed a reputation over the past two decades as the innovator among educational institutions.[28] Nowhere is innovation more evident than in the introduction and implementation of new technologies. The result is transformation of work through technology and managerial change in and around network enterprises.[29] Identifying with businesses, the community college is an eager participant in conducting its business electronically. The rise of distance education, on-line learning, as well as computer-based management systems such as Banner and web-based information dissemination, marks the community college as a progressive enterprise, altering to keep up with business and consumers.[30] Indeed, community colleges are arguably the exemplar of educational institutions that cater to consumers, from their low-cost price structure for their services to students to their goals of fitting curriculum to the demands of the labor market, thereby satisfying two classes of consumers—students and employers.

At the beginning of the twenty-first century community colleges have not only multiple and possibly conflicting missions[31] but also new alliances and a new identity. The alliances are with economic entities such as business and industry and political affiliations with neo-liberal proponents such as those elements of government and business that foster economic development and competition.[32]

If we examine the institutions' self-characterizations as well as those of the state and the national organization of community colleges, the emphasis upon neo-liberal values is evident. Here, first, is the vision statement for the national organization of the American Association of Community Colleges (AACC):

> AACC will be a bold leader in creating a nation where all have access to the learning needed to participate productively in their communities and in the economy. Through AACC's leadership, community colleges will increasingly be recognized as the gateway to the American dream—the learning resource needed to sustain America's economic viability and productivity. (American Association of Community Colleges, January 17, 2005, http://www.aacc.nche.edu/Content/NavigationMenu/AboutAACC/Mission/OurMissionStatement.htm)

The economic orientation is the central theme here: the assumption is that one learns to earn and that the American economy requires these learners. Another national organization—The League for Innovation in the Community College—characterizes itself as an innovative and dynamic organization, "leading community college organizations in the application of information technology to improve teaching and learning, student services, and institutional management."[33] There are a considerable number of connections between the League and AACC and between the League and private sector business, including advanced technology corporations.

On a system level, within Texas, for example, the Houston Community College System, with five separate colleges and a total student enrollment of over 53,000 students, notes in its mission statement in 2005:

> The Houston Community College System is an open-admission, public institution of higher education offering opportunities for academic advancement, workforce training, career development, and lifelong learning that prepare individuals in our diverse communities for life and work in a global and technological society.

Worker preparation is aimed at the New Economy, a "global and technological society."

On the one hand, legislation and statutes at the state level for community colleges continue to refer to these institutions as public, comprehensive community colleges with a primary and main focus upon education in its broadest sense. On the other hand, less legal language stemming from institutions and district systems as well as from associations such as AACC opt for a focus on economic matters, in addition to language that indicates that teaching students is part of the mix.

Numerous colleges' mission statements reflect a corporate identity consistent with neo-liberalism and economic markets. In a recent examination, David Ayers analyzed a sample of 144 community colleges with current membership in the American Association of Community Colleges. He then retrieved mission statements from the internet sites of each institution in the sample. He subjected these statements to critical discourse analysis. Ayers found that discursive practices of neo-liberalism within the community college mission "(a) subordinates workers/learners to employers, thereby constituting identities of servitude, and (b) displaces the community and faculty in planning educational programs, placing instead representatives of business and industry as the chief designers of curricula."[34]

This is not to suggest, however, that all community colleges have evolved to a position of serving a neo-liberal ideology. Indeed, numerous community colleges continue to cling to the open access, comprehensive, student-centered focus, as exemplified by Dutchess Community College in Poughkeepsie, New York.

> The mission of Dutchess Community College is to provide open access to affordable, quality post-secondary education to citizens of Dutchess County and others. As a comprehensive community college, DCC offers college transfer and occupational/technical degree programs, certificate programs, lifelong learning opportunities, and service to the community. The College provides educational experiences that enable qualified students to expand their academic capabilities and further develop thinking and decision making skills. By providing a full collegiate experience, the College seeks to ensure that all students achieve their individual potential.

Dutchess' mission statement is not unlike countless other community colleges throughout the United States; there is no emphasis on economic or workforce development. Indeed, Dutchess' programs, its sponsored activities, such as a lecture series, even its "award winning" campus landscaping, are reflective of a junior college, where the goals of the college are set on preparing students primarily for academic work at four-year colleges and universities or for employment. There is no language here about preparing a globally competitive workforce or for supporting the economic development needs of the state. While a similar orientation can be noted at Pasadena City College in California, their mission statement does add an economic goal.

> The mission of Pasadena City College is successful student learning. The College provides high-quality, academically rigorous instruction in a comprehensive transfer and vocational curriculum, as well as learning activities designed to improve the economic condition and quality of life of the diverse communities within the College service area.

However, none of their stated mission activities or actions directly suggests actions that will address economic conditions. Instead, the language notes courses and programs that "reflect academic excellence and professional integrity" and "foster a creative learning environment that is technologically challenging and intellectually and culturally stimulating." All actions are underscored by "we serve our students."

Thus from these examples and others, we can see the stark contrasts between those institutions that have adopted a decidedly economic market orientation—one that serves the needs of business and industry—and those that have either maintained the traditional comprehensive mission, with emphasis on education, or clung to the junior college characteristics of academic preparation for further education at a four-year college or university.

During the late twentieth and early twenty-first centuries community colleges became or are becoming globalized institutions. As such, community colleges embrace neo-liberal political philosophy and adopt business practices of the New Economy (these theoretical bases will be explored and discussed in chapter 3). Both neo-liberalism and the New Economy focus on serving the needs and interests of government and business, and not those of individuals. By aligning themselves with these interests community colleges direct their behaviors not to the needs and desires of their students and local communities, but to external forces, and as institutions, they respond to the demands of business and industry, governments, and multinational corporations, as well as to the requirements of information technology. The first part of our new discourse on community colleges, then, gives emphasis to external interests and the influence they wield on community colleges. Given this responsiveness to outside agencies, community colleges function as service providers with their faculty as public service professionals. As one of many service organizations in the neo-liberal, New Economy, and global market nexus, community colleges seek to sell their products (curriculum and programs) to as many customers as possible. Meeting the needs of government or large business interests offers them the opportunity for the largest sales—these two, then, are the most important markets for community colleges. Like any diversified corporation in the twenty-first century, community colleges continually seek to reach new markets and sources of revenue. With each new market, new service professionals must be found to meet the market's needs.

In *nouveau* college faculty are more than teachers—they are consultants, salespeople, account representatives, troubleshooters—the human connection between the organization and markets. As such, community college faculty work encompasses much more than teaching. Faculty are more involved in governance; they are the "floor models" for new technological products as well as the educational experimenters of information technology; and they are expected to interact with external interests ranging from contract training, to business partnerships, and to granting agencies. They train workers for industry; they participate in ventures with business, and they write proposals for grants and contracts. In short, they are expected to be more entrepreneurial in their practices, and their entrepreneurial behaviors are focused on economic efficiency, not necessarily educational quality.

From the perspective of the first part of our discourse, faculty are viewed more as instruments than as autonomous professionals. They are clearly in that class of "managed professionals" referenced by Gary Rhoades in his examination of unionized faculty in the United States.[35] Indeed, community college faculty are a highly managed and stratified workforce within the field of academic labor. To the extent that community college faculty align themselves with the views and values of a corporate like organization, they have become colonized, with behaviors as extensions of the corporate ethos.[36]

In chapters 4, 5, 6, and 7, we elaborate on the condition of community college faculty in the New Economy.

From the perspective of the second part of our discourse, one where we intend to be instructive if not uplifting, faculty are accorded a professional identity and are central to the educational efficacy of the community college. We develop this first in chapter 8 and then in chapter 9 where we address both faculty and *nouveau* college, with suggestions for their future.

In chapter 3, we detail the scholarly literature and theoretical bases that we rely upon for our examination of faculty. We also outline the research methods we have employed to investigate community college faculty and their work.

# 3

# THE SCHOLARLY LITERATURE, THE THEORETICAL BASES, AND RESEARCH METHODS

Existing literature on the subjects of globalization, neo-liberalism, and community college faculty is extensive and diverse. However, the connection between and among these subjects has little precedent, with some exceptions.[1] In the literature on universities and four-year colleges, the past decade has produced several instructive works that integrate globalization, neo-liberalism, and academic faculty.[2] Of these only Sheila Slaughter and Gary Rhoades make the leap beyond universities to include community college faculty.[3] *Community College Faculty: At Work in the New Economy* is the first work to focus primarily on this connection and to use the concepts of neo-liberalism and globalization to explain faculty work in community colleges.

To simplify our presentation of relevant scholarship, this chapter classifies into sub-sections the themes and problems introduced in chapters 1 and 2. Using Cooper's categorization,[4] we use an integrative model for this literature review, which isolates and summarizes the relevant themes within existing scholarship on globalization, neo-liberalism, and community college faculty. We approach globalization as the paradigmatic condition shaping contemporary educational transformations and subsequently effecting social values, including higher education. Our specific object is to explore the effects of the new isomorphic, global norms of productivity, efficiency, and competition—all components of economic globalization in the late twentieth and early twenty-first century—on community college faculty. We develop a network of interrelated concepts, with the purpose of explaining spaces—cultural, psychical, social, and even physical—in which globalization and community college faculty interact.

We begin with globalization, which we view as a borderless economic, social, and cultural condition and then we move to related concepts including neo-liberalism, corporatism, postindustrialism, new capitalism, and the New Economy. Explaining the popular interest in *globalization* and its effects on economics, sociology, and education, Malcolm Waters suggests that geography is no longer a significant boundary to cross-cultural influence.[5] Roland Robertson elegantly conceptualizes globalization as "the compression of the world and the intensification of consciousness of the world as a whole."[6] The globalization process represents the unification and assimilation of our economic and social realities. Identifying a "problem of globality," Robertson explores the latent conflict when the presence of divergent identities calls into question this new homogeneity of norms, values, and principles. The opposition requires the "comparative interaction of different forms of life."[7] The world has moved toward "unicity"—"a relatively specific path that the world has taken in the direction of it becoming singular."[8] Although economic globalization is arguably oriented toward unitary systems and homogeneity of economic behaviors, which some suggest spill over to cultural and social behaviors,[9] there is also evidence that globalization results in diversity and differentiation.[10] Catherine Kingfisher discusses cultural hybridity, or the mixing of cultural or social characteristics, as a product of globalization.[11] Local or regional behaviors are not always subordinate to global pressures for unification and homogeneity; accordingly Rosemary Deem[12] and William Sites[13] promote the importance of maintaining local factors within the internationalization of ideas and educational practices. Sites refers to "primitive globalization," that is the exploration of how localities function within a broader national and international context.

Discussion about globalization and its effects on human societies illustrates a variety of economic, political, sociological, and educational priorities, of which we highlight only a few. Gary Teeple recognizes that globalization is not just a transformed political vision, but also an expression of the internationalization of capital, which is arguably the advent of the global economy. Capital has no national home: because it is distinguished by interconnected trade and investment, capital has become denationalized.[14]

Arguing that globalization represents a shift to a postmodern, radical transformation of society, Scott[15] asserts that globalization will challenge the resilience of higher education. Alderman[16] agrees: the globalization of education should cause some apprehension over educational quality and education's responsiveness to particular cultural identities. From a critical perspective, Kwiek[17] asks whether the university must challenge the latent assumptions about the function of government in a globalized world. Should higher education function as an objective witness to or evaluator of such sociopolitical trends as the gradual elimination of the welfare state? Similarly, Nadesan[18] opposes the general "celebratory" treatment of globalization, arguing that observers, especially those in higher education, must remain responsive and responsible to those sectors of society adversely affected by the globalization of the local economy.

Not surprisingly, much of the literature on globalization and its ideological derivatives is comparative in orientation. Using Australia as a case study, McBurnie[19] approaches globalization as a policy paradigm, affecting universities economically, culturally, politically, and technologically. Such effects include new governmental management tools used to exert greater control over higher education. Levin[20] investigates government policy toward community colleges in the United States and Canada in the 1990s and examines the way colleges responded to such interventions. Despite differences in research locations, he observed greater government managerial interventions in the administration of higher education. Government policies generally addressed regional, state, and provincial economic competitiveness, job training, efficiency, productivity, accountability, and responsiveness to industry.

*Neo-liberalism* could be described as the ideological complement to the mechanics of globalization. Our review of the literature shows that critics of neo-liberalism and globalization are more forthright in their discussions of its economic, political, and societal effects. Chomsky,[21] for example, argues that neo-liberals justify the development of international financial institutions for the domination of vulnerable nations and societies through the dissemination of such norms as the liberalization of trade, market price-setting, and privatization. Because they control much of the international economy, dictate policy development, and influence public opinion, large corporations are the architects of the neo-liberal project. Michael Apple summarizes the ideological commitments and ideal behaviors of neo-liberalism.[22] These include, among others: the expansion of open, economic markets; the reduction of government responsibility for social needs; the reinforcement of a competitive structure for economic behaviors; and, the lowering of social expectations for economic security. He concludes that neo-liberal policies are framed as market solutions that serve to reproduce traditional hierarchies, such as race and class.

Within the context of neo-liberalism, the economic marketplace is deified and thus institutions are valued by their relationship to this deity. Neo-liberal critics have a different message: the valorization of the economic marketplace with relatively unfettered competition induces inequality.[23] Social and educational mobility for some ultimately excludes others.[24] The collective good is suppressed and individual advancement, often justified under the guise of merit, is vaunted.[25] Such norms have spilled over to education with serious and likely long-range effects. Schools are viewed as corporations,[26] with private interests replacing the public good.[27] For higher education, the charge of neo-liberal critics is that learners are defined as or indeed reduced to economic entities and curriculum is surrendered to economic markets.[28]

Barnet and Cavanaugh outline the evolution of corporations as having replaced national governing authority. Because they can control communications, economic transactions, and the distribution of material objects, corporations dominate global, national, and local activities. Corporations are increasingly unaccountable to public authorities. Barnet and Cavanaugh note that "political agreement on the global level, whether on the environment, immigration, labor standards, human rights, trade, or investment is proceeding slowly."[29] More abstractly, Saul[30] defines *corporatism* as an ideology in which rationality is central and essential. Critical of the postmodern acceptance of the corporatist ideology, Saul argues that it undermines the legitimacy of democratic citizenship. In other words, legitimacy in the ideology of corporatism is found in the private group, rather than in the individual agent. Casey[31] also studies group versus individual behavior, discussing corporatism as the methods through which workers and managers deal with rapid technological changes within the work organization. Thus, corporatism represents a movement away from individual agency and toward the incorporation of decision-making processes within an economic entity.

The workforce in colleges and universities is increasingly framed by managers and government and private sector interests as corporate employees who support competition and entrepreneurialism even though higher education historically existed in a sphere separate from business and industry. Scholars note these differences based upon cultural and social values found in academe.[32] In this sense, universities and colleges have transformed, conceptually though perhaps not in practice, from earlier functions, even if they are not, using Readings' term, "ruined."[33] The neo-liberal university is now clearly established;[34] it remains to be seen if the community college is advancing to this condition, resisting it, or instead has already adopted that role.[35]

In explaining the advent of *postindustrialism* as a fundamental transformation of the global economy, Rifkin[36] argues that human labor is undergoing systematic elimination from economic transactions. Such a revolution, toward sophisticated information and communication technologies at the expense of meaningful human activity, requires every nation and locality to reconsider old beliefs about government, politics, and individual citizenship. Rifkin asks, which individuals have the right to participate in and benefit from the productivity benefits of this information and communication technology revolution? This discussion of the postindustrial economy's tendency to supersede individual rights and agency is especially topical for this text. Casey[37] notes that postindustrial corporations exercise considerable pedagogical acumen in designing new cultures for employees: these corporations use advanced automation and information technologies as both tools of indoctrination and surveillance. Indeed, Manuel Castells[38] links the transformation of work to technological and managerial change and the development of network structures. These networks are dominated by governments and corporations and "[pertain] to a space of flows that links them up around the world, while fragmenting subordinate functions, and people, in the multiple spaces of places, made of locales increasingly segregated and disconnected from each other."[39] While Castells overstates the case for the dominance of network structures,[40] his observations identify sources of power in a globalized economy and the structuring of work around information technologies.

In extending postindustrialism, Richard Sennett examines work and its effects on people in *the new capitalism*.[41] In the new capitalism, particularly in the Anglo-American model of capitalism, the work ethic is shaped to fit assumptions of those in positions of power on the needs of a flexible economy, which includes rapid change in skills and the development of teamwork. These actions result in discontinuity of the workforce and group practices that are necessarily superficial. Although some operational practices alter, and workers are discarded or "re-tooled," the production system does not change. The implications for faculty work include conformity or obsolescence as well as a rejection of the routine of labor. Past practices, such as face-to-face interactions and educating for the public good, lose their value.

According to Carnoy,[42] the *New Economy* is characterized by cutthroat global competition, increased organizational flexibility, and the separation of workers from the social institutions that reproduce human capital and social capital, such as universities and colleges. Economic growth is technologically dependent; and production is more reliant upon knowledge than labor, unless the labor is low-cost. Carnoy argues that the New Economy, ironically, derives its key workforce from the very institutions that replicate the economy's most important asset—knowledge. Suggesting that local communities have been stressed by incompatible job and labor markets, Carnoy requires that higher education provide measures to increase access to knowledge, to bridge the current divide between available labor and job skill requirements in the New Economy. We suggest that this is a critical function of higher education institutions generally and community colleges specifically.

There are significant implications for higher education stemming from the globalization process. A number of salient concepts also serve as derivatives of globalization. Of the numerous connections between globalization and higher education, the customary association is with economic globalization and the financing of higher education. This may be simply a result of the high level of dependency that higher education institutions have on external sources of funds.[43] Or it may be a result of a mission shift for higher education institutions to economic survival. In their discussion of *funding patterns* and institutional dependencies, Pfeffer and Salancik[44] assert a survivalist perspective of higher education. To survive, an organization must acquire resources from its environment, usually in competition with other entities. The instability and unpredictability of the environment cause transaction inefficiencies in the acquisition of resources. Pfeffer and Salancik define interdependence as "whenever one actor does not entirely control all of the conditions necessary for the achievement of an action or for obtaining the outcome desired from the action."[45] In a globalized economy, institutional actors are necessarily interdependent and competitive.[46]

In explaining *resource dependence* theory, Slaughter and Leslie argue that organizational change may be shaped by the conditions in which essential resources are appropriated to organizations.[47] Influence, bargaining, and creative alliances prove critical in resource negotiations. Strauss[48] discovers a proliferation of programs and initiatives at the community college leading to more frequent competition among these programs and initiatives for state appropriations. She recommends an entrepreneurial model for acquiring external monies, rather than continue with the institution's dependence on state funding. In addition, colleges are urged to clarify their missions to defend against cuts in subsidies. Palmer[49] agrees, arguing that fiscal conditions affect the multipurpose character of the community college, and its advocates must therefore resolve conflicting institutional priorities. Palmer differentiates competing priorities: curricular flexibility, student transfer, and social service. In a study of community college presidents' perceptions of funding, Fonte[50] finds that educational access and partnerships with local business should be institutions' highest priorities; and given real and perceived budget constraints, social services receive the least attention by presidents. Organizational priorities, and not fiscal scarcity, shape and influence funding sources and allocations.

*Competition* for resources is a common theme throughout recent literature on globalization and higher education. Lubienski[51] describes the market-driven behavioral characteristics of universities and colleges at the end of the twentieth century. Dissatisfaction with bureaucratic educational monopolies has spawned competitive, consumer-choice educational models. Lubienski asks if choice and competition foster innovation, quality, and improvement? Competitive institutional environments are not solely a North American phenomenon: Marris[52] argues that institutions in the United Kingdom face significant internal competition for resources, as do Marginson and Considine for Australia.[53]

The result of competition is the tendency toward intra-institutional *entrepreneurialism*, articulated most notably by Slaughter and Leslie.[54] Marginson and Considine,[55] in their late 1990s study of higher education in Australia, also notice an increasing scarcity of public funds and competition between institutions. This competition is facilitated intentionally by public policy, promoting institutional isomorphism. The internal economy is defined by quasi-market relationships: internal allocations are unequal, determined by performance and zero-sum competition. The institutions investigated by Marginson and Considine exhibit strong executive control and encourage the developmental enterprises external to the institution. They also recognize the increasing displacement of traditional academic governance by executive groups and consulting agencies. In discussing nontraditional workforce development programs, Grubb, Badway, Bell, Bragg, and Russman describe such initiatives as "entrepreneurial."[56] External and internal influences, such as institutional missions, faculty philosophies, localized economic demands, and state policy, directly and indirectly, affect management priorities. In a study of New Zealand institutions, Roche and Berg[57] find that the competitive capitalist model creates structural inequalities unrepresentative of the traditional college mission. Attempting to reconcile the traditional and new functions of higher education, Meyer[58] considers the role of the entrepreneurial university within a knowledge economy. Together, these pieces identify the emerging problem of deteriorating institutional and academic identities within institutions of higher education.

Studying Canadian universities in the 1980s, which suffered from declining enrollment and budgets restrictions, Hardy[59] describes *managerialism* as the application of managerial techniques that demand increased accountability, centralized decision making and authority, and objective resource allocation. Her study focused on competition for scarce resources when public pressure for increased fiscal accountability began to direct institutional management methods. As early as 1958, Mason[60] refers to the changing motivations of those in control of the corporation as "managerial" capitalism. According to Levin, colleges experiencing decreases in state funding in the late 1980s were required to secure alternate sources of funding or reallocate budget expenditures to manage costs.[61] Robst[62] looked at revenue and cost structures, noticing the reduced importance of state appropriations for institutional budgets; however, by the early 1990s tuition revenue began to supplant state subsidies to higher education. Despite declining appropriations, state and local governments encouraged productivity through performance measures. Universities and colleges responded by restructuring managerial practices and engaging in academic capitalism.[63] Deem[64] also recognizes the ways in which global and local stimuli can affect management practices. The globalization and internationalization of market forces encourage managerialism or administrative tendencies to increase accountability, productivity, flexibility, and centralized authority. While this phenomenon of greater governmental intervention in the management and administration of higher education seems initially problematic, Simkins cautions against making generalizations about the suitability of new managerial practices and infrastructures.[65] He advises that different organizational contexts will produce different managerial outcomes. This is consistent with Marginson and Considine's observation about diverse approaches of institutions to the acquisition of new revenue streams.[66]

The pressure of *productivity* is a specific constraint imposed by corporatism, managerialism, and entrepreneurialism, which are all expressions of a neo-liberal economic paradigm within a globalized economy. Productivity is discussed within the context of administrative outputs, student learning, and faculty scholarship. Dundar and Lewis[67] suggest exploring the relationship between research productivity and institutional factors. Massy[68] suggests that certain factors internal to the institution raise costs and limit productivity; one solution is the introduction of labor saving technologies and automation. Questioning the appropriateness of technological innovations in higher education, Massy and Zemsky[69] ask if the perpetual search for increasing productivity requires continual transformations of educational functions and processes. Massy and Wilger[70] add that technologies are likely to increase productivity in those areas serving a high volume of students, offering a standardized curriculum, and where faculty are less possessive of course content.

Jalongo,[71] exploring the reasons why some faculty choose not to engage in original scholarship, provides a model of professional development which defines productivity as research output. Investigating measures of faculty productivity, Denton, Tsai, and Cloud[72] quantify productivity as both contributions to annual meetings of large professional associations and the number of papers published in major journals. Studying a Southern, mid-sized public university, Baldwin[73] describes an accountability framework and productivity analysis based on institutions securing external research and public service funds. The terms productivity and accountability imply an industrial model of higher education; Shupe[74] even characterizes faculty, students, and businesses as customers of the institution.

The concept of institutional *efficiency* is closely related, in the literature, to productivity. Ferris[75] admits that outsourcing and contracting are often useful mechanisms of increasing efficiency within the university. He does, however, acknowledge the trade-off between production costs and managerial incentives with flexibility and transaction costs. As early as the mid-1970s, Hoos[76] discovers that the progressive use of technology in education is justified by the expectation of increased efficiency. Like Ferris, she notes that industrial modes of efficiency may be inappropriate and thus costly for higher education. In a similar sense, Cowan[77] distinguishes between institutional efficiency and effectiveness, arguing that researchers must measure individual educational programs rather than apply global values arbitrarily. More recent attention to efficiency in higher education notes the use of management tools such as Total Quality Management or the infusion of information technology into all operations of the institutions, including instruction.[78]

Related to this conversation on institutional efficiency, effectiveness, and the community college mission is an institution's responsiveness to the needs of welfare recipients or other marginalized individuals. Globalization and its subsequent emphasis on productivity and efficiency have affected states' philosophical and budgetary commitments to maintaining educational access for those on welfare. Davies and Guppy argue that "globalization's effect on education is a simultaneous centralization and devolution of authority that squeezes power from middle levels of educational administration and redistributes it upward to more central states and downward to individual schools and reform groups."[79] Mazzeo, Rab, and Alssid[80] and Dever and Templin[81] recognize that policy makers attempt to adjust workforce and educational priorities to match changing local and regional economic conditions, in which flexibility and adaptability are priorities. Bragg and Layton[82] also explore how the community college represents educational reform, particularly with regard to vocational education. In promoting a fundamental change in the community college's mission, Lorenzo and LeCroy[83] recommend a conceptual renewal of the essential functions of the community college based on critical societal pressures. Lorenzo and LeCroy's position is representative of the postindustrial trend toward institutional efficiency and productivity. Among their suggestions are more efficient governance, greater faculty specialization and flexibility, the incorporation of new technologies, and the establishment of new inter-institutional partnerships.

Sturgeon[84] suggests that intra- and inter-institutional *partnerships* can be implemented to enhance services at lower costs. Similarly, Nixon and Lundquist[85] describe a new organizational culture of collaboration, which they call a "partnership paradigm." Examining partnerships between a North Carolina community college and twelve local, nonprofit organizations, Sink and Jackson[86] describe the creation of successful partnerships between higher education and industry: such liaisons require accessibility, shared goals, open communication, and effective coordination. Using case study methods, Johnson[87] also explains the strategies that community colleges use to satisfy the needs of their corporate partners.

The emphasis upon *information technology* in higher education literature reflects the association of higher education institutions with business and industry, suggesting a network of organizations that are adaptive and responsive, as well as current. DeNoia and Swearingen[88] advocate effective and efficient college administration, suggesting that information technology may be a particularly valuable resource if tied to administrative productivity and stated institutional outcomes. Applications of technology are encouraged to be strategic and their organizational effects immediately assessed. Bullock and Ory[89] argue that assessments of instructional technology should measure the degree of technological integration, perhaps as a proxy for effectiveness. According to Ely,[90] eight conditions promote the effective application of managerial and instructional innovations. These include dissatisfaction with the *status quo*, suitable skill levels among workers, adequate resources, sufficient time to learn the processes, rewards and incentives, participation, commitments, and effective leadership. Adequate resources for the implementation of technology, however, may be a challenge in the New Economy: Green[91] notes that 2001 survey data indicate significant declines in technology spending in 2000–2001. Specific to a study of community college faculty and their acceptance of new technologies, Mitra, Steffensmeier, and Lenzmeier[92] suggest that faculty members, with their increased computer use and altering attitudes, need adequate computer training and infrastructural support to sustain use of such technology. Carnevale[93] explains that many faculty are ill-equipped to convert traditional classroom curricula into online or distance educational courses. To streamline the transformation of curricular formats, many colleges and industries have developed systems and processes for the efficient transfer of course materials.

March and Cohen,[94] with some distinction, conceptualize technology as not only the physical tools and programs used to decrease manual labor, but also as the ability to innovate, describe, and replicate important processes. In this sense, partnerships may constitute a labor saving alternative technology for community colleges. Rogers[95] presents a similarly abstract concept of technology-as-innovation. Diffusion is the process by which a technological innovation is communicated through established channels throughout a system of interrelated units sharing a common goal.

In recognizing the importance of control for the dissemination of a technology, Vallas[96] describes how technological trends reflect various managerial structures. In effect, technology becomes a mechanism of control and marginalization. Attempting to introduce questions of value, meaning, and morals to this conversation over the role of technology in higher education, Winner[97] addresses the sociopolitical and ideological consequences of technological innovation. He notes that power, control, autonomy, and equity are necessarily embedded in both technology and managers' attempts to implement new technologies. Roe,[98] investigating community college faculty's adoption of electronic technologies for instruction, concludes that the use of technology structures faculty work. More generally, Tapscott[99] concludes that the New Economy and the new technology are connected and mutually enabling.

Several scholars approach the community college as a *cultural institution*, wherein cultural norms and values are reflected and through which they are transmitted. Commenting on management-faculty relationships, Baker[100] concludes that the creation of a jointly determined institutional culture is essential for the performance success of community colleges. More critically, Shaw, Valadez, and Rhoads[101] treat the community college as a cultural text, asking whether institutions actually promote the upward mobility that has been an historical priority of the institution. In a similar vein, Griffith and Connor[102] investigate the ability of open door colleges to pursue their traditional missions, given severe budget cuts and public misperceptions about the educational functions of community colleges. Addressing the conflict between critics and advocates of the community college, Dougherty[103] condenses the argument to several key points. What is the impact of the community college on students and industry? Why have community colleges developed in the manner observed? Why have community colleges transformed their original missions into largely vocational education? These questions, and the disagreements they generate, reflect a broader conversation on the social function and significance of the community college. Herideen[104] also contextualizes the "controversiality" of the community college's social role. Because of the community college's mission of providing access and equalizing educational opportunity, and because of its role in promoting the state's welfare agenda, the community college is immediately affected by this shift toward postindustrial economic and social attitudes, as equality and welfare become less prominent under neo-liberalism.

Students' *access* to postsecondary education has been a salient topic in studies of higher education, particularly for community colleges because their mission gives high priority to equity and to further educational opportunities. Valadez[105] examines how students reach critical decisions about their lives, education, and career. Studying the impact of social class as a determinant of success in higher education, Valadez asserts that social position represents an important cultural capital. The community college is best able to serve middle-class students who have a basic level of cultural capital, the resources necessary to make use of college resources. Valadez argues that lower class and underrepresented populations face more significant obstacles in the community college because they do not possess that cultural capital. On the other hand, Smith and Vellani[106] suggest that the community college presents a unique opportunity for a variety of students to gain cross-cultural understanding, in addition to professional training. Along these lines, the "new student majority" in community colleges is comprised of a broad spectrum of non-traditional students, many of whom seek to acquire the social and cultural capital required for upward mobility.[107]

It is within this complex context described and discussed thus far in the chapter that we view the community college and community college faculty. Our contextualized understanding includes the political economy, with neo-liberalism and globalization as foreground, as well as organizational behaviors which are themselves a product of history, culture, and the political economy.

We turn now to the characteristics of community college faculty.[108] Who are they? Our understandings to date are limited largely to several comparative data sets of four-year and two-year faculty from the National Center for Educational Studies (NCES) and the 1993 and 1999 versions of the National Study of Postsecondary Faculty (NSOPF), a handful of other quantitative studies of community college faculty,[109] and W. Norton Grubb's examination of instruction.[110] The 1993 and 1999 versions of the National Study of Postsecondary Faculty (NSOPF) offer useful demographic data on community college faculty. For example, NSOPF 93 reports that, in 1992, public, two-year institutions represent 31.9 percent of all institutions of higher education. NSOPF 99 is particularly useful for our purposes and this data set provides a number of comparative observations comparing four-year and community college faculty in 1998.

We describe these demographic and professional characteristics through comparisons with faculty at four-year institutions because, historically, the four-year institution has been the focus of research and critical reflection. Our readers may be less familiar with the features of the contemporary community college. Thus, it may be helpful to characterize the institution and its faculty through relevant contrasts with the four-year institutions, a more familiar institutional type. A number of categories of comparison are used to differentiate the two faculty groups. Examples of these are displayed in table 3.1.

Of special import in these characteristics of faculty is that in 1998, 170,000 faculty in public, two-year institutions worked part-time, representing 62.5 percent of the total faculty labor force in community colleges. There

**Table 3.1** Faculty comparisons: community colleges and four-year colleges

| Category | |
|---|---|
| Gender | Women are more likely to teach at public, community colleges, compared to four-year institutions, than men. |
| Race | The faculties of both two-year and four-year institutions were predominantly white: 90.5% white at community colleges and 88.9% at four-year institutions. |
| Age | The average age of faculty at community colleges was 48.3, compared to an average age of 48.9 for faculty at four-year institutions. |
| Degree attainment | The most prevalent highest-degree for faculty at community colleges was the master's degree (53.5% hold the MA as their highest earned degree). 19.2% hold the bachelor's degree as their highest earned degree, and 11.8% hold the doctoral degree as their highest earned degree. Faculty at four-year institutions predominantly hold doctoral degrees (51.8%) and master's degrees (25.7%). |
| Work | Compared to their peers at four-year institutions, faculty at community colleges spent more time teaching and less time engaged in research and administrative responsibilities. |
| Use of technology | Faculty at community colleges rated lower in their general use of instructional technology than their peers at four-year institutions. |
| Employment satisfaction | A large majority (79.1%) of faculty at community colleges report being somewhat satisfied or very satisfied with their workload, compared to 72.4% of faculty at four-year institutions. |

**Table 3.2** NSOPF 1999 faculty characteristics[a]

| | All | Academic | Professional | Vocational | Developmental Remedial | Librarian Counselor |
|---|---|---|---|---|---|---|
| *Mean Figures* | | | | | | |
| Female | 53% | 49% | 57% | 36% | 77% | 73% |
| Age | 48.7 | 49.4 | 48.0 | 48.4 | 49.5 | 47.7 |
| *Field Categories* | | | | | | |
| Academic | 47% | | | | | |
| Professional | 40% | | | | | |
| Vocational | 8% | | | | | |
| Developmental Remedial | 4% | | | | | |
| Librarian Counselor | 2% | | | | | |
| *Age Categories* | | | | | | |
| Less than 35 | 10% | 10% | 8% | 9% | 10% | 10% |
| 35–39 | 10% | 9% | 11% | 11% | 6% | 8% |
| 40–44 | 13% | 11% | 16% | 13% | 11% | 16% |
| 45–49 | 18% | 16% | 20% | 21% | 17% | 16% |
| 50–54 | 20% | 21% | 20% | 18% | 29% | 27% |
| 55–59 | 15% | 17% | 14% | 17% | 15% | 11% |
| 60 and above | 13% | 16% | 11% | 11% | 12% | 11% |
| *Race Categories* | | | | | | |
| American Indian | 1% | 1% | 1% | 1% | 0% | 0% |
| Asian | 3% | 3% | 3% | 1% | 8% | 3% |
| Black | 9% | 7% | 9% | 9% | 11% | 26% |
| Hispanic | 8% | 9% | 7% | 7% | 9% | 8% |
| White | 79% | 80% | 81% | 81% | 72% | 63% |

*Note*: [a]NSOPF data under-represents part-time faculty in all categories.

are more faculty at community colleges who work part-time than at any other institutional type as described by the Carnegie Classification. The NSOPF 93 and NSOPF 99 surveys provide a wealth of data on community college faculty. We display in table 3.2 the distribution of faculty at community colleges based upon the results of the Fall 1999 NSOPF survey. Our modifications of the full NSOPF survey results include dropping faculty members reported in a field of "other" or "not applicable" and thus our figures in table 3.2 differ somewhat from those in table 3.1. We use five broad categories for faculty: Academic, Professional, Vocational, Development/Remedial, and Librarians/Counselors. For the academic category we include faculty in such areas as Humanities, Social Sciences, and Sciences. For the professional category, we include faculty in such areas as Business, Computing, and Nursing. For the vocational category, we include faculty in such areas as Industrial Arts, Drafting, and Personal services such as early childcare and nurse's aide. For the Developmental/Remedial category we include faculty in such areas as Basic Skills, Special Education, and English as a Second Language. Finally, for the Librarian and Counselor category, we include all faculty who perform librarian and counseling functions within the institution. The academic and professional categories contain the largest number of faculty, with 87 percent of all faculty affiliated with these. This way of configuring faculty work refutes earlier arguments and views of the community college as a largely vocational institution.[111] With 40 percent of faculty working in programs that have occupational/professional goals for students—Nursing, Business Management, Systems Analysis, Accounting—and 47 percent working in disciplines with decidedly university parallel curricula—Psychology, English Literature, Composition, Biology, Chemistry, Physics, Economics, and Languages—there is a considerable stretch to support the vocational argument of the 1980s.

The claim that community colleges are multicultural institutions with diverse populations applies to the institution's students but not to the faculty.[112] Seventy-nine percent of faculty—both part-time and full-time combined—are categorized as "white." Minority faculty are scarce, particularly evident in programs where minority students are found in large numbers: for example, American Indian faculty constitute 0 percent of faculty in developmental education and 1 percent of total faculty.

Finally, the view of an aging faculty, common in discussions among institutional leaders, is somewhat exaggerated, with 13 percent of faculty over 60 years of age and 28 percent over 55. Indeed, 48 percent are under 50 and 20 percent of these are under 40.

However, quantitative data do not tell the whole story of community college faculty experience. We use considerable qualitative data to supplement our explanation. Additionally, we discuss literature on four-year as well as community college faculty whenever the literature on four-year faculty has salience for our understanding of community college faculty.

Of all the themes and constructs that are gleaned from national databases, *satisfaction* is among the most frequently discussed and likely relevant to our examination of faculty as a labor force. Discussing the analytical importance of studying *satisfaction*, Wagoner argues that faculty satisfaction represents their orientation and dedication to the profession and the changing institutional cultures in which the profession is located. Community college faculty satisfaction is based on a number of related factors, including such abstract concepts as autonomy, management practice, perceptions of changing status, the flexibility of labor, and faculty roles in governance.[113]

The majority of examinations of faculty satisfaction depend heavily upon faculty at four-year colleges and universities as their units of analysis. In 1977, Moxley[114] argued that such hygiene factors as policies, practices, salary, budgets, and supervision were categories of actions that led to faculty dissatisfaction. Actions connected to achievement, recognition, and growth opportunities, on the other hand, promoted faculty satisfaction. However, by 1991, Bowen and Radhakrishna[115] found that demographic and situational variables, as defined by Moxley, are not good indicators of satisfaction. Similarly, Plascak-Craig and Bean[116] determined that perceptions of faculty autonomy, opportunities for creativity, participation in institutional governance, fairness, and esteem positively affect faculty satisfaction. In short, the most predictive variables for faculty satisfaction relate to perceptions of professionalism and self-governance within the academy. Using the NSOPF 93 data, Finkelstein, Seal, and Schuster[117]argue that college and university faculty demonstrate substantial pessimism about their professional status and opportunities. They indicate that the culture of the contemporary college and university does not promote satisfaction through the non-hygienic—ideational and attitudinal—indicators highlighted by the Plascak-Craig and Bean study.

Most importantly, Finkelstein, Seal, and Schuster discovered that new faculty professionals are significantly less satisfied than more experienced faculty with regard to job security and other cultural characteristics. Additionally, women are less satisfied than men with their academic jobs; faculty at liberal arts colleges are least satisfied. Those in the natural science fields tend to be the most satisfied and those working in the humanities the least satisfied. Of significance to our examination, Finkelstein, Seal, and Schuster found that these relationships pertain across institutional types, including community colleges. Valadez and Antony[118] found that part-time faculty members at community colleges are increasingly concerned with such issues as job security, salary, and benefits. Wagoner[119] also noticed that levels of satisfaction vary significantly between different demographic populations within part-time faculty. Two observations are of special interest. First is the division within community colleges of part-time faculty: part-time instructors in vocational disciplines and programs were significantly more satisfied than part-time instructors from the academic groups. Second is that results of full-time faculty satisfaction measures show much less variation than those for part-time faculty, indicating that full-time faculty were much more homogenous in their opinions of satisfaction.

Despite the breadth of these data, the survey questions asked of participants may not reveal more subtle indications of satisfaction or dissatisfaction. The NSOPF 93 and NSOPF 99 surveys attempted to capture faculty satisfaction through twenty-two indicators. Given several prominent researchers' conceptualization of satisfaction as predominantly determined by the degree of professionalism and self-governance,[120] we expect the subthemes of autonomy, managed professionalism, labor flexibility, and institutional governance, all of which are affected by the growing globalization of higher education, to help explain trends in faculty satisfaction.

Defining satisfaction as the degree to which faculty perceive that the institution provides a climate corresponding to their professional expertise, Pollicino[121] and Ferrara[122] acknowledge the importance of an institutional climate respectful of *autonomy*, collegiality, and faculty workloads. Ferrara, in particular, argues that management policies affecting autonomy have a significant effect on faculty satisfaction and morale. Nickerson and Schaefer[123] observed that faculty are often attracted to work at branch campuses, rather than main campuses, because of the greater autonomy and flexibility such positions offer. In a study of faculty perceptions of administrative and government influence on curricula, Mazzoli[124] found that faculty believe out-groups to have the proper amount of influence over courses and faculty work. Despite observations of general satisfaction with the type and degree of external influence, Mazzoli recognizes that unwelcome influence may affect faculty satisfaction negatively. In short, the faculty attitudes under examination in Mazzoli's research indicate the importance of autonomy, even if out-group interventions have not compromised it.

Nixon suggests that changes in higher education, particularly transformations of faculty autonomy and the introduction of new technologies, inevitably affect professional identity.[125] Ferrara[126] noticed that an institution's technological climate can affect faculty job satisfaction. One might understand this observation by contrasting the aforementioned conceptualizations of autonomy with the concept of the *managed professional or knowledge worker.* Vallas argued that technology may reflect a trend in managerial authority, wherein technological automation undermines human labor.[127] Acknowledging a larger trend in higher education, Gary Rhoades commented on the decline of faculty autonomy through increasing administrative demands and pressures, one of which is the use of technology. Technology represents a mechanism through which faculty decisions can be controlled and, more ominously, as a means of displacing traditional professionals with "flexible" labor, a topic we address shortly.[128] Rhoades related faculty labor to other historical forms of labor exploitation, wherein technology supplanted worker autonomy and control. The expansion of managerialism and corporatism into higher education creates an ethos of professional insecurity, wherein faculty professionals espouse collective bargaining to protect their status and the quality of education they provide.[129] Providing an abstract, feminist critique of this trend, Connole[130] treats the knowledge worker as a "cyborg," in which the relationship between human labor and technology is blurred.

To promote greater efficiency and productivity within higher education, academic managers increasingly pursue *flexible instructional labor*, which is the trend toward replacing professional faculty with lower-cost, disposable part-time and adjunct instructors. The data from the NSOPF surveys indicate an increasing institutional reliance on part-time faculty. A related NCES report, *A Profile of Part-Time Faculty: Fall 1998*,[131] acknowledges the benefits and hazards of institutional reliance on flexible labor. Part-time instructors provide the institution considerable flexibility: institutions can hire instructors for the short-term, as and when needed to fulfill curricular needs. Part-time opportunities may benefit the instructor as well, especially if that individual lacks professional credentials or simply enjoys teaching as an avocation. Part-time faculty, who are paid less and receive fewer benefits than full-time faculty, may provide financial savings for the institution, but the disadvantages are numerous.[132] Part-time faculty may not possess the highest possible degrees for their fields, perform research, spend time with students outside the classroom, or be fully committed to the teaching profession.

They may also suffer financially and emotionally from reduced salaries and job security. Moreover, there are significant gender differences in the demographic composition of part-time faculty.

Exploring the economic value of labor flexibility and its associated organizational hazards, Gappa and Leslie present dozens of specific suggestions for institutions to utilize and integrate their part-time labor force effectively within the organization. Interviews with hundreds of institutional officers reveal the diversity of casual, flexible labor: the identities of part-time faculty and their relationships with the institution and its management vary significantly.[133] Benjamin[134] agrees: the use of flexible or casual labor varies within institutions, between departments and organizational divisions.

Despite these observations and cautions, Rhoades, through a content analysis of the collective bargaining agreements of 183 institutions of higher education, found significant managerial discretion in the use of part-time faculty.[135] Ultimately, according to Morgan,[136] the worker in order to survive must adapt to the changing academic climate. Morgan admits that these employees must remain occupationally and professionally flexible, and develop a comprehensive understanding of the organizational trends affecting higher education.

Smith[137] provides a broad, neo-Marxist indictment of the sociocultural hegemony and domination that the casualization of academic labor represents. Although she does not investigate higher education specifically, she does recognize that disposable workers are not served by the current shift toward the contingency of employment on productivity. Noting the decline of stability and the growing prevalence of risk in academic employment, Smith pursues an alternative employment model characterized by recognition, protection, commitment, and dignity. However, Roueche, Roueche, and Milliron argue that the existence and utilization of a part-time labor force is not an abstract philosophical idea, but an economic and organizational reality.[138] Like Gappa and Leslie, they attempt to address the problem of integration, specifically into the culture of the community college. According to Roueche, Roueche, and Milliron, all other discussions of part-time or flexible labor are secondary to issues of inequity of compensation, inequity of benefits, political marginalization within governance, and the inadequacy of tools and resources.

The transition away from hierarchically controlled structures toward the casualization of labor has important consequences for power relationships within the organization. It ultimately may challenge the capacity of academic professionals to participate in the short- and long-term decision-making processes in their institutions. Lucey argues that community colleges and their agents should model citizenship and engagement; shared governance is one way to promote those values.[139] Studying trends in community college *governance*, Kater and Levin isolated a number of governance areas, including budgeting, curricular planning, and tenure decisions.[140] They conclude that the centralization of governance has not undermined faculty participation in institutional decision making. Employment contracts actually enlarged faculty's influence, possibly indicating the increasing importance of collective bargaining for the contemporary academic laborer.

Lovell and Trought illustrate several emerging issues of community college governance, including seamless education and the integration of technology.[141] Federal financial aid policies, welfare reform legislation, and state budgetary patterns have significant implications for community college governance, but they are understudied. Levin admits that researchers need an improved understanding of the relationship between external political influences, internal governance, and faculty participation.[142] Finkelstein, Seal, and Schuster[143] agree that scholars lack reliable information about faculty's roles in institutional governance, as well as whether faculty collaboration has been supplanted by a hierarchical model of management. Students of globalization and its effects on higher education may surmise that a casualized faculty, pressured by postindustrial managerialism to prioritize labor productivity, is not permitted or does not take advantage of shared governance. Faculty transformations from autonomous professionals into lower-level human labor may pose a major challenge to labor participation in academic governance; however, current research is inconclusive.

There are, no doubt, several intangible indicators of faculty satisfaction within community colleges. Moreover, one might predict that variables are highly likely to be intensified by neo-liberal or postindustrial trends. Before one can continue to hypothesize the relationship between globalization and community college faculty, one must understand the *ethos, values, and self-identity* of the community college. Using "culture" as a proxy for organizational climate and structures, Martin and Meyerson and Smircich comprehend organizations as patterns of meaning, values, and behavior.[144] Tierney and others have applied this understanding to higher education institutions.[145] This approach helps in the understanding of the reflective relationship between the ethos of the community college and the organizational structures it implements. As external, globalizing forces, such as legislative or economic contingencies, assert themselves within higher education, one might expect the ethos or culture of the community college to evolve in tandem with its specific organizational structures.[146]

Kempner defines cultural conflict "as the opposition or antagonism among individuals over the beliefs and values they hold. When beliefs, values, and symbols of one group clash with what is significant for another group, we find cultural conflict."[147] Community colleges are foci of cultural conflict: they attempt to blend competing social values, such as social mobility and social reproduction and social justice and capitalistic production.[148] These social values also expose globalizing influences and provide another avenue through which the mechanics of globalization will reach the community college.

While there are divergent viewpoints about community college identity, the literature, in spite of Cohen and Brawer's caution that generalizations about community colleges are nearly impossible given the diversity of program offerings and the students they attract,[149] frames a rather unified vision.

Grubb notes that, compared to other institutional types, "community colleges are certainly the most varied in their students and purposes."[150] Cohen and Brawer admit that the community college, with its under-prepared students and scant opportunities for research, suffers from negative perceptions within the general public. It is frequently perceived to be an unattractive employment prospect for those immersed in the general snobbery of higher education.[151] Howard London charges that the community college bears some responsibility for educators' disinterest in employment at these institutions. According to London, the multiplication of community colleges has been a "gangling, awkward, adolescent one complete with problems of self-consciousness and self-identity."[152] Faculty have not adopted clear roles and responsibilities, which would distinguish them from high school and university faculty. Frye[153] furthers the subservient role of the community college, noting that the four-year university remains the organizational model and primary unit of analysis in studies of higher education.[154] McGrath and Spear provide an identity of the community college that indicates it is a failed four-year institution.[155]

In some distinction from traditional understandings of the community college, we view the community college as a more complex institution as it develops in the context of a political economy and within a neo-liberal framework. While it continues to serve the educational needs of a broad spectrum of students, the community college is also an instrument of the state,[156] as well as a servant of business and industry—its multiple functions[157] militate against simple or reductive identity categories. Our multiple inquiry methods into the understanding of community college faculty reflect this complexity.

We use not only a variety of research methods, referred to as mixed methods, but also a methodology that is eclectic and draws upon both qualitative and quantitative research traditions. We view these methods as complementary. Our overall approach is similar to an embedded case study. "In an embedded case study, the starting and ending points are the comprehension of the case as a whole in its real-world context. However, in the course of the analysis, the case will be faceted either by different perspectives of inquiry or by several subunits."[158] Scholz and Tietje suggest a three-tiered architecture for an embedded case study. These three levels include understanding, conceptualizing, and explaining. Understanding relates to the case itself and is tied to empathetic and intuitive methods to describe the case. In terms of *Community College Faculty: At Work in the New Economy*, this connects to our backgrounds—we are all experts of one kind or another on community college faculty work based on our own personal and professional experience and this gives us an empathetic or intuitive sense of what faculty work is and what it means. This is one of the beginning points of our study, contributing to a holistic perspective.

Conceptualizing seeks a system or model view of the case. That is, at the second level we seek theories that conceptualize the holistic perspective from the first stage. In our chapters 2 and 3 we look to other scholars for theories and concepts about community colleges, their faculty, and how both are situated in and affected by globalization, the New Economy, and neo-liberalism.

The third tier, explaining, is what we do in chapters 4, 5, 6, 7, and 8. With these chapters we explain important and valid facets of the case. These three tiers work together, defining and influencing each other. An embedded case study works in both directions through these three tiers—holistic picture of the case, conceptualizing the case, individual facets explained, with those explanations leading to new conceptualizing, which provides us with a new holistic picture. We trust that in chapter 9 we accomplish this new conceptualization.

The integration of knowledge is a central concern for embedded case studies. Given the various subprojects (both qualitative and quantitative) of an embedded case, a transparent, explicit means of integrating that knowledge must be incorporated. Scholz and Tietje offer four types of knowledge integration: disciplines, systems, interests, and modes of thought. We rely upon different disciplinary and multidisciplinary discourses and methods. We also acknowledge differing systems within community colleges. As well, there are certainly various interests that work to help integrate the book—ours as researchers and authors, those of different faculty groups, students, administrators, and policy makers. Finally, we incorporate intuitive, integrative, creative, and analytical modes of thought in the book.

Consistent with embedded case studies, Eisenhardt focuses on how to build theory from case studies.[159] The qualitative case study contributes to the discovery of new phenomena; reflects the need for a more in-depth understanding of naturalistic settings; underscores the importance of understanding context; and reveals the complexity of implementing organizational and technological change. Case studies are a valid method of analysis if the case is complex and highly contextualized and the case of community college faculty work is both complex and contextualized. Therefore, we could define *Community College Faculty: At Work in the New Economy* as a form of embedded case study.

Our research employs a variety of quantitative methods. Our examination of part-time faculty uses differences between means for various faculty groups (ANOVA, or analysis of variance) as well as weighted least squares regressions focused on job satisfaction of those same faculty groups. Our rationale for this approach derives from a particular fault line in the scholarly literature regarding part-time faculty. Qualitative studies tend to focus on faculty from traditional academic subjects, such as the humanities and social sciences. In general, part-time faculty in these areas desire full-time positions and their resulting pay, prestige, and related acceptance lead to findings of widespread exploitation and/or dissatisfaction.[160] On the other hand, quantitative analysis, with the exception of Benjamin,[161] includes part-time faculty as one group. As such, the subtleties are lost in a gross aggregate. Our work attempts to disaggregate large data sets—NSOPF 99 and 93—to illuminate more subtlety and nuance while employing quantitative analysis to capture a national picture. The motivation for disaggregation is a combination of the globalized community college and theories and descriptions of faculty labor in the New Economy.

For our work on faculty use of technology, we use data on community college faculty from the 1999 National Study of Postsecondary Faculty

(NSOPF) to describe the level of technology use by faculty and to investigate what factors are associated with greater levels. We measure technology use in three ways: use of e-mail to correspond with students, use of course websites, and the use of distance education as the means for delivery.

We then turn to regression analysis to identify which faculty characteristics, fields, and institutional characteristics are associated with greater use of technology by faculty in instruction. Our specific methods result from the form of the data used. Because our outcome variables simply take values between 0 and 1, we use logit regressions and report the odds ratio as commonly done in the higher education literature.[162] In addition, as we have multiple faculty members at each college, we use robust standard errors with clustering in all regressions to allow for correlations across observations within each college.[163]

Our research on governance utilizes document analysis and interview data from public community colleges across the United States and Canada. Consistent with an earlier study of shared governance by Levin,[164] the methodology of utilizing document analysis in a comparative case study differs from the traditional case study methodology suggested by other scholars, but is appropriate for addressing the current research. Through document analysis of collective bargaining agreements, we use cross-sectional data indexing across the data set to evaluate faculty participation in governance. Cross-sectional data indexing allows the researcher to use the same lens across the data in an effort to describe patterns and themes.[165]

Contracts representing faculty at over 300 public community colleges in the United States and Canada were reviewed. The primary data sources for the documents were the 1995–1996 and 1998–1999 and Spring 2003 Higher Education Contract Analysis System (HECAS) CD-ROMs made available by the National Education Association. Additional contracts representing colleges in the study states but not available from HECAS were obtained directly from the institutions. Different HECAS databases were utilized (NEA, 1995–1996, 1998–1999, Spring 2003) due to the time frame in which the contract analysis took place and our interest in looking at faculty participation in governance in the 1990s and beyond.

In addition to document analysis for governance, we used open-ended interviews with faculty, part-time faculty, administrators, and faculty union representatives regarding governance issues. We used two sites for these interviews in 2004, and we checked interview data against our observations on document data.

Qualitative research methods, used most notably in chapter 7, adhere to mainstream qualitative field methods for collecting and analyzing data: to ensure that data are authentic, not manufactured; representative of a sample set, whether individuals or groups or sites, and meaningful; and that findings and conclusions are both credible and coherent.[166] In data collection, we ensure that the language of documents and the words of organizational members and participants are captured accurately; in our observations, we record these and endeavor to confirm our understandings and our impressions.

We collected data from seven sites over a period of six years. These sites are given pseudonyms in order to provide anonymity for those whom we interviewed. In data analysis, we are both systematic and thorough, using such techniques as coding and clustering, in pursuit of conceptual coherence as well as seeking alternate explanations for our observations and conclusions.

We now move to the explanation of our examination of community college faculty within the context of a new, global economy. In chapter 4, we begin that explanation by addressing the role of faculty in the governance of the institution.

# 4

# Faculty and Institutional Management and Governance

The changing face of management and governance is one of the major implications of a workforce in higher education that is structured by global economic competition. As community colleges continue to respond to local economic needs and employer demands, relying more heavily on workplace efficiencies such as the increasing use of part-time labor, they have the potential to turn themselves into businesses to the detriment of their social and educational missions. An environment of high productivity, dynamic change, and competition has become the norm. Community college faculty are not only working inside the classroom but at many institutions, they are also participating with the management in institutional governance. Although governance "is the mechanism through which higher education's major stakeholders actively participate in the decisions that affect their lives within the campus community,"[1] faculty participation may be furthering the interests of the management in increasing the productivity of the institution's workforce.

In the past decade, there has been a resurgence of interest in governance primarily as the result of the effects of corporatization and globalization in higher education.[2] Corporate or bureaucratic authority threatens the professional and collegial authority of higher education faculty. Community college faculty are not immune to such pressures as commercialization, productivity and efficiency initiatives, and accountability measures generated from within their institutions. Labor relations within community colleges are undergoing alteration in response to global forces.[3] Community colleges are increasingly directing their operations toward the economic marketplace in order to acquire fiscal resources or to generate student numbers, which lead to government resources.[4] Described by John Levin as economizing behaviors, institutional shifts in strategic and operational planning that change from a focus on expanding educational and training opportunities for the local community to achieving economic goals motivated by values of efficiency and productivity have affected the governance of community colleges. "The academic world is collapsing in on itself [in the form of] job training for a consumer society" notes a faculty member at Suburban Valley Community College in California,[5] an institution that continues to weather ongoing budget cuts. Economizing behaviors do include increased faculty participation in governance because such participation entails sharing in the workload of managers—a behavior consistent with community colleges' integration into the global economy.[6] Management, in an effort to improve productivity and efficiency, has attempted to increase employee participation in governance. This shift from labor and management competition to increased cooperation among stakeholders in governance through collective bargaining has been evident in recent years.[7]

In this chapter, we consider how globalization has shaped shared governance in the community college by examining how the faculty-management contract shapes faculty work in the new economy. Because there is sparse research on community college governance, we aspire to describe shared governance in community colleges in the 1990s and into the 2000s. Governance is a complex dynamic, involving formal and informal behaviors, multiple parties, shifting structures and a myriad of rules and rituals.[8] Thus our discussion is limited. We chose unionized community colleges because of their formal, legal, contractual agreements, bargained between two parties—faculty and management. These agreements reflect at least the negotiated intentions of the two parties within the context of government legislation that both defines the institutions, legally, and sets up the parameters of the role of faculty and their relationship with management.

Although we use the term "shared governance" as do other scholars and practitioners, "shared governance" is a misnomer.[9] Legal powers are held by boards and for public institutions by boards and governments. Even in practice, this is recognized, as a faculty member in a Canadian college notes: "As a community college in Alberta [according to] legislation, faculty have very little role or authority in [the] governance of the institution . . . The only real authority is the board." Legal authority vested in management is consistent throughout public community colleges in both Canada and the United States. Managers are the legal arms of boards and governments. Yet, what we found through talking with faculty in the United States and Canada is that the term "shared governance" is used by faculty to describe institutional governance. As one faculty member involved in institutional governance at a California community college noted, "the reality is we have shared governance around here and it works pretty well." However, the term is seldom found in collective agreements—the legal documents that formalize the relationship between faculty and their college. While there is some evidence to indicate that community college faculty are not only legally permitted to participate in institutional governance but also required to participate, there is also evidence that this participation, with only a few exceptions, does not constitute authority in decision making. Indeed, with one rare exception—the legal framework of governance in British Columbia—faculty professional rights are structured by state or provincial government legislation which vests institutional authority in government, governing boards, and chief executive officers. Governance, including shared governance, in community colleges is the prerogative of management.

Recently, professional work in higher education institutions has been described as controlled by managerialism,[10] with increased emphasis on professional management, formal planning, accountability, centralized resource allocation, and directive leadership. Rosemary Deem uses the term "new managerialism" to refer to management practices and values commonly associated with the private sector.[11] In higher education, new managerialism focuses planning and operations on market-oriented behaviors, with an emphasis on entrepreneurialism.[12] Institutional behaviors are increasingly oriented to generating revenues and reducing costs, economizing behaviors which are becoming customary in community colleges.[13]

An organizational emphasis on productivity and efficiency and an orientation to the economic marketplace impact both faculty work and faculty values. One of the characteristics of professionals is their exercise of control over their working conditions. Autonomy in what work is and how it is to be accomplished is a defining characteristic of professionals.[14] Organizational patterns of new managerialism, with emphasis on productivity and efficiency, threaten faculty autonomy. The current environment of high productivity, dynamic change, and competition has become the norm for community colleges. Catherine Casey[15] suggests that an environment of increasing workloads, rapid change, and competition is an adaptive strategy for organizations and their employees in an era of postindustrial production.

We are interested in exploring how new managerialism in the current environment affects faculty work through their participation in institutional governance. Community colleges operate as professional bureaucracies where decision-making processes function as political processes of exchange.[16] We view new managerialism and its effects on shared governance in community colleges as grounded in neo-liberal ideology and altering the formal roles of faculty. Traditionally in the collective bargaining process, management and faculty have exchanged monetary rewards for productivity (teaching). We suggest that neo-liberalism enacted through new managerialism has created a new pattern of exchange—participation in governance for productivity. By viewing shared governance not only as an academic tradition but also as an exchange of goods and services, we theorize a new concept of shared governance indicative of the commodification of cooperation. In conjunction with pressures for economy and efficiency during a period of declining resources, management may be willing to share operational decision making with faculty in return for faculty productivity. Traditionally faculty have accepted the condition of higher productivity with the reward of higher salaries—"the faculty . . . has been willing to trade that high level of productivity for better salaries" notes a part-time faculty member at Suburban Valley Community College in California. But the promise of salary and benefit increases is waning under new economic imperatives. Faculty, we suspect, are accepting an increasing role in managing the institution in lieu of resource rewards.

Under a neo-liberal lens, we focus on the faculty-management relationship in institutional governance. We examine the rights, roles, and responsibilities of faculty in unionized institutions throughout the United States and Canada. We suggest that faculty are increasingly asked to take on managerial roles through participation in governance—over and above their normal teaching loads. "There are increasing expectations for faculty to participate in governance," observed a faculty member an at Alberta college. Through collective bargaining, faculty have collaborated with management in increasing their workload by participating in governance through their work on committees such as faculty hiring committees, budget committees, and long-range planning committees. While faculty unions may have assumed that they were extending the rights of faculty, they may have agreed to simply participation in a neo-liberal regime. Thus, shared governance in the community college may not be advancement in joint decision making but instead an increase in faculty work and responsibility for the management of the institution.

The traditional concept of shared governance is more of an ideal than a practice in community colleges even though organizational members may confuse sharing in decision making with faculty participation in decision making. We define *shared governance as the organizational work in public community colleges which is shared between faculty and administration*, with the role of faculty going above and beyond their traditional teaching roles. From the more traditional perspective, John Corson[17] is credited with applying the term "governance" to higher education and identifying the bicameral system of dividing decision making between faculty, who had authority over curricula, instruction, research and classroom issues, and administration, who had authority over other institutional operations such as finance, student affairs, physical plant, and public relations.[18] For community colleges, the concept of governance was more applicable to governing boards and not to the role of faculty. Unionization in the 1970s and its resultant behaviors in the 1980s pushed issues of governance off to the side, replaced by rights and responsibilities of the two parties—labor and management. Shared governance issues were eclipsed by monetary and workload concerns in collective bargaining.[19] For all of higher education, including community colleges, the end of the 1980s as well as the decade of the 1990s brought the effects of globalization, with resulting economizing behaviors such as increased emphasis on productivity and efficiency and an expanding market orientation to higher education institutions.[20] Globalization, academic capitalism, increasing governmental interaction, and organizational turbulence have affected internal and external governance patterns throughout higher education organizations.[21] This is especially the case for the community college.[22]

In examining shared governance we focus primarily on full-time faculty contracts (of which almost half include part-time faculty policies) in effect in the 1990s and early 2000s. We concentrate on full-time faculty in unionized institutions because most—94 percent—community college faculty are represented by bargaining agents of some type.[23] The language of collective agreements forms the basis of our analysis of faculty work related to governance in that the core of the legal relationship between an institution and its faculty is typically a contractual agreement, governed by contract law, which varies considerably by state and province. While describing governance issues outlined in collective agreements, we acknowledge that the agreements may not include all the terms of the contract as "employee handbooks and oral promises have been ruled to create binding contracts in some states."[24] Or, in the absence of specific language, the courts may rely on "academic custom and usage"[25] for faculty employment terms (customary practices and tradition) within higher education generally. We focus on collective agreements and the faculty–management relationship as the units of analysis for examining governance because of our interest in faculty work. While there are multiple levels and structures of governance, our emphasis is on faculty work; thus we limit our inquiry to codified language of decision making found in collective agreements.

In our research on faculty governance, we reviewed contracts representing community college faculty in 308 public institutions across 22 states in the United States and 3 Canadian provinces. We also interviewed full-time faculty, adjunct or part-time faculty, sessional faculty, and administrators in the United States and Canada. We found that as part of the new managerialism, faculty participate in institutional governance in areas including, but not limited to, those traditionally considered to be academic decisions in the framework of shared governance—where faculty retain primary responsibility for academic decisions and administration for fiscal decisions.[26]

Almost half of the collective agreements covered both full-time and part-time faculty at their respective institutions, with slightly more than half covering only full-time faculty. The large number of contracts representative of part-time faculty members is significant because part-time faculty are often considered a silent minority who bear an increasing load of teaching contact hours in community colleges.[27] While a considerable number of the contracts specifically define differences in salaries and benefits between full-time and part-time faculty, for the most part the general stipulations do not—according to the language in the documents—limit committees to full-time faculty (only) participation, although financial aspects and scheduling conflicts may create *de facto* biases toward the use of full-time faculty in governance decisions.

In order to evaluate the faculty–management relationship in shared governance we undertook a qualitative analysis of collective agreements utilizing an analytical framework developed by John Levin.[28] The process allowed us to categorize authority for decision making in contractual language as "joint action, (JA)" indicating shared decision making by faculty and management in decisions; "faculty participation, (FP)" utilized in clauses where faculty have an advisory role; "management, (M)" indicating when management and/or board representatives appear in the language as the sole decision-makers, and "silent (S)" to code issues where the issue is not addressed in the contract or the responsibility for the decision-making process is not clearly delineated. The result of the qualitative analysis is displayed in table 4.1, which allows for the creation of a descriptive explanation[29] with the

**Table 4.1** Governance areas and authority for decision making

| | FP N | JA N | % of total contracts | | M N | S N | % of total contracts |
|---|---|---|---|---|---|---|---|
| Grievance | 33 | 254 | 93 | New Positions | 15 | 267 | 92 |
| Curriculum | 166 | 3 | 55 | Program Changes | 19 | 251 | 88 |
| Evaluation | 153 | 8 | 52 | Management Hiring | 62 | 195 | 84 |
| Sabbatical | 148 | 0 | 48 | Budget | 32 | 198 | 75 |
| Retrenchment | 144 | 0 | 47 | Professional Development | 35 | 176 | 69 |
| Calendar | 123 | 3 | 41 | Tenure | 13 | 193 | 67 |
| Faculty Hiring | 116 | 1 | 38 | Faculty Hiring | 63 | 128 | 62 |
| Discipline | 116 | 1 | 38 | Discipline | 43 | 148 | 62 |
| Tenure | 102 | 0 | 33 | Calendar | 15 | 167 | 59 |
| Professional Development | 94 | 3 | 31 | Retrenchment | 100 | 64 | 53 |
| Budget | 78 | 0 | 25 | Sabbatical | 72 | 88 | 52 |
| Management Hiring | 50 | 0 | 16 | Evaluation | 61 | 86 | 48 |
| Program Changes | 38 | 0 | 12 | Curriculum | 11 | 128 | 45 |
| New Positions | 26 | 0 | 8 | Grievance | 19 | 2 | 7 |

*Note*
FP = Faculty Participation
JA = Joint Action
M = Management
S = Silent

construction of an inventory of shared governance in the community college. As described in greater detail later in the chapter, the contracts indicate a role for faculty in all areas queried in the contracts, with the largest concentration of participation in articles related to grievance proceedings, curriculum design and development, faculty evaluations, sabbatical recommendations, retrenchment proceedings, and faculty hiring.

In examining faculty work, we acknowledge that "the legal relationship between a college and its faculty is defined by an increasingly complex web of principles and authorities."[30] We suggest that untangling this web requires constant attention to the changing face of shared governance in higher education. What little research has been done on the governance of community colleges focuses primarily on the bureaucratic nature of the institution and the contentious nature of bargaining, or the effects of unionization.[31]

The early movement of faculty toward unionization in higher education began in community colleges[32] but the professional nature of faculty work with emphasis on independent thought and action was contradictory to the notion of consolidation through union activity, as centralization of decision making through collective bargaining theoretically limits faculty in their participation in governance. Unionization was seen as a threat to this participation—"employers have sought to alter the definition of working conditions as to remove many of the areas of decision-making which have, in the past, been determined by joint faculty-administrative participation, and more recently with student involvement."[33] But the rapid growth of enrollments and institutions and favorable economic and legal conditions created a positive growth environment for unionism within higher education in the mid-1960s through the 1970s.

A second phase in the history of faculty unionism began in the 1980s following the U.S. Supreme Court's *Yeshiva* decision, which sounded the death knell to private sector bargaining within academe. Political actions against unions by President Ronald Reagan continued what *Yeshiva* had started—a reduction in union activity within higher education.[34] The late 1990s marked the third and current phase in union history within higher education—a resurgence and transformation of collective bargaining with an increasing trend toward labor–management partnerships and collaborative processes as parallel systems to collective bargaining. One preceptor of increased cooperative labor–management relations has been the rise of international competition and the dominance of foreign firms in U.S. markets overseas and at home.[35]

Over the past thirty years there have been changes in bargaining issues within faculty contracts, with movement from priorities of monetary compensation (which ebbed with declining enrollments in the face of budget cuts) to personnel matters such as formalizing tenure policies and strengthening the role of faculty in institutional governance. "Faculty members desired a greater degree of participation in decision-making and sought entry into formal decision-making structures when collegial governance mechanisms were unable to satisfy their needs."[36]

Community college governance has been described as having an "emphasis on control and efficiency [which] reflects a top-down approach to decision-making . . . developed by central administrators."[37] But an autocratic system does not reflect the reality of governance that community college faculty experience at many institutions. The unique mission, culture, and identity of the community college within the postsecondary landscape suggest an appropriate use of a mixed model for describing governance in community colleges.[38] Participation in governance may be seen as a move to collegial decision-making processes within the professional bureaucracy of community colleges, where common interests motivate outcomes and shared norms dictate how decisions are translated into action.[39] Faculty in the United States and Canada reiterate their part in institutional governance. "Faculty have historically been involved in governance" noted a faculty member at an Alberta college.

Our research on faculty involvement in governance has implications for the expansion of the concept of shared governance within the framework of globalization. Our governance research focuses on a sample of areas where work between faculty and administration is shared: faculty are an integral part of the operations of the institutions through their participation in governance. These behaviors, if viewed as economizing behaviors, provide a framework for reconceptualizing shared governance as a behavior responsive to and consistent with the global economy.[40] Organizational behaviors driven by economic values and rationalized by improvement in efficiency and productivity are described as economizing behaviors and are desired outcomes of bureaucratic decision-making processes.[41]

Economizing behaviors are codified into the legal language of collective bargaining agreements most commonly through language in the Management Rights clauses which speak of management's right to direct personnel and use resources to ensure effective operation of the institution or district. An example is Brevard (Florida) Community College's 1999 contract: "*the Employer Exclusively retains and reserves the rights to . . . take such measures as management may consider to be reasonably necessary to the orderly, efficient, and economical operation of the College*" (NEA, 1998–99, Article 7). The bargaining agreement for Blackhawk Technical College in Illinois states "*the purpose of the Agreement is to promote harmony, cooperation and efficiency in the working relationship between the parties . . .*" (NEA, 1998–99, Article II). It seems that labor relations within institutions have been altered to meet the economic, social, political, and cultural changes facing community colleges.

In looking broadly—both conceptually and geographically—we see that community college faculty are engaged in shared governance in both the traditional academic areas such as faculty evaluation, curriculum, sabbatical and tenure recommendations, and in nontraditional areas such as budget and retrenchment decisions. Faculty engagement in decision making across all areas of the institution suggests that the boundaries within the academic dualism of governance[42] are less rigid than the literature implies.

Community college faculty, based on the legal language of the contracts, which "are primary factors establishing the legal parameters of managerial direction and of professional autonomy, involvement, and constraint in the academic work place,"[43] are engaged in institutional governance. The historical conception of the community college as a bureaucratic and autocratic institution[44] places faculty in a position of limited power in institutional decision making. However, we find that centralization of decision making through collective bargaining has not limited faculty in their participation in governance, but rather through contractual agreements they have expanded their influence and their participation in governance in a number of areas.[45]

Community college faculty involvement in governance extends beyond the traditional limitation of participation in academic decisions. While it was beyond the scope of this book to determine the structural configuration of participation in governance (through academic senates, advisory councils), collective bargaining has codified the actions of faculty in their participation in governance. The authority of faculty and administration, no doubt, varies according to the governance issue at hand, especially given the ideals of shared governance.[46] Over half of the contracts outlined a process for faculty participation in traditional areas of shared governance such as curriculum and faculty evaluation, areas of primary faculty responsibility as suggested in the joint statement on college and university governance by the AAUP/AGE/AGB.[47] Almost half of the contracts stipulated a role for faculty in decisions outside of the traditional academic areas, such as retrenchment. In ancillary areas of governance such as the college calendar, grievance, and discipline, over one-third of the institutions represented by the contracts involved faculty in decision making in these governance areas.

The primary areas of faculty input based on collective agreements are in curriculum, evaluation, grievance, sabbatical leaves, and retrenchment decisions. Grievance was the most common category coded as "joint action." Where the contract language called for both sides to commit to binding arbitration as the final step in the grievance process, both sides argue with equal representation and surrender authority to an impartial arbitrator. While the majority of "joint action" articles pertained to binding arbitration, there are instances outside of the grievance process where faculty and management participate jointly in decision making. An example is Brevard County (Florida) Community College's contract in effect through June, 1999 where a joint committee of six faculty and six administrators were given joint authority to modify a faculty performance plan.

One-quarter to one-half of the contracts contained language that specified faculty involvement in faculty hiring, calendar, disciplinary hearings, tenure, professional development, and budget decisions. Budgetary input ranged from department-level input to general institutional recommendations in determining short and long-range fiscal priorities: "*the allocation of resources among competing demands is central in the formal responsibility of the governing board, in the administrative authority of the President, and in the educational function of the Faculty. These three components should therefore have a voice in the determination of short and long-range priorities*" (Camden County Community College, NEA, 1998–99). Suburban Valley Community College in California has joint labor and management development processes and forums where people meet together on specific issues. As one member of the joint committee at Suburban Valley notes "we might meet to talk together about the budget process, not necessarily who gets the dollars, but how you make that decision."

There are regional and institutional differences between faculty participation as specified by the collective agreements and validated by faculty interviews. As shown in figure 4.1, provinces and states with institutions having a higher percentage of faculty participation in governance are found more often in the east and west regions of the United States and in British Columbia, Canada. The states with the highest percentage of artifacts coded for faculty participation include Minnesota, Washington, Massachusetts, Maryland, Rhode Island, Oregon, Michigan, New York, and California in the United States, and in British Columbia in Canada—where the Education Council, with faculty as of the major group of its members, has legislative authority in decision making.

These findings are consistent with Richard Hurd, Jennifer Bloom, and Beth Johnson's evaluation of the top ten states for faculty union membership in higher education (combining two-year and four-year institutions, public and private) which include eight of the states listed above.[48]

The concentration of faculty participation represented by contracts in western institutions, representing California, Oregon, and Washington, may also be the result of isomorphism,[49] with California having enacted AB 1725 in 1988, designed to introduce more collegial governance practices into

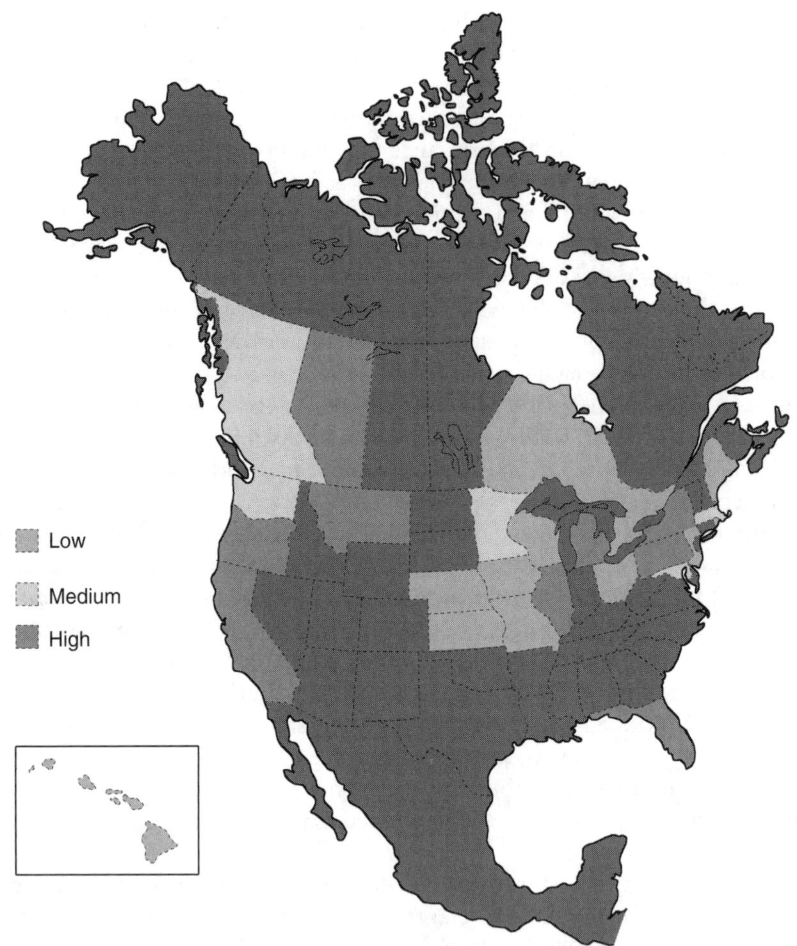


**Figure 4.1** Highest concentration of faculty participation in governance by jurisdiction

California's community colleges.[50] However, while Washington, Oregon, and California are among the higher tier states in the degree of faculty participation in governance prescribed by the contracts, Hawaii, which may be considered a western state, ranks near the bottom of the list in faculty participation, and was noted as a state in which the appointed Board of Regents of the University of Hawaii (which has legal responsibility for all public institutions of higher education in the state) serves at the pleasure of the governor, and whose collective agreement indicates little faculty involvement in governance.[51]

Although the term "shared governance" is rarely used, a majority of contracts refer to faculty participation in decision making and provide formal structures to implement governance processes. In the one North American exception (British Columbia), faculty in this province actually do share in the governance of the colleges, as already noted. Collective agreements in British Columbia have a clearly identified role for faculty to participate in institutional governance. Furthermore, legislation in the province has clearly set roles for faculty, not just to participate in institutional governance but to share authority with management in several domains. Faculty members constitute the largest sub-group of the twenty member group on the Education Council—an institutional decision-making body. Faculty also have representation on the governing board. The Council has an advisory role on all educational policy matters and the power to set academic standards, set curriculum content for courses (provided that actions do not contravene the government minister's policies for postsecondary education or training). In British Columbia, which is an exception to other Canadian provinces and the United States, collective agreements and legislation recognize that faculty have a considerable role in institutional governance.[52]

Other examples of participatory language include Lower Columbia College's (Washington) 1994–97 contract which states "*the Governance Council shall advise the Board of Trustees and the College administration on all matters which may significantly affect faculty-board, faculty-administration, faculty-faculty, or faculty-student interaction*" (NEA, 1995–96, Article CVII, 107 B. f.). The contract for Grant MacEwan College in Alberta specifically notes that the college endorses participation in decision making. Less formally, Bellevue Community College's (Washington) 1991–93 contract states "*it is agreed that administrative structures shall provide for faculty involvement and participation in institutional affairs*" (NEA, 1995–96, Article VI, Section II) but does not specifically define the governance structures.

In addition to regional differences in faculty participation, there are variances related to traditional, nontraditional, and ancillary areas of shared governance. The traditional areas of shared governance include peer review, curriculum, and academic decisions. Contractually we found that faculty are participants either in the faculty performance evaluation process via peer review or in design and implementation of the evaluation instruments. For example, the Maine Technical College System contract stipulates that the "*evaluation process shall be developed by Administrative Faculty Development Committee with the approval of the college faculty president*" (Article 5B, NEA, 1998–99). Flathead Valley Community College's (Montana) contract states "*the College and Association agree to implement an instructor evaluation process for pro and post-tenured faculty that is developed jointly and mutually agreed upon*" (Article 11.00 B, NEA, 1998–99). Brevard Community College's contract specifies committee membership, meeting schedules, and committee responsibilities and authority.

> *A joint committee of six (6) faculty appointed by UFF-BCC [United Faculty of Florida—Brevard Community College] and six (6) BCC Administrators/ Professionals chaired by the faculty and administration will meet at least once a year to review the Performance Enhancement Plan and its forms. Any changes in*

> *the Performance Enhancement Plan must be agreed to by more than two-thirds (⅔) of the entire twelve (12) person committee.* (Article 13, section 3, NEA, 1998–99)

In the province of Alberta, the collective agreement for Lethbridge Community College requires faculty participation in faculty evaluation. The participatory nature of these clauses can be contrasted with the stronger management position found in other contracts, such as "*teaching faculty members shall be evaluated whenever deemed necessary by the administration*" (Finger Lakes Community College, New York, Article VII, NEA, 1998–99).

In the tradition of shared governance the assumption is that faculty, due to their status as professionals, have the responsibility of determining the delivery and content of curricular offerings within institutions. Within contracts with provisions for faculty involvement in curriculum development, the language tends to be stronger than in other governance areas in which faculty are involved. Often delineated under "Faculty Rights" articles, phrases such as "*faculty are expected to participate*" (NEA, 1998–99, Gogebic Community College, Michigan), the "*District shall consult,*" "*curriculum development is a shared responsibility*" (NEA, 1995–96, McHenry Community College, Illinois), and "*faculty have the right to determine curriculum policy*" (NEA, 1998–99, Sullivan Community College, New York) are frequently descriptions of the role of faculty in curricular matters.

Numerous contracts contain language which specifies a role for faculty in general institutional decision making as demonstrated by Broward County (Florida) Community College's 1995–98 contract which states "*wherever possible, campus decisions shall be the result of dialogues between relevant administrative, departmental, and affected faculty and staff*" (Article 2.92, NEA, 1998–99). Massachusetts Community College Council's contract, in effect between 1990 and 1993, stipulates the creation of a "*Joint Study Committee to resolve matters of concern, contract issues, identify root causes of problems*" (Article IIA. 01) and outlines a governance structure that "*shall provide for an open forum for discussion and information sharing for the purpose of providing the President of the college with advisory input prior to the promulgation of college policy*" (Article IVA.01, NEA, 1998–99).

The hiring of new faculty is another traditional area of shared governance. Over one-third of the contracts allow for, at a minimum, an advisory role for faculty in the hiring of new faculty either through recommendations and advice to administration or through more active participation via participation on selection committees (although the contracts often do not stipulate the breakdown of committee members in terms of numbers or percentage of faculty/administration). Camden County Community College in New Jersey provides an example of strong faculty participation in the selection of faculty.

> *Faculty status and related matters are shared responsibility. The faculty in each academic department shall annually elect three of its tenured members to serve as a committee which shall share equal responsibility with departmental chairpersons who shall be a member of it, and with the President or his designee, in the*

> *interviewing and selection of new faculty in that academic department.* (Article XXVI, NEA, 1998–99)

Finally, in traditional areas of shared governance, language requiring promotion and tenure recommendations by faculty appear contractually in slightly over one-third of the artifacts. Most commonly, the contracts describe tenure review or promotion and tenure committee functions, providing an avenue for faculty to make formal recommendations to administration for promotion and retention of peers.

Faculty are involved not only in the traditional areas of academic governance such as curriculum and faculty evaluation but also in other (nontraditional) areas traditionally reserved for administration, such as retrenchment, budget, long-term planning, and management hiring. Washington State's Lower Columbia Community College's contract serves as an example of contractual language that gives faculty advisory responsibility for areas outside of the traditional academic decisions. Lower Columbia's Governance Council consists of members of the College Faculty Association's Executive Council and equal numbers of administrators appointed by the president. The charge of the council is to serve as an advisory body to the Board on all matters of shared governance, extending beyond faculty–management relations.

> *Advise the Board of Trustees and the College administration on all matters which may significantly affect faculty-board, faculty-administration, faculty-faculty or faculty-student interaction. Such matters will include but not be limited to changes in educational policies and or/procedures . . . remodeling or construction of physical facilities, new or modified fiscal, budgetary, long-range planning, etc.* (Article 107 C, NEA, 1995–96)

Budget decisions at the institutional and/or departmental levels are actions not necessarily attached to traditional understandings of academic governance, yet approximately one-quarter of the contracts refer to faculty involvement in budget processes. Consistent with other governance issues, the state of faculty input varies from relatively weak language such as "*faculty shall be allowed to participate*" in budgetary decisions (Southwestern Community College, Iowa, NEA, 1995–96) and "*the role of such Faculty at these [budget] meetings shall normally be limited to observing, clarifying, advising, and providing a Faculty perspective*" (NEA, 1998–99, Broward County Community College, Florida, Article 2.91 D) to the stronger position as seen in colleges where faculty are involved in developing institutional budgets.

Almost half of the contracts stipulate involvement of the faculty association or senate in retrenchment proceedings. The 1995–98 faculty contract for Edison State Community College in Ohio states that as a result of financial exigency or discontinuation or curtailment of an academic program, a preliminary report shall be submitted to the affected unit(s) and to the president of the Association (Article XVIII, a., b., NEA, 1998–99). Central Ohio Technical College's 1993–95 contract, consistent with many other institutions with faculty participation in retrenchment, states that faculty recommendations regarding proposed retrenchment "*shall be considered by the College administration before implementing a reduction in staff*" (Article XII, B. 3, NEA, 1998–99).

The other areas where faculty participate in governance outside of traditional academic decisions include long-term planning, management hiring, and policy recommendations. An example of language codifying faculty participation in long-term planning is found in Jackson Community College's (Michigan) contract which states "*long-range institutional planning shall be conducted cooperatively by the Administration and the Faculty*" (Jackson Community College, Article XIII, NEA, 1998–99). Mid-Michigan's 1996–99 contract states that the Faculty Senate will be "*involved in all long-range planning*" (NEA, 1998–99, Article XIII). Another area of faculty participation noted contractually is policy making, for which the Minnesota State Colleges and Universities agreement with United Technical College Educators (1995–97) outlines the governance role of the senate: "*the purpose of the Senate is to provide a forum for campus faculty to act in full partnership with campus administration in determination of campus operations, policy and planning prior to decision making*" (Article 9, NEA, 1998–99). Indeed, the faculty senate provides the formal structure for faculty participation in governance at many institutions.

Consistent with their role in the hiring of personnel, faculty in a number of institutions contractually are expected to participate in the selection of management employees. Faculty may be required to serve on selection committees for varying levels of administrators and also may be involved in the development of criteria for selection of management employees as evidenced by Washington State's Whatcom Community College's 1991–93 contract (NEA, 1995–96). Overall, in management hiring decisions, 16 percent of the contracts called for faculty involvement.

Outside of the traditional and nontraditional areas for shared governance, faculty are expected to participate in governance in other areas such as calendar decisions, disciplinary actions, and grievance. One-hundred twenty-five of the contracts stipulated that faculty had at a minimum advisory input into scheduling of the annual academic calendar with some (for example, the Community College of Spokane, Washington State's) stating that the academic calendar must be developed by mutual agreement of the faculty association and the board of trustees (NEA, 1995–96).

While faculty participate in governance in traditional, nontraditional, and ancillary areas of governance, management typically retains a broad spectrum of rights specifically stated in "management rights" clauses and by state statute or provincial legislation. Management rights clauses in contracts range from the broad, "*it is the responsibility of the Board to administer the schools within the district in accordance with Wisconsin Statutes, Chapter 38, and in conformance with the Constitution and Laws of the State of Wisconsin and the Constitution and Laws of the United States of America*" of Madison Area Technical College's (Wisconsin) 1992–2000 contract (Article II, NEA,

1998–99), to the very specific. In Florida, Brevard Community College's (1999) management rights "and prerogatives" exemplify the specificity of management's authority.

> The Employer expressly reserves and retains, to the maximum extent permitted by law, each and every right and prerogative that it has ever had and enjoyed at any time in the absence of any collective bargaining relationship whatsoever, whether exercised or not, and as if the collective bargaining relationship did not in fact exist . . .

Overall, in 55 percent of the contracts, the variables for governance areas were not addressed nor was there any indication of the process for decision making. We suggest that the absence of any contract language in many governance areas in collective agreements gives management broad rights and supports the characteristics of new managerialism.

Management, in an effort to improve productivity and efficiency, has attempted to increase employee participation in governance.[53] Although governance is viewed as a collaborative process"[54] and there is a pronounced shift from a condition of faculty and management competition to collaboration,[55] the ends of collaboration and cooperation are largely those of management. Thus we suspect that collective agreement language that specifies faculty responsibilities does not so much enable faculty to exercise their expertise as it compels faculty to act for managerial ends. In this sense, community college faculty are "managed professionals."[56]

We argue that, formally, community college faculty are expected to increase their participation in institutional governance largely to fit the institution to the requirements of a globally competitive economy. As resources decline in public institutions of higher education, an emerging commodity available to management in exchange for increased production by faculty may be participation in decision making. Thus, we now question whether shared governance in the community college is an academic ideal which upholds the professionalization of the workforce or a neo-liberal activity imposed by management to foster efficiency and effectiveness by engaging faculty in management work.

# 5

# Faculty Use of Instructional Technology and Distributed Learning

*Veronica Diaz and John Cheslock*

Community colleges are increasing the learning options offered to students in an effort to respond to new markets for networked and remote learning. Such alterations have implications for faculty and for faculty work as new educational technologies are embraced and institutional behaviors evolve. Educational technology has grown and evolved from correspondence in the early 1900s to more sophisticated delivery systems including videotapes, television, satellite, and eventually the Internet and the World Wide Web by the 1990s.[1] Through the 1990s, however, colleges and universities underwent a major change: a shift in emphasis from the computer as a desktop tool to the computer as the communications gateway to colleagues and "content" (databases, image and text libraries, video, and the like) made increasingly accessible via computer networks.[2] These developments were applied to instruction and student learning became decentralized from traditional formats, such as classroom instruction, labs, and lectures. These learning developments are expected to continue in the next decade to the extent that potentially profound and unavoidable advances in technology—particularly in computing capability, connectivity, bandwidth, software development, and digitized content—are expected to be vehicles of change for higher education.[3]

In this chapter, we examine the utilization of technology in instruction by faculty at community colleges. Reflecting the theme of this book, we argue that one must consider the context of the New Economy in performing such an examination. For example, economic pressures will influence how much and what type of technology is chosen. In addition, these pressures will influence where the technology is situated within the community college and which faculty members actually staff courses using technology.

In addition to outlining the possible influences of the New Economy on how technology is integrated into instruction at community colleges, we also provide empirical evidence using the 1998–99 National Study of

Postsecondary Faculty (NSOPF). We start by describing the level of use of technology among community college faculty. Such descriptions are important because, as we later discuss in more detail, technology structures the work life of faculty in important ways.[4] In addition, we examine differences in technology use across faculty to see whether their work reflects pressures from the New Economy. We are particularly interested in the differences in community college faculty on the basis of their disciplines and work status.

As a prelude to our discussion of how the New Economy influences the use of technologically enhanced instruction at community colleges, we introduce the concept of distributed learning. Distributed learning is a broad category of activity descriptive of the intersection between instructional processes and technology. This intersection has produced an instructional model that allows instructors, students, and content to be located in different, noncentralized locations so that instruction and learning can occur independent of time and place.

Such a model deviates from the traditional classroom model that has historically dominated instruction. The traditional model consists of one instructor and students within the same physical space. The customary reliance upon this method of instruction is one reason why there is debate and discussion indicating that higher education faces a "cost disease" relative to other industries.[5] Higher education has experienced slow growth in productivity due to the labor requirements of instruction. In the traditional classroom, the quality of instruction is difficult to maintain if the amount of labor is reduced over time, or if the number of students served increases. A rather different setting exists for the production of automobiles and food, for example, where technological improvements have allowed the same number of workers to produce a larger number of goods. Consequently, these other industries are able to offer their products at much lower costs and increase the wages of their workers, which forces higher education institutions to also increase wages to attract quality personnel to the profession.[6] If colleges simply rely upon the traditional classroom model of instruction, then their costs will rise as salaries increase and the size of the workforce does not decrease.

The use of technology, however, allows community colleges to change the production process in instruction in fundamental ways. A discussion of distributed learning in the aggregate, however, hides the diversity of options available within this category. Table 5.1 displays eight different forms of distributed learning constructed from various sources of literature on the growth of distributed learning activities.[7] Each of these categorized activities utilizes varying degrees of institutional resources, technical skill, instructional and curricular expertise, and involves various constituents.

The first category, basic technology used for instructional purposes (table 5.1, activity #1), supplements the traditional classroom model through the use of the Internet and projection camera within the classroom or the use of e-mail and course websites outside of the classroom. The latter tools allow additional communication and instruction to take place independent of time and location. Because these forms of technology are not used to replace the

**Table 5.1** The distributed learning continuum

| Distributed learning activity | Example/Description | Use of institutional resources | Technical expertise required |
|---|---|---|---|
| 1. Basic technology used for instructional purposes | Projection cameras, electronic presentations, Internet, e-mail, video | Low (varies depending on medium) | Low/ medium |
| 2. Instructional labs | Discipline-based labs in which faculty members develop (commercially unavailable) software to be used in converted instructional environments (from lecture to a self-paced, on-line format) | High | High |
| 3. On-line courses (faculty-produced/hosted) | Courses conducted using faculty-developed web pages/hosted on faculty or institutional site | Low/ medium | Very high |
| 4. On-line courses (institutionally-hosted) | Courses conducted using commercially-developed course management systems (i.e., WebCT, Blackboard) or institutionally-developed products | High | Medium |
| 5. Learning Management Systems (LMS) | LMS typically provide capabilities for all types of learning events: home pages for students, classroom resource management, on-line student enrollment, records and content keeping, integration of third party content, testing, and delivery of electronic courses | High | Very high |
| 6. Content Management Systems (CMS) | The CMS's objective is to simplify the creation and administration of on-line content (articles, text, images, audio) used in the instructional process | High | High |
| 7. Learning Content Management Systems (LCMS) | The LCMS (mostly web-based) are used to author, approve, publish, and manage (learning content more specifically referred to as learning objects) | High | Very high |
| 8. Digital Repositories | Multimedia Educational Resource for Learning and On-line Teaching (MERLOT): a free and open resource designed primarily for faculty and students of higher education with links to on-line learning materials along with annotations, such as peer reviews and assignments | High | Very high |

classroom model but simply to augment traditional instruction, the primary benefit is intended to be increased quality of instruction, and not cost savings. Indeed, expenses will rise due to the cost of the technological infrastructure required to support such activities. These infrastructure costs are likely to be non-trivial if community colleges expect that course websites will be used widely. A course management system, which requires an investment of institutional resources, will be needed for faculty members to upload documents or enter content directly into a web template, with ease.

Another type of distributed learning (activity #3 and #4), on-line courses, is a more substantial deviation from the traditional classroom model of instruction. In this setting, most if not all of the entire course takes place on-line, and thus the method of instruction is less dependent upon time and location. This mode of instruction is more far-reaching in its implications. Perhaps, the principal impact occurs through increased access by students who find the available traditional classroom instruction difficult to attend due to geographical or time constraints. Consequently, community colleges can reach additional students and gain access to a different set of revenues through the use of on-line courses.[8]

Instruction at a distance that uses on-line courses has a substantial impact on the production process for instruction. In this setting, course materials take on greater importance than in a traditional one. In a physical classroom, an instructor can meet students without instructional materials beyond the lecture and continue to be able to deliver the course. In cyberspace, this becomes more difficult and course materials begin to embody or encapsulate many of the processes of the physical classroom. Because creating course material for an on-line course can be a time-intensive endeavor, community colleges will likely seek to avoid the high costs of course development by using the same material for numerous courses. Consequently, when community colleges establish their distance education programs to the point where efficiency adjustments can be instituted, these courses will often have separate instructors for the development of the course materials and the actual instruction of the students.

This alternative production process may have important financial implications for community colleges. First, the costs of instruction may change. The digitization and standardization of content would allow institutions to rely upon fewer full-time faculty members to develop the course material and then supervise numerous part-time instructors who teach the courses. Such staffing patterns reduce labor costs due to the greater reliance on part-time instructors. On-line courses can also reduce expenditures by decreasing the need for physical classrooms to house instruction. The extent to which overall cost savings are realized, however, depends upon the degree to which these savings are outweighed by the labor and equipment costs needed to maintain the technological infrastructure required to support on-line courses. The potentially high costs of this infrastructure are demonstrated by the proliferation of learning technology managers and support staff housed in centers with teams of highly skilled professionals including instructional technologists, media technicians, visual and web designers, web programmers, and accessibility specialists.[9]

Without a substantial investment in the required infrastructure, community colleges have difficulty creating a large number of distance education courses. An institution can make a substantial investment and rely upon individual faculty members to produce, develop, and host the on-line courses only with a faculty that possesses a high level of technical expertise. Indeed, if an institution expects widespread implementation of on-line courses or programs, it will need to provide commercially developed course management systems or institutionally developed products (table 5.1, #4 activity) along with support personnel so that faculty with lower levels of technical expertise can participate.[10] Such an approach may generate greater revenue and increase access for certain types of students through the widespread use of technology, but it may be expensive and not reduce the costs of instruction significantly.

On-line education can also impact the revenue generated by a community college. Because some students cannot enroll in on-campus courses due to time and geographical considerations, on-line courses allow community colleges to gain access to a new set of students and their associated tuition and state appropriation dollars. Colleges can generate revenues from the creation of standardized course material that can be sold to other schools. Institutions of higher education are increasingly purchasing already established on-line courses from other institutions or from for-profit businesses rather than develop their own on-line courses.[11] To facilitate this activity, the Monterey Institute for Technology and Education is developing the National Repository of On-line Courses. In addition, the League for Innovation in the Community College helps institutions trade courses through its Specialty Asynchronous Industry Learning project.[12] The extent to which community colleges can generate revenue through selling their courses is not clearly established; however, this opportunity will likely have implications for resource-stressed schools.

In line with production processes and revenue generation, the broader sociopolitical context is an important influence on the use of instructional technology within community colleges. While technology has modified the instructional options available to community colleges over the past two decades, the rapid rate of technological progress has also reshaped the broader economy in several ways that have affected community colleges. Rapid reductions in transportation and communication costs result in companies becoming much more geographically mobile, pressuring federal and state governments to reduce government spending to attract employers. Concurrently, institutions of higher education face greater student demand because the return to education has grown substantially. The growth in the payoff to education is part of a general trend toward greater income inequality, which some economists partially attribute to rapid technological change.[13] In addition to increasing the general return to education, the fast pace of technological change rapidly alters the skills required to compete in the workforce. Consequently, more students seek to take courses periodically for specific training, behaviors especially important for community colleges that often provide these services. Together, these trends point to the pressures from the New Economy that have forced community colleges to educate more students without increased resources from the government.

Manuel Castells identifies the New Economy as informational in that the productivity and competitiveness of units or agents in this economy depend upon their capacity to generate, process, and apply knowledge-based information efficiently.[14] Because higher education institutions are the premier knowledge-based producers, and disseminators of knowledge in the case of community colleges, the new economic context will provide these institutions with considerable pressures and challenges. Increased global competitiveness and an increasing focus on productivity are altering community colleges in important ways.[15] Castells notes that the "generalization of knowledge-based production and management to the whole realm of economic processes on a global scale requires fundamental social, cultural, and institutional transformations."[16]

In *Globalizing the Community College: Strategies for Change in the Twenty-First Century*, John Levin echoes Castells' perspective in discussing the role of globalization on the actions of community colleges.[17] Consistent with the trend of stagnant government funding along with greater student demand, community colleges are asked to serve more students without the provision of additional resources. At the same time, the mission of the community college has shifted from student and community betterment to a workforce development model that seeks to serve the "global economy."[18] In such an environment, increased emphasis on productivity and efficiency and further restructuring, marketization, and commodification are expected. Levin notes numerous changes, such as colleges' participation in contract training partnerships with local and foreign businesses and governments, rising tuition and fees, increased reliance upon donations from the private sector, a new focus on vocational programs (that is, allied health, business technology, and manufacturing), and a greater reliance on part-time faculty.[19]

Levin also presents evidence to show that the implementation of distributed learning is spreading rapidly in public community colleges and suggests that this growth reflects pressures from the greater economy.[20] Cristie Roe outlines three factors that impact the selection and implementation of information technology within community colleges.[21] The first involves government policies that provide incentives for community colleges to generate revenue, become more efficient, and meet the needs of business and industry for skilled labor. With respect to the provision of a skilled workforce, community colleges are under pressure to produce graduates who are employable[22] especially in the numerous jobs recently created that require mid-level management or technical skills.[23] Levin finds that state and provincial governments directly promoted the use of information technologies in teaching and learning because their officials and leaders make a number of assumptions about students and the needs of the economy.

> [T]here are new students with different learning styles and needs from the past; there are fewer or at least not increasing funds available for public institutions, and therefore higher productivity or greater efficiencies or both must be realized by institutions; and the world of work—business and industry—requires well-trained and technologically savvy workers.[24]

As discussed earlier, the general infrastructure costs associated with the use of technology in instruction cast doubt on the proposition that greater use of technology will result in greater efficiencies and lower costs. However, little doubt exists that the hope of possible efficiencies partially propels the increasing use of technology in instruction.

The second factor driving the use of information technology identified by Roe is the demands by community college constituents who want training in specific areas and flexibility in time, location, and pedagogical methods.[25] These demands are both for greater use of technology within the classroom as well as increased course offerings through distance education, and they are especially important when considered in combination with two additional trends. First, community colleges are increasingly making instructional decisions based on the preferences of their "consumers."[26] Second, the number of individuals who want additional education is rising steadily. As discussed earlier, the growing financial return on education as well as the imperative for updating one's skills to meet the changing requirements of the labor market should increase the number of students who seek college admissions. In addition, demographic trends in many states (especially those in the southeast and southwest) result in a significant increase in the number of high-school graduates.[27] Given the limited availability of space at four-year institutions, considerable pressure will be placed on community colleges to accommodate these additional students.

The final factor driving the use of technology identified by Roe is the response by community colleges to the expanding demands of their socioeconomic environment.[28] Of special interest is the movement within community colleges to a more managerial or business-like culture, and the focus of community colleges on the needs of business and industry rather than the local community.[29] Within that context, the promise of a new instructional approach that can increase efficiency and improve workforce development is and will continue to be attractive.

We have thus far discussed the community college as a whole rather than as an organization that contains multiple units and departments that differ in important ways. This aggregate analysis hides several complexities regarding how the use of instructional technology is impacted by the increasing focus on workforce development, student preferences, and the needs of business and industry. Within community colleges, these trends should result in growth for those fields that teach courses that provide skills rewarded in the marketplace; this growth occurs at the expense of those fields that teach courses less directly tied to the workplace.[30]

Fields closer to the economic marketplace, however, may enjoy an even greater advantage in distance education courses. First, community colleges seeking to use technology to reach the goal of improved workforce development will invest resources in those courses and programs that provide material viewed as vital to the greater economy.[31] For example, fields that teach skills in demand by business and industry will be considered for investment, especially if community colleges can establish profitable contracts with employers to train their workers at a distance. In addition, fields that support industry such as education and nursing, which are required for future workforce development and lower health care costs, are also likely to be favored, although their stature as feminized fields may work against them.[32] A second reason for substantial differences across fields involves varying student demand. Students who seek courses containing content more directly tied to the workplace may be constrained by time and place as a result of their current employment.

Several practical considerations also contribute to differences across disciplinary fields in the use of instructional technology. For example, course content in some subject areas is more or less amenable to the use of technology. That is, students require technology in engineering courses where its use facilitates and enhances the learning process and future employability of students. In addition, the faculty within certain fields may have greater knowledge and training in technology, which would make it easier for these faculty members to use technology in instruction. Kenneth Green finds evidence that among community college faculty, those in occupational programs, business, and biological and physical sciences are better prepared to participate in distributed learning activities while those in education, humanities, and social sciences are the least prepared.[33] These differences across fields exist for three reasons. First, the nature of undergraduate and graduate education varies across subject areas with some fields more likely to use technology and consequently expose future faculty members to technology. Second, the self-selection of individuals interested and experienced in various forms of technology into fields of study where technology is more heavily used will also contribute to differences. Third, community colleges may exert greater effort, for a variety of reasons such as student demand, into training faculty in some fields relative to others.

Some limited evidence suggests that important differences across fields do exist. Early distance education programs served high technology professionals who could not attend courses on campus but needed to stay current in their field.[34] Levin finds that technology was not used extensively in traditional arts and sciences fields, but was more common in fields such as nursing and business.[35] Gary Rhoades provides additional evidence that faculty in the humanities and social sciences fared poorly because resources in these fields were diverted toward investment in educational hardware and software.[36]

We end this discussion of how pressures from the new economy influence the use of instructional technology by examining which faculty by employment status (full and part-time), discipline, and other characteristics produce distance education courses. On-line courses could be staffed in ways similar to those in the traditional classroom setting where the instructor plays an important role in all aspects of producing the course. But as discussed earlier, the enhanced importance of course materials within distance education increases the likelihood that the production of instruction will be unbundled with different instructors handling different aspects of the course. Karen Paulson disaggregates instruction into five activities: designing the course and curriculum, developing the course and curriculum, delivering the subject material, mediating the learning process, and assessing individual student learning.[37] In table 5.2, we illustrate how instruction may be disaggregated and how distributed learning mechanisms discussed in table 5.1 are used to facilitate this function.

**Table 5.2** The disaggregation of the instructional function via distributed learning

| Instructional function |
|---|
| *Designing* the course or curriculum |
| *Developing* the course or curriculum by selecting appropriate instructional methods and course materials, or creating those course materials |
| *Delivering* the subject matter previously selected either in person (lectures, etc.) or through the use of various forms of media |
| *Mediating* (also called "tutoring") the learning process, which helps students understand materials in ways tailored to their individual learning styles and levels of understanding |
| *Assessing* individual student learning through appropriate methods and assignments designed to certify the attainment of a given level of competence |

*Source*: Karen Paulson, "Refiguring Faculty Roles for Virtual Settings," *Journal of Higher Education* 73, no. 1 (2002): 123–140.

The first two activities—*designing* the course or curriculum and *developing* the course or curriculum—could be unbundled from the last three—*delivering* the subject matter, *mediating* the learning process, and *assessing* individual student learning—so that an instructor could perform the first two steps and then supervise numerous part-time instructors who staff separate sections of the course and perform the final three steps. Similarly, an institution could outsource some of the instructional activities.[38] Outsourcing is consistent with community college behaviors already noted by Levin as patterns of globalization.[39] Now, there is privatization not only for such services as janitorial, food services, and groundskeeping but also for the core function, which is teaching. The implications for faculty are both serious and legion.

Given the movement toward a more managerial and business-like culture, the pressure to reduce labor costs is considerable at community colleges.[40] These institutions have increasingly relied upon part-time faculty to reduce costs for education in general,[41] but there is less evidence regarding the use of part-time faculty for distance education specifically. However, heavy reliance upon part-time faculty for on-line education is likely for the reasons noted above as well as for the geographical flexibility inherent in distance education. For the part-time faculty member, whose only activity on campus is a single course, options that eliminate the time and cost of commuting are attractive, especially if that faculty member holds positions at multiple institutions.

While we have argued that technology has affected faculty work and instructional practices, the impact of technology on faculty does vary according to faculty characteristics. We use data from the 1998–99 National Study of Postsecondary Faculty to provide empirical evidence on the use of instructional technology by community college faculty. Our first contribution is to describe the share of faculty who use technology. Such a description is important because the use of technology alters the work life of faculty members in several important ways. The literature describes and promotes a shift from delivering instruction to facilitating learning.[42] Although subtle in definition, this trend has had major implications in the institutional expectations placed on faculty members and the way that they participate in the instructional process. New instructional roles proposed for faculty include instructional designer, coach or facilitator, classroom instructional researcher, interdisciplinary team member, and broker of educational experiences.[43] Indeed, increased workload is one change not only for faculty in the educational technology environment that has become the norm at community colleges but also for students and administrators. An Alberta college Dean reflects upon this condition in 2004.

> We have a number of faculty involved in applications of technology, so they spend quite a bit of time with websites and such. That's a bit of a double-edge sword for them and for the students. I get some feedback from students that the courses are getting too much—too much reading, too many exercises to do, and such. Many of the faculty members get release time to get these things started, but that stops because it becomes a lot of work to keep it updated. The administration of it becomes very difficult. It's made it very difficult to set-up and operate multi-section courses.

Through extensive interviews with community college faculty, Cristie Roe finds evidence that the use of technology in instruction has a complicated effect on the workload of faculty.[44] Specifically, the responses of faculty members suggest a paradox.

> [A] common thread can be discerned running through most of the comments in the efficiency and time/workload subcategories. This thread is that, on the one hand, computer technology creates more work for faculty, and that, on the other hand, it facilitates the accomplishment of the extra work. Respondents in both these subcategories insisted that they had more work to do since incorporating technology into their work lives, yet they also found that the technology permitted them to accomplish more in a shorter amount of time.[45]

One reason why many instructors indicated that technology increased workload was the absence of release time granted to most faculty members to develop a technology-enhanced course. Another workload related concern was the increasing disintegration of the boundary between work-time and free-time. Responses to e-mail were often made at home rather than at work.

The use of instructional technology can impact community college faculty in areas other than workload. For example, the autonomy and power of faculty can be changed fundamentally.[46] Roe finds limited evidence supporting such concerns,[47] but several implicit attributes of the use of technology in instruction suggest that these concerns are valid. First, the use of e-mail (which some community colleges claim they can monitor as a managerial prerogative) and course websites makes the instruction process more public, allowing colleges to monitor their faculty more closely than in the past.[48] Second, as discussed earlier, distance education increases the likelihood that the instructional role will be unbundled with different instructors delivering specific aspects of the instructional process. If the roles were unbundled, the few faculty members who design and develop the course curriculum and the computer technicians who design the software that will house the content will probably see their roles expanded within the institution. However, other faculty members who actually staff individual courses will have less control over the content of the courses and may become more marginalized as a class of employees.[49]

In order to understand how much faculty work life is changing, estimates of the extent to which faculty are using instructional technology are needed. Norton Grubb found only minor technological innovation in his study of thirty-two colleges in eleven states while Roe found much more activity at several community colleges in the southwest, although her sample contained a disproportionate share of early adopters.[50] Past research, however, has not produced national estimates of technology use at community colleges, and we fill this void using the most recent National Study of Postsecondary Faculty (NSOPF). This survey contains a large sample of community college faculty—3,968 reported information on the use of technology—that is nationally representative. However, the most recent NSOPF survey only covered courses in the fall of 1998, thus the estimates we present would probably underestimate current levels of instructional technology use, given advances in use over time.

Table 5.3 contains estimates for three types of technological activity: use of e-mail to communicate with students, course websites, and distance education. Consequently, we can examine the use of technology that supports classroom-based education (e-mails and course websites) and technology that allows much of the class to be taught independently of time and location (distance education). The results in table 5.3 indicate that slightly more than a third of faculty use technology to support classroom instruction.

**Table 5.3** Average faculty distributed learning activity in fall 1998[a]

| | |
|---|---|
| *Percentage of faculty who:* | |
| used electronic mail to communicate with students in their class | 38.9 |
| used a course website | 33.2 |
| taught a distance education course | 7.6 |
| *Average percentage of their students a faculty member communicated with over e-mail:* | |
| Full sample | 8.7 |
| Sample reporting any e-mail activity | 22.4 |
| *Percentage of faculty who used their course website for:* | |
| Posting general classroom information, such as the syllabus and office hours | 24.9 |
| Posting information on homework assignments or readings | 21.5 |
| Posting practice exams or exercises that provide immediate scoring | 10.3 |
| Posting exams or exam results | 8.8 |
| Providing links to other information | 26.7 |
| Other uses | 7.9 |
| Number of observations | 3968 |

*Note*: [a] All figures are weighted.

Thirty-nine (39) percent of faculty members used e-mail to communicate with students in their classes and 33 percent used a course website. These figures are substantially lower than corresponding figures from Veronica Diaz and John Cheslock for four-year faculty, which were 70 and 41 percent, respectively.[51] In general, one should expect this different level of technology use at four-year institutions because four-year schools employ faculty members with more education, have stronger technological infrastructures due to research activities, and employ smaller shares of part-time faculty. Therefore, the greater use of technology to support classroom instruction at four-year institutions may simply reflect the above disparities rather than differences in institutional effort to promote technology.

The estimates for distance education indicate that while only a small percentage of community college instructors teach distance education courses, the share is substantially higher than found by Diaz and Cheslock for four-year institutions (7.6 versus 5 percent).[52] Given the greater resources enjoyed by four-year institutions mentioned above, this finding suggests that community colleges may be more aggressively encouraging faculty members to engage in distance education.

Table 5.3 also contains information on the intensity of e-mail and website use, rather than simple descriptions of the share of faculty engaged in those activities. The results for e-mail indicate that faculty members who do use e-mail in instruction interact with 22 percent of their students using that technology. The results for course websites demonstrate that most faculty members simply post general information or provide links to other websites. A smaller percentage of faculty (10 percent) use course websites to post exams and exercises, but those estimates are identical to figures for four-year institutions found by Diaz and Cheslock indicating that no difference exists across institutional type in more meaningful utilization of course websites.[53]

There are differences across faculty groups in their use of technology. Table 5.4 contains the share of faculty participating in distributed learning activities for different groups of faculty. The first set of results displays differences across various demographic characteristics such as gender, race/ethnicity, and age. Given the important manner in which a faculty member's work life is altered by the use of technology, these results indicate which type of faculty members are most affected. No differences on the basis of gender exist for the use of e-mail, but female faculty members are less likely to utilize course websites (30 percent relative to 36 percent) and more likely to teach distance education courses (8.8 percent to 6.5 percent) than their male counterparts.

No consistent pattern exists across the racial or ethnic groups for the two categories of technology that support classroom instruction. For distance education, white faculty members have the highest participation rates while African- and Asian-American faculty members have the lowest. Age is often assumed to be an important determinant of technology use because younger cohorts of faculty received much greater instruction in technology during their education. The results for e-mail and course websites provide evidence that such differential educational experiences may result in different patterns

**Table 5.4** Percentage of faculty reporting use of technology in instruction

| | # Obs. | E-mail % | Website % | Dist. Ed % |
|---|---|---|---|---|
| All | 3968 | 38.9 | 33.2 | 7.6 |
| Male | 1922 | 38.8 | 36.3 | 6.5 |
| Female | 2046 | 39.0 | 30.0 | 8.8 |
| American Indian | 33 | 49.9 | 35.9 | 6.1 |
| Asian American | 126 | 49.6 | 23.8 | 5.1 |
| African American | 329 | 32.9 | 41.7 | 4.8 |
| Hispanic | 298 | 42.7 | 43.7 | 7.0 |
| White | 3182 | 38.7 | 32.4 | 7.9 |
| Age: <35 | 381 | 44.4 | 28.8 | 8.8 |
| Age: 35–39 | 391 | 45.0 | 41.2 | 4.8 |
| Age: 40–44 | 513 | 43.9 | 36.5 | 7.0 |
| Age: 45–49 | 739 | 39.9 | 35.2 | 6.2 |
| Age: 50–54 | 806 | 41.2 | 32.6 | 8.9 |
| Age: 55–59 | 625 | 34.4 | 29.9 | 8.8 |
| Age: ≥ = 60 | 513 | 24.6 | 28.4 | 8.6 |
| Arts & Humanities | 908 | 40.0 | 36.3 | 5.7 |
| Social & Behavioral Sciences | 451 | 39.0 | 33.1 | 14.7 |
| Physical & Biological Sciences | 602 | 42.8 | 27.8 | 8.4 |
| Computing & Technology | 367 | 56.5 | 42.4 | 5.4 |
| Professional | 562 | 37.7 | 37.7 | 7.8 |
| Trades & Services | 338 | 24.8 | 33.2 | 3.7 |
| Low Status Professionals | 609 | 30.2 | 25.0 | 8.2 |
| Doctorate | 567 | 50.5 | 34.9 | 7.4 |
| Masters or 1st Professional | 2469 | 39.8 | 33.4 | 8.5 |
| Baccalaureate, Associate, or No Degree | 932 | 31.1 | 31.9 | 5.6 |
| Full-Time | 2141 | 48.5 | 34.1 | 10.1 |
| Part-Time | 1827 | 33.0 | 32.7 | 6.1 |

*Note*: [a] All figures are weighted.

of the use of technology. Starting with the age category of 35–39 year old faculty, the participation rates almost always drop as one examines older and older groups of faculty. Surprisingly, the opposite relationship exists for distance education, as faculty over fifty years of age have some of the highest participation levels. We note, however, that faculty under thirty-five use websites less than all other faculty but for one age group, and faculty under thirty-five do not have significantly higher use of e-mail for instruction than the thirty-five to thirty-nine age range and just slightly more than the forty to forty-four age range. These results may reflect the influence of part-time status upon these younger faculty as we have observed that part-time faculty have less access to institutional resources than full-time faculty (see chapter 6).

We now turn to examining differences across faculty on the basis of field, education level, and work status. Our earlier discussion suggested that pressures from the new economy, as well as other factors, might drive differences across these faculty characteristics. To examine the differences by field, we use the field classification system developed by Richard Wagoner[54] that allocates faculty into groups that should experience similar pressures from the greater economy. The seven groupings (with the two largest fields following in parenthesis) are: arts and humanities (general education and English composition and creative writing), social and behavioral sciences (Psychology, History), physical and biological sciences (Mathematics, Biology), computing and technology (Computer and Information Sciences and Allied Health Technologies and Services), professional (Business Administration/ Management and Accounting), trades and services (Protective Services/ Criminal Justice and Vehicle Equipment Mechanics), and lesser-status professionals (Nursing, Physical Education).

First, we examine the results for distance education because much of our earlier discussion of differences on the basis of field focused on technology that reduces constraints associated with time and place. We do find some evidence indicating that community college faculty members are more likely to teach distance education courses when the content of the course is more closely tied to workforce development. Of the four groups showing the highest participation rates, three are in areas considered important in the New Economy: physical and biological sciences, professional, and lesser-status professional. Additional evidence supporting concerns for workforce preparation includes the low levels in arts and sciences, which have weak ties to workforce development in the New Economy, and trades and services, which contain fields that are not currently in ascension.

Not all of the results on the basis of field, however, support the claim that differences in the use of distance education are driven by workforce development concerns. Faculty members in computing and technology, a growing area within the new economy, demonstrate the second lowest rate of participation. This result is especially surprising because faculty members in this area are likely to possess strong computing skills, which would make conducting a distance education course easier for the instructor. A second surprising result is the extremely high participation rates within social and behavioral sciences, which is almost twice as large as any other field. Such a finding may indicate that many of the students who are using distance education are seeking general education courses toward a specific credential, such as the Associate's, or a program requirement rather than a few specific courses to update their skills. Because physical and biological sciences contain large numbers of Mathematics faculty within Wagoner's classification scheme, the high levels of technology use in that field, in part, support this conclusion.

The differences across the fields in faculty use of e-mail and course websites indicate the importance of faculty skills, course content, and student preferences. Computing and technology faculty members have the highest participation rates, which is expected given the likely technological preparedness among these instructors, the preference for technology among their students, and the need to use technology to deliver some of the instructional material. Additionally, lesser-status professional and trades and services, two fields that probably have less-technologically savvy faculty and course content that does not require the use of technology, have the lowest participation rates.

Earlier, we discussed the ability of community colleges to unbundle the role of faculty into separate activities. If a premium is placed upon lowering costs, community colleges may rely upon less educated and part-time faculty to implement distance education courses. The results in table 5.4, however, demonstrate that a larger share of full-time faculty members participates in distance education courses than part-timers. In addition, less educated faculty are not more likely to participate in distance education. Such a finding may indicate that community colleges place special importance on distance education courses and consequently staff them with full-time faculty.

But other explanations for this finding can be offered, most notably the possibility that by the fall of 1998, community colleges were in the early stages of a major effort to adopt distance education courses. At that moment "early adopters" who were producing and hosting their own courses taught most of the on-line classes. As community colleges increasingly host the distance education courses themselves, different models of instruction may emerge. When future NSOPF surveys become available, longitudinal analysis can determine the extent to which part-time faculty members increasingly deliver on-line courses.

For both e-mail and course website use, more educated and full-time instructors have higher participation rates, although the difference is not substantial for the use of course websites. The differences across educational level may simply represent the knowledge gained in graduate school about technology. For work status, the differences may be due to part-time faculty being less integrated into the campus community and receiving less professional development.[55] In some cases, part-time faculty do not have access to campus e-mail as Levin observed.[56] In addition, part-time instructors may have less of an incentive to learn about existing instructional technology because their expected employment is short term and unpredictable.

Thus far, we have simply examined the correlation between each faculty member characteristic and instructional technology use. Some of these relationships, however, may simply be due to a third variable that is correlated with the faculty characteristic as well as with the level of instructional technology use. To examine this possibility, we turn to estimates of logistic regressions that include all of the variables in table 5.4, as well as several characteristics of the institution. The institutional characteristics reflect that the use of technology in instruction likely varies on the basis of the institution's wealth, location, control, and size. The regression sample of 3645 community college faculty members is slightly smaller than the sample used in tables 5.3 and 5.4 because some data are missing for key institutional variables. The results in tables 5.3 and 5.4 are similar when this smaller sample is used.

Table 5.5 contains results for three logistic regressions that are identical except for the different dependent variables: use of e-mail to communicate with students, course websites, and distance education. For each regression, odds ratios are reported in addition to the coefficient and standard error to provide meaningful estimates of the size of the relationships with each independent variable and the use of technology. In general, the results indicate that most of the main findings from table 5.4 are not altered once controls

**Table 5.5** Logistic regressions explaining faculty use of technology in instruction[a]

| | E-mail | | | Course websites | | | Distance education | | |
|---|---|---|---|---|---|---|---|---|---|
| | Coeff. | Std Err. | Odds Rat. | Coeff. | Std Err. | Odds Rat. | Coeff. | Std Err. | Odds Rat. |
| Female | −0.084 | 0.103 | 0.919 | −0.302** | 0.135 | 0.740 | 0.336 | 0.238 | 1.400 |
| American Indian | −0.026 | 0.405 | 0.974 | −0.514 | 0.560 | 0.598 | −0.209 | 0.771 | 0.812 |
| Asian American | 0.329 | 0.259 | 1.390 | −0.347 | 0.304 | 0.707 | −0.794* | 0.453 | 0.452 |
| African American | −0.219 | 0.185 | 0.803 | 0.495** | 0.174 | 1.640 | −0.653* | 0.361 | 0.521 |
| Hispanic | −0.081 | 0.237 | 0.922 | 0.344 | 0.268 | 1.411 | −0.094 | 0.455 | 0.910 |
| Age | −0.033** | 0.005 | 0.968 | −0.009 | 0.006 | 0.991 | 0.002 | 0.011 | 1.002 |
| Doctorate | 0.729** | 0.173 | 2.073 | 0.169 | 0.193 | 1.184 | −0.102 | 0.321 | 0.903 |
| Masters or 1st Professional | 0.309** | 0.134 | 1.362 | 0.078 | 0.164 | 1.081 | 0.190 | 0.268 | 1.210 |
| Part-Time | −0.796** | 0.095 | 0.451 | −0.239** | 0.119 | 0.787 | −0.621** | 0.261 | 0.538 |
| Arts & Humanities | −0.786** | 0.194 | 0.456 | −0.346 | 0.211 | 0.708 | 0.177 | 0.267 | 1.194 |
| Social & Behavioral Sciences | −0.710** | 0.231 | 0.492 | −0.710** | 0.244 | 0.492 | 1.418** | 0.410 | 4.130 |
| Physical & Biological Sciences | −0.737** | 0.213 | 0.479 | −0.798** | 0.236 | 0.450 | 0.606* | 0.352 | 1.833 |
| Professional | −0.806** | 0.210 | 0.447 | −0.253 | 0.215 | 0.776 | 0.388 | 0.358 | 1.475 |
| Trades and Services | −1.474** | 0.224 | 0.229 | −0.639** | 0.260 | 0.528 | −0.224 | 0.461 | 0.799 |
| Low Status Professionals | −1.091** | 0.222 | 0.336 | −0.813** | 0.232 | 0.443 | 0.146 | 0.389 | 1.157 |
| Other Fields | −0.650* | 0.374 | 0.522 | −1.120** | 0.429 | 0.326 | 0.499 | 0.495 | 1.647 |

*Note*: [a]N = 3645. All regressions include the appropriate weights and robust standard errors with clusters. In all regressions, the omitted race/ethnicity group is white, the omitted education group is Baccalaureate, Associate, or No Degree, and the omitted field is Computing and Technology. All regressions also include an intercept, a private dummy, location dummy variables, educational expenditures per student, and full-time equivalent enrollment as independent variables.

**, * indicates significance at the 5 and 10 percent level of significance, respectively.

are added for other determinants of technology use. Some of the differences, however, are not statistically significant at conventional levels because of large standard errors, especially in the case of distance education.

Female faculty members use course websites at lower levels and distance education at higher levels, although the latter result is insignificant due to high standard errors. Based on the coefficient for the female dummy variable, which equals one for females and zero for males, male faculty members are 1.35 times more likely than females to use course websites, but female faculty members are 1.4 times more likely to participate in distance education. Similar patterns also exist for the race or ethnicity of the faculty as white faculty members are 2.21 and 1.92 times more likely to participate in distance education than Asian American and African American faculty members, respectively.

The results for age change slightly when examined in the regression format, partially because we use a continuous measure rather than the age categories used in table 5.4. For both course websites and distance education, age appears to have little effect on the use of technology with regard to the size of the relationship or statistical significance. However, age continues to be an important predictor of e-mail usage.

The education of a faculty member is similar to age in that the only substantial differences appear to be in the use of e-mail, where those with a doctorate are two times more likely and those with a Master's or first professional degree are 1.4 times more likely to use that form of technology than those without a graduate degree. The much lower rates of technology usage among part-time faculty continue once controls are added for other determinants. Full-time faculty are 2.2 times more likely to use e-mail to communicate with students, 1.3 times more likely to use course websites, and 1.9 times more likely to participate in distance education.

The results are similar for field, as well. For e-mail and course websites, computing and technology faculty members continue to demonstrate much higher participation rates than other fields; in many cases, they are twice as likely as other faculty to use technology to support classroom instruction. For distance education, social and behavioral science faculty members continue to demonstrate substantially higher participation rates than other faculty, and faculty in the physical and biological sciences as well as those in professional fields demonstrate slightly higher rates. Thus, the use of specific forms of technology and the instructional use of technology differ on the basis of faculty characteristics. We observe, then, considerable stratification of technology use within community colleges. With respect to faculty work, we can conclude that faculty characterized by the use of technology is not homogenous.

As discussed throughout this chapter, the growth of distributed learning activities has the potential to change the production of instruction substantially. Relative to the traditional classroom model that relies upon one instructor, a greater number of personnel will be involved in the creation of a course using instructional technology. Community colleges employ workers in a variety of new positions such as instructional technologists, media technicians, visual and web designers, and web programmers.[57]

Because extensive course materials are required for on-line courses and are costly to create, community colleges will find it less expensive to separate the tasks of creating the material and directly instructing the class. Such a division of labor would substantially alter the nature of work for many instructors. For those faculty members who simply instruct a course using materials created by others, their job will be reduced in status. Donald Wagner, the chairman of the American Association of University Professors' (AAUP) distance-education committee, highlights this point when discussing the implications for faculty when community colleges purchase course materials from another organization. "If it's something you haven't developed yourself, you're simply a talking head. It may be a cost-saving measure in the short term, but in the long term it reduces what the faculty member is."[58]

Of course, for community colleges not solely concerned with reducing costs, they may staff on-line courses with other goals in mind, such as enhancing educational quality. As Cristie Roe points out, such efforts will no doubt alter work for full-time faculty as the use of technology for instructional purposes structures how faculty teach and how they conduct their professional lives.[59] However, given the growth in the area of distributed learning, as well as limited finances and increasing demand for education and training at community colleges, low-cost labor is one way to meet colleges' efforts to maintain and expand access. Part-time faculty are not only one way for community colleges to achieve productivity—serving students efficiently—but also the preferred way. We examine this labor force in chapter 6.

# 6

# Part-Time Community College Faculty as New Economy Temporary Labor

Both strikingly and significantly, over the past thirty years, part-time faculty have become the majority of community college faculty.[1] During the same period this condition paralleled that of temporary labor generally in organizations in what is referred to as the New Economy.[2] In this sense, part-timers can be understood as a direct link between labor in the New Economy and community colleges.[3] According to the American Association of Community Colleges, 64 percent of all community college faculty were part-time in 1998.[4] While part-time faculty have traditionally been part of the community college labor pool, their use increased precipitously in the 1980s and 1990s. This alteration is consistent with the community college's emphasis during this period on economic competitiveness, including the relative decline in government funding and the increasing resource acquisition behaviors of institutional members as well as privatization of services.[5] That is, the increased reliance on part-time faculty is directly related to the globalization of community colleges and the ascendancy of New Economy management principles.

Part-time labor is now used as the key labor force to undertake the core activity of the community college, suggesting that community college part-time faculty resemble part-time labor in the New Economy. We view this condition and the identity of part-time faculty through the perceptions of faculty and administrators and through national data sets that point to the presence of two distinct strata of part-time employment. These distinct categories of employment frame how faculty membership in those strata affect income, employment perceptions, and work satisfaction. There are indeed serious implications arising from the central role of this labor force in the community college.

As early as the beginning of the 1980s, scholars and practitioners began to discuss part-time faculty labor at community colleges from an instrumentalist perspective. "The adult who turns to the two-year college for skills and/or credentials needs instant service—community colleges must be ready to provide work skills to match the changing requirements of the job market.

A static faculty cannot provide this."[6] Carol Eliason argued for those institutional practices as well as part-time faculty integration in 1980; these were called for again seventeen years later by Judith Gappa and David Leslie.[7] Furthermore, Eliason endeavors to legitimize the notion of the New Economy/postindustrial model which has served to increase the use and, for some, exploitation of part-time faculty. Her language is key to understanding how the New Economy has come to dominate thinking about part-time faculty at community colleges.

Eliason ignores the transfer or academic function in her statement; instead she suggests that the institution is oriented to vocations or jobs. Whether a student seeks to obtain a GED, to acquire a better job, to train to become a computer network engineer, or to be retrained for a new position in their current company, the nontransfer functions of the community college have all come to be viewed as skills training and access to employment. Eliason refers to work skills, the job market, and credentials. While credentials could conceivably refer to an associate's degree and transfer to a university, given the context of the rest of the statement, it seems likely that she refers to employment credentials, not academic ones. Students are described as customers who must be given immediate service and resultant marketable skills. And, most important for this chapter, Eliason states that a static faculty is not up to the task. Static is a particularly interesting word in this context because it can refer both to an individual full-time faculty member who has not grown professionally to meet these new demands and it can also refer to a tenured or permanent faculty that cannot readily be rearranged to meet changing demands. Ultimately, Eliason presents the community college and its faculty as a postindustrial business: a lean, flexible organization ready to exploit and profit from a constantly changing marketplace that demands instantaneous service. Eliason's language is permeated by its ideology. It is akin to what we refer to as neo-liberalism. Over the past two decades, scholars have documented the results of a neo-liberal ideology on labor. These results include "job shift," "the end of work" as we have customarily understood work, and constant retraining, as well as more tenuous working conditions and benefits, and a dwindling social safety net.[8]

The influence of the New Economy has isolated individual workers and allowed institutions to increase efficiency and flexibility in a form of hyper-capitalism. Manuel Castells discusses how work has been transformed by the New Economy. He argues that the most "fundamental transformation" in work and employment is "the individualization of work and the fragmentation of societies."[9] This is also a central concern of Martin Carnoy. If individuals must fend for themselves with no protection, either from the government or from unions, in the economic marketplace, there is the potential for a fortunate few to reap considerable rewards, but many others will be exploited.[10] Vicki Smith equates the differences in potential rewards to a "great divide": in order to cross this divide, workers must be willing to take increased individual risks.[11] This idea is in direct contrast to the social contract that governed employee and employer relations throughout the mid- and late twentieth century.[12]

Along with Carnoy, both Castells and Smith suggest that this form of individualization and the divide it creates has resulted in two distinct types of part-time labor in the New Economy.[13] Some temporary laborers are valued by the companies and institutions that hire them because of their skill and expertise as well as their personal networks—the contacts and connections they have with other experts and organizations. This group has numerous options outside of the employing institution to capitalize on its skills and expertise. On the other side of the gulf of temporary labor are those who do not possess rare, highly valued skills and abilities. These part-timers do not have numerous opportunities in multiple industries. This lack of employment options causes these part-timers to seek, sometimes in desperation, full-time, stable employment with the institution where they are employed. Their predicament is exacerbated by a condition of a surplus of labor that can perform their duties. Companies and institutions, in an effort to embody the values of efficiency and flexibility central to globalized institutions, are reluctant to promote these part-timers to full-time status. Both Castells and Smith suggest that both of these groups coexist in the New Economy. They are not mutually exclusive; indeed, both types of part-timers can be found in the same institution simultaneously.

Part-time faculty at community colleges have also been described in similar terms. Frederic Jacobs points out that, traditionally, the use of part-time faculty increases the prestige of institutions because part-timers bring skills, abilities, and talents to the institution not possessed by its regular faculty.[14] Part-timers in this category are identified by their impressive experience and/or their highly valued skills—experience and skills that full-time faculty do not possess. Generally, the majority of these individuals either have full-time employment outside the college or are retired.

Jacobs and others have suggested that the rising problem of part-time faculty in higher education does not center on this traditional use of part-timers, but rather as convenient and expedient means to lower costs and increase flexibility for institutions.[15] This practice has increased dramatically as the percentage of part-time faculty has grown over the last thirty years. These part-time faculty members are frequently viewed as less skilled and trained than full-time faculty; the quality of their instruction and their dedication to the institution are questioned as well.

These two opposing views of the use of part-time faculty reveal an important contradiction: part-time faculty as highly skilled and trained assets and part-time faculty as a less-skilled means to achieve efficiency, flexibility, and control. This contradiction is tied to the transfer and vocational functions of community colleges. Those who are not academics but who have an educational background in academic disciplines do not necessarily possess skills and training beyond those of full-time faculty in community colleges, but those with advanced training and experience in specific vocational areas who are not full-time faculty are likely to possess skills that full-time vocational faculty do not. That is, it is reasonable to assume that on average a higher percentage of part-time faculty from vocational fields bring both rare and valued skills to community colleges than do part-time faculty from academic fields. From this perspective, vocational faculty who are part-time fit the highly valued, traditional definition of part-timer, while transfer faculty who are part-time fit the definition of part-timers as a means to efficiency, flexibility, and control.

From the perspective of managerialism,[16] part-time faculty are clearly at a lower stratum of professional labor when compared to full-time faculty in the New Economy. Although clearly a lower stratum of professional labor, part-timers have also become crucial to the strategic plans of modern organizations. The use of part-time employees in recurrent tasks that have traditionally been fulfilled by permanent employees is promoted in current management principles. Smith sees this stance as a "paradigmatic shift" in the way managers view the employment of part-time employees.[17] This paradigm shift is evident in the increased, and now institutionalized, use of part-time faculty in community colleges. Upper level administrators at community colleges are willing to accept the continuing exploitation of part-time faculty—even though they may not understand their institution's behaviors as exploitation—if it allows them to achieve those goals they deem essential for their colleges.[18] This exploitative use of part-timers enables colleges to increase efficiency and productivity while simultaneously increasing the authority and control of managers.[19]

This drive toward efficiency and control exhibited by managers has affected the individual perceptions of part-time faculty. Emily Abel and Kathleen Barker have documented an important shift in the locus of control and motivation for part-time faculty.[20] Abel argues that until the early 1980s motivation and control for part-time faculty was mostly intrinsic and based upon a belief in meritocracy. Barker noted that motives had become considerably more extrinsic by the mid-1990s. She found that part-timers were acutely aware of the new business efficiency model and its exploitation of part-time faculty. As a result, part-timers no longer blamed themselves for not having a full-time position, but instead blamed the unjust system, a strong indication that the nature of part-time work in community colleges has changed and with it the perceptions and responses of part-timers as well. Barker rejects the idealism of Gappa and Leslie, who argue that part-time and full-time faculty can form one faculty in the guise of a collegium.

> The contradiction of workplace transformation in higher education is that it institutionalizes privilege for one set of citizens (tenured and tenure track faculty) at a cost to others. The failure of inclusion within academe, or the success of exclusive membership, is revealed when a system of layered citizenship is constructed, made coherent, and legitimated.[21]

This is precisely the problem with proposed solutions to solve the part-time problem offered by Gappa and Leslie, as well as by John Roueche, Suanne Roueche, and Mark Milliron:[22] best practices will not be implemented because they are not viable economically. Our evidence to date, and collected a decade after the proffered solutions of Gappa and Leslie and

Roueche, Roueche, and Milliron, indicates that part-time faculty conditions are more dire than in the past.[23] The essence of the new economic use of part-timers depends on their increased exploitation, and unless there is a major crisis within community colleges resulting from the high level of reliance on part-time labor, behaviors are unlikely to change. That is, as long as community colleges are tied to economic development and private interests, and they employ the business models preferred by those interests, they will continue to view part-timers as a central means to controlling production costs. Managerialism and the New Economy business practices it fosters have led to a contradictory labor market where temporary employees exist side by side with permanent employees. Both groups serve similar functions.[24] Part-time employees are then forced to negotiate this potentially exploitative market on their own; those with rare skills and abilities may be valued commodities in numerous markets, while those with common skills will find themselves on the wrong side of a labor market chasm.[25]

In our observations and interviews at community colleges as recently as 2004, we were continually struck by how both part-time faculty themselves and college administrators would present the contradictions stated above. Some part-time faculty would speak freely about feeling exploited and marginalized, while others would indicate satisfaction with their positions. The theme of exploitation frequently centered on salary. Nearly everyone we have interviewed—faculty and administrators alike—has agreed that part-time faculty are paid too little, but the importance of this situation has varied depending on the interviewee. Those part-timers who were dependent on their salaries to survive voiced the loudest complaints. Perhaps the most striking example of this in our interviews came from a part-time faculty member at Suburban Valley Community College in California[26] who was running a large monthly deficit due to an inability to obtain full-time employment and was able to exist only by using a reverse mortgage on a current house. While many other part-timers did not have problems as severe as this, those who relied on their wages for the majority of their income voiced highly negative opinions about their pay. Those part-timers who did not rely on their part-time salaries for survival did not express the same negativity. While we did find that individuals had a wide variety of reasons for not relying on their teaching salaries for their livelihoods, most of these reasons revolved around some form of achievement in the private (nonacademic) sector. Those part-time faculty members without this type of nonacademic opportunity tended to be most troubled by their academic salaries.

Employment ties to the private sector were correlated with satisfactory financial situations for part-time faculty members because those ties also added nonacademic motivations for teaching at community colleges, resulting in more satisfaction. Part-time faculty with strong ties to business and industry tended not to portray themselves as alienated at campuses because they taught for reasons that had little to do with an academic career. For these part-timers teaching was a means to advancing their nonacademic careers. As one part-time technology instructor noted: "[in my business] teaching is a feather in my cap." Because these faculty members receive increased standing in their nonacademic careers by teaching at community colleges and are not focused on becoming full-time academics, they are not preoccupied by perceptions of a lack of full integration in the campus community.

Community college administrators also presented us with a weighted contradiction. While they were frequently enthusiastic about the quality of some part-time faculty members and the advanced skills some part-timers brought to college programs, administrators were nearly unanimous in their belief that the level of efficiency and control they needed to manage their institutions could only come with the use of a large percentage of part-time faculty. Economic efficiency was central to many of these interviews. Almost all administrators we spoke to during the period of 2001 to 2004—and there were thirty-two of these at three colleges, including one in Arizona (Cactus College), one in California (Suburban Valley Community College), and one in Alberta, Canada (North Mountain College)—indicated that they could not afford to run programs without the cost savings of part-time faculty. For many of these administrators their obligation was to their local community. One dean indicated that "the mission is to serve the community . . . we couldn't be at every place for the whole community without adjunct faculty."

Several administrators go further than stating that part-timers allowed them to serve their communities better, indicating that colleges are not obligated to part-time faculty. One dean was fairly succinct, "We can expand with adjuncts, or we can reduce what we are doing with adjuncts; and we don't hurt the programs; we don't hurt the full-time faculty." Here, the paradigmatic shift from full-time labor to part-time labor has become entrenched in the perceptions of community college administrators.[27] This dean also highlights that full-time positions are both privileged and protected by the tenuous status of part-timers. From this perspective, then, part-time positions are important only for the flexibility they offer institutions, not as means for part-time faculty to earn a living wage or receive reasonable employment benefits. This extreme view was bluntly presented by one college president: "We are not a social service agency. We are not here to hand out jobs."

Arguably, the economic savings made possible by part-time faculty have a negative impact on instruction at community colleges. Data from the National Study of Postsecondary Faculty of 1993 and 1999 on the availability of professional development opportunities illuminate the lack of resources dedicated to part-time faculty in community colleges.[28] In both years, professional development opportunities were available to full-time faculty at a rate at least twice that of part-time faculty. The data also indicate that, on average, support increased for full-timers and decreased for part-timers from 1993 to 1999. This disparity is particularly important because community colleges are teaching institutions where quality of instruction is viewed as sacrosanct.[29] To deny the opportunity for professional development to such a large percentage of faculty could have a negative impact on the quality of instruction at community colleges. What is particularly ironic with this finding is that during the same period scholars expounded on the importance of increased professional support for part-time faculty.[30] We conclude that the decision to exclude part-time faculty in professional development activities must be based on a desire to conserve resources, rather than to improve the quality of instruction.

These assertions and observations indicated that there were at least two bifurcations in community college faculty—one between full-time and part-time faculty and one among various types of part-timers—and those bifurcations resembled the types of bifurcations in New Economy labor indicated by other scholars.[31] We found that not only were full-time faculty privileged when compared to part-time faculty, but also that those part-time faculty who had full-time careers in or strong ties to business and industry possessed skills and personal networks that were held in high regard by colleges. These faculty in particular were also much less dependent on income gained from teaching for their livelihoods. Specifically, those part-time faculty members with ties to business and industry tended to resemble the highly valued stratum of temporary labor in the New Economy, while those part-timers whose focus and abilities were more traditionally academic tended to resemble the exploited and less valued stratum of labor in the New Economy. A logical extension of the trends we had found in our qualitative work was to see if they existed at a national level.

We constructed a profile of the two types of part-time faculty we encountered at our study colleges and hypothesized what traits each group might include. Resembling the stratum of temporary labor in the New Economy who possess rare and highly valued skills, the first type of part-time faculty at community colleges are those faculty members with strong employment options outside of their academic institution. These close ties to the private sector create a distinct profile. These faculty members are less dependent on their income from colleges because of well-paying employment outside of academe. As a result, they do not perceive themselves as exploited financially. Professional careers and contacts outside of academe also contribute to less alienation and higher levels of satisfaction for these faculty members because they do not require their college employment to fulfill their need for an active professional life. Given this general profile, we expected that we would find evidence in national data sets that these part-timers earned a majority of their income from nonacademic sources, earned more income from all sources than other part-timers, would tend to be employed full-time in a position outside of academe, and would be more satisfied overall with the demands and rewards of their part-time faculty positions.

On the other hand, the second stratum of part-time faculty we assumed would resemble the type of New Economy temporary labor that does not possess rare and highly valued skills, causing them to be employed as a means for the institution to achieve increased managerial control through economic efficiency and labor force flexibility. We expected to find in national data sets that this group of part-time faculty would be a mirror image of the first. That is, these part-time faculty would be dependent primarily on academic careers both for their livelihoods and their professional identities. Therefore, we expected this group to be dependent on income from academic employment, to work part-time at other academic institutions, and to be less satisfied with their part-time faculty positions because of the need to have those positions fulfill all professional identity needs.

Beyond these two general profiles and the hypotheses they invite, our intention was to add nuance to what appear to be dichotomous categories. In that case, we disaggregate community college faculty into seven groups based on academic program and relative employment opportunities outside of academe. While this disaggregation is based in part on the work of Benjamin,[32] our intention is to add detail to the simple dichotomy of liberal arts versus vocational programs and to include as many fields as possible into the disaggregation to capture as complete a picture of all part-time faculty in community colleges as possible. It is not our intention to change in radical fashion how fields are grouped, or even to abandon the transfer versus training tensions in community colleges. We do, however, refine groupings within transfer programs and training programs with three separate groups for transfer programs and three groups for training programs and a seventh group that has aspects in common with both areas. The seven groups include: arts and humanities, social and behavioral sciences, physical and biological sciences, computing and technology, professional programs, trades and services, and low status professional programs.

The first three groups are composed of programs generally considered in academic or transfer curriculum, but there are several compelling reasons to separate the groups. First, the general literature on higher education faculty indicates that there are differences between these three categories; therefore, it is valuable to discover if there are differences between these groups in community colleges. Second, the literature on exploited part-time faculty generally portrays faculty from either the arts and humanities group (especially English faculty) or from the social and behavioral sciences, not the hard sciences.[33] These first two reasons focus primarily on academic programs: the final reason is concerned with career opportunities outside of academe. Traditionally, members of the arts and humanities group have been associated with and found employment in academe. While academic employment is important to members of the social and behavioral sciences group, its members do have more numerous employment opportunities available outside of academe than do members of the arts and humanities. Similarly, those trained in the physical and biological sciences traditionally have had numerous employment opportunities outside of academe with government agencies and with the research and development departments of private corporations.

These general trends in employment opportunities outside of the academy were intensified in some cases during the 1990s.[34] Private companies that once would hire people trained in the arts and humanities for sales and marketing positions and for entry-level management positions began to demand specialized degrees focused on these areas for new employees, decreasing employment opportunities for arts and humanities students. In contrast, the biotech boom and a general increase in new technologies developed in part by physical scientists in the 1990s increased the opportunities outside of academe for faculty members from the physical and biological sciences group.[35]

The next three groups in the disaggregation—computing and technology, professional programs, and trades and services—might all be considered vocational or training programs, but each of these groups, similar to the three transfer program groups, experience varying employment opportunities outside of the academy. Traditionally, those trained in the computing and technology fields were able to find employment at large corporations and government agencies, but many smaller organizations could not afford, or perhaps did not see the need for, large, complex, and expensive mainframe computers. Those trained in professional programs generally experience numerous, well-paid opportunities outside of higher education. While employment opportunities in the trades and services sectors tend to ebb and flow with the general economy, employment opportunities in these areas have been numerous during the twentieth century.[36] As with the transfer function groups, opportunities for these three groups did change throughout the 1990s and, therefore, deserve to be analyzed separately. Computing and related technologies have fueled globalization and the New Economy, and all enterprises, of all sizes, rely on computers.[37] Therefore, faculty members from this group should have had numerous and well-paying career opportunities outside of academe. Conversely, faculty members from the professional group tend to have quality opportunities available to them which are not necessarily dependent on the New Economy. The third group from training and vocational programs—trades and services—is problematical. Some of these fields are tied to globalization and the New Economy, for example, air transportation, while other fields, such as building trades, are more traditional and less associated with employment in a postindustrial society.

Employment opportunities outside of community colleges are not the only reason to divide these three groups. As John Levin has discussed, training programs at community colleges have evolved during the 1990s.[38] While there continue to be numerous training programs designed to meet the needs of less demanding fields, there has been a marked increase in training and certification programs at community colleges for highly skilled and technologically based careers, with some of these programs requiring college degrees or similar training as a requirement for admission. Such programs are more represented in the computing and technology and professional groups than they are in the trades and services group. Not only do outside employment opportunities separate these three groups, but there is also a potential hierarchy in the status of these programs within community colleges. The experiences and perceptions of faculty in these groups, then, could show marked differences from the aggregate.

The final group in the disaggregation—low status professional programs—has elements in common with the academic groups and with the vocational groups. Many of the fields in this group do have a long-standing place in the academy, for example, education programs, and employment possibilities outside of academe. The problem is that whether opportunities are available inside the academic world or in the private sector, the relative status and pay of these fields is low in comparison with other fields. There are numerous opportunities for people with education backgrounds in the K-12 system in the United States, but teaching is not seen as a prestigious profession, particularly at the elementary and secondary levels. Nursing is a high demand profession in health care, but traditionally it has not only been less a prestigious area than other health care professions, it also has been a field with lower overall compensation. The fields in this final aggregation are also highly feminized, which has been linked to decreased disciplinary salaries in higher education.[39] Therefore, because of the hybrid nature of the fields included in this last group, we combine them as a separate category to decrease the possibility that the individual fields might distort results in the other academic and vocational divisions.

Given our general faculty profile and the seven group disaggregation that stems from it, we now turn to a discussion of the results of quantitative analysis we conducted with both the 1993 and 1999 National Studies of Postsecondary Faculty (NSOPF 93 and NSOPF 99). As we are only concerned here with the community college labor market, the NSOPF data sets were cleaned to include only faculty members from community colleges, both private and public, who identified themselves as either full or part-time (table 6.1). NSOPF 99 included responses from 4,560 faculty at 269 community colleges; 8,435 faculty from 266 institutions responded to the NSOPF 93 questionnaire. To insure consistency in the data for the study only faculty members who provided valid responses to all questions included in the study are included in the analysis. For NSOPF 99 this results in a total of 4,283 faculty—1,572 full-time and 2,711 part-time. For NSOPF 93 this results in a total of 8,151 faculty—3,113 full-time and 5,038 part-time.

Although we incorporate all seven disaggregated groups in our analysis, we frequently refer to results for the broad categories indicated by our general profiles: the traditional arts and sciences (arts and humanities, social and behavioral sciences, physical and biological sciences) and vocational and technical training (computing and technology, professions, trades and services). At the most basic level, we interpret the three groups that comprise the traditional arts and sciences as the type of New Economy temporary labor that possesses training and abilities that are neither rare nor highly valued, resulting in few employment options and relatively low pay. That is, this stratum of New Economy labor is exploited in the pursuit of efficiency and flexibility. Conversely, we view the three groups that comprise the vocational and technical area as the upper stratum of New Economy temporary labor because of their employment options outside of academe, their more valued skills and training within colleges, and the relatively high level of their income. We further discuss results from our analysis based on the hypotheses that rose from our general profiles—specifically, part-time faculty income,

**Table 6.1** NSOPF 1999 community college faculty labor market conditions

| | | Mean Income | | Other Employment | |
|---|---|---|---|---|---|
| | | Total | % Academic | % Full-time | Academic |
| All | | | | | |
| | Part-time | 40,226 | 45.0 | 37.7 | 63.8 |
| | Full-time | 53,989 | | | |
| Arts & Humanities | | | | | |
| | Part-time | 31,968 | 59.2 | 30.3 | 77.1 |
| | Full-time | 52,168 | | | |
| Social Science | | | | | |
| | Part-time | 44,891 | 41.8 | 27.7 | 69.1 |
| | Full-time | 58,504 | | | |
| Hard Sciences | | | | | |
| | Part-time | 41,775 | 58.5 | 31.7 | 71.5 |
| | Full-time | 54,401 | | | |
| Computer/Technology | | | | | |
| | Part-time | 43,729 | 30.4 | 48.8 | 47.6 |
| | Full-time | 55,521 | | | |
| Professions | | | | | |
| | Part-time | 50,599 | 26.8 | 54.5 | 45.4 |
| | Full-time | 55,587 | | | |
| Trades | | | | | |
| | Part-time | 45,473 | 34.7 | 39.8 | 42.6 |
| | Full-time | 54,408 | | | |
| Low Status Pros | | | | | |
| | Part-time | 33,901 | 55.5 | 41.8 | 64.5 |
| | Full-time | 50,989 | | | |

*Notes*

1. All results in the table incorporate weights to model a representative sample. The number of faculty members for each group are as follows: All Part-time 2,711, All Full-time 1,572, Arts and Humanities Part-time 731, Arts and Humanities Full-time 353, Social and Behavioral Sciences Part-time 323, Social and Behavioral Sciences Full-time 161, Physical and Biological Sciences Part-time 404, Physical and Biological Sciences Full-time 241, Computing and Technology Part-time 288, Computing and Technology Full-time 129, Professional Programs Part-time 389, Professional Programs Full-time 243, Trades and Services Part-time 216, Trades and Services Full-time 165, Low Status Professionals Part-time 360, Low Status Professionals Full-time 280.
2. Income figures are stated in dollars (as per its value in 1998).
3. The Academic Income category is based on all academic income, including income from other higher education institutions as well as the study institution.

including total income and sources of income; part-time faculty perceptions of their community college position; their desire for a full-time academic position; the status and sector of their outside employment; and their satisfaction.

The data for mean total earned income demonstrate important results themselves. While the overall aggregate incomes for part and full-time faculty are significantly different, they appear to be reasonably close to one another, a point supported by Gappa and Leslie.[40] But, when community college faculty are disaggregated, a different picture appears. Part-timers from the three academic groups earn less than the average of all part-timers and earn proportionally less when compared to full-time faculty in their groups.

Conversely, part-time faculty from the three vocational groups on average earn more than all part-timers and earn a higher proportion of income when compared to full-time faculty. Taken together, these three income variables clearly illuminate the differences in total earned income. Members of the three vocationally oriented groups earn significantly more income than members of the three academic groups. The source of the majority of the income earned by the vocational groups is work conducted outside of an academic setting. In fact, members of the part-time faculty from the professional group earn more nonacademic income than part-time faculty from the arts and humanities and the low status professional groups earn from all sources. The three academic groups earn much more of their total income from academic sources, but they also rely on additional nonacademic income to earn a living. Simply put, groups from the academically related groups rely on academic employment for their livelihoods, while members of the vocational groups supplement their incomes with academic work.

Results from the income data also indicate a striking trend regarding gender. First, women are disproportionately represented in groups that have the lowest personal incomes in community colleges. Women are a majority in the arts and humanities and social and behavioral sciences part-time groups and in both categories of the low status professionals group. These are all groups that tend to have the lowest individual incomes. The second reason concerns both income and status. Men tend to be employed more as full-time faculty in areas where a full-time faculty position would be considered desirable, and they are also employed more as part-timers in areas that tend to have higher paying options outside of academe. In each of the three academic transfer groups men are more likely to be hired as full-time instructors than as part-time instructors. In contrast, women are more likely to be hired as full-time instructors in the areas that offer more lucrative options outside of academe. Women are 37 percent (sixteen percentage points) more likely to be hired as full-time instructors in the computing and technology area than as part-timers. They also comprise a clear majority in that area. Women are 16 percent (seven percentage points) more likely to be hired as full-time faculty in the professional area. Finally, women are an extreme minority in both the full- and part-time categories in the trades and services area. As discussed earlier in the chapter, nonacademic income for each of these three groups is significantly higher than the other four groups. Thus, women employed as full-time faculty in these areas could be considered at a disadvantage because they are less likely to benefit from the opportunities available to them outside of academe.

The differences demonstrated by the results for income are also reflected in part-time faculty members' responses to questions about how they perceive their positions at community colleges and in their desire for full-time employment at those colleges. When asked if they view the study institution as their primary employer, members of the academic groups, particularly those in the arts and humanities and the social and behavioral sciences, were almost twice as likely to respond that they did view the study institution as their primary employer when compared to part-timers from the three vocational and professional groups. Similar findings resulted from part-time faculty members' response to their employment as part-timer at the institution. Once again, part-timers from the academic groups were almost twice as likely to indicate that they desired full-time employment but none was available when compared to their counterparts from the vocational and professional groups. These results add credence to the assumption that part-time faculty from the traditional academic areas identify themselves primarily as academics, while part-time faculty from the vocational and training areas of community colleges gain their professional identity outside of academe.

The source of the professional identity for part-time faculty in the training and vocational fields is evident in the results for the status of employment outside the study institution and the sector of that employment. Part-timers from the training and vocational areas were approximately 65 percent more likely to work in a full-time position outside of their study institution than were part-time faculty from the academic groups. With respect to the sector in which part-time faculty work outside their community college, members of the vocational and training groups were approximately 80 percent more likely to work in a nonacademic setting. Again, there is strong evidence to suggest that part-time faculty members from the training and vocational areas of community colleges gain their professional identity from nonacademic employment.

We examined four elements of the part-time faculty labor market in an effort to distinguish between part-time faculty and full-time faculty in a number of areas. These include earned income and professional development opportunities. Additionally we examined for those two variables among part-timers as well as the nature and perceptions that part-time faculty hold for their positions at community colleges and the status and employment sector of positions part-time faculty hold outside of the study institution. The income data indicate that there is a significant difference in the incomes of full- and part-time faculty, even in the aggregate. Furthermore, these differences are more acute for members of the academic groups than they are for members of the vocational groups. While all full-time faculty groups earn the overwhelming majority of their income from the study institution, the results are different for part-time faculty. Members of the vocational groups tend to earn much more of their income in nonacademic jobs and they tend to hold full-time positions in this employment. Part-time members of the academic groups, who earn significantly less than the vocational groups, tend to earn the majority of their income from postsecondary employment and they also tend to have part-time status in these positions. There would seem to be, then, a substantial divide among part-time faculty regarding how, where, and to what level they earn a living. While others have suggested that these differences are much more a function of the taxonomy of motivation for employment of part-time faculty members,[41] we suggest that the field of the part-time faculty member is an important factor as well.

Our analysis to this point supports the assertion that there are two distinct bifurcations for community college faculty members: one among part-time and full-time faculty with regard to income and professional development opportunities, and one among academically oriented and vocationally oriented part-time faculty with regard to their incomes and the status and sector of their outside employment. Given these labor market differences, it can be assumed that there are significant differences between these groups concerning their satisfaction with the demands and rewards of their community college positions (table 6.2).

Our analysis explores faculty satisfaction in the area that James Valadez and James Antony describe as demands and rewards.[42] Data for five specific satisfaction variables—overall satisfaction, job security, advancement opportunities, salary, and benefits—were included. In addition to these five variables, responses to the question of whether faculty would choose an academic career again were analyzed. We begin with a discussion of the mean responses of both full- and part-time faculty for each of the variables and conclude with results from weighted least squares regression analysis of the satisfaction data. While six variables are included two are particularly important to our analysis: overall satisfaction and the desire to pursue an academic career again. Overall satisfaction is valuable because it presents faculty members' perceptions of their positions as a whole; the desire to choose an academic career again not only indicates faculty members' willingness to experience the demands and rewards of academe, but also, in a larger sense, measures their overall orientation and dedication to an academic life.

Part-timers in the academic groups displayed the lowest levels of overall satisfaction and in each of the other four demand and reward variables as well. However, they did have the highest mean score in response to the question of whether or not they would be willing to pursue an academic career again. This exception is revealing and at first glance appears to be counterintuitive. That is, if part-timers from the academic groups were less satisfied overall and in each of the other areas of demands and rewards, it would be reasonable to assume that they, therefore, would be less willing to pursue an academic career again. However, they were more willing than any of the vocational groups to pursue an academic career again. Even with their overall dissatisfaction, members of these groups were willing to pursue academic employment; they viewed their primary careers as academically oriented, even if they were less than satisfying. This point adds considerable evidence to explain why there is an oversupply of labor for academic jobs: academics appear to be willing to face greater than average dissatisfaction in pursuit of their aspirations. The opposite applies to part-time vocational faculty. While members of these groups were more satisfied overall and in each of the four areas of demands and rewards, they were significantly less willing to pursue an academic career again. That is, they were not willing to accept the challenges of an academic career.

This trend is reinforced by the differences in means between part-time and full-time faculty for each group. Part-time members of the academic groups had lower means than full-time faculty in the same groups, and the difference in the mean responses between part-timers and full-timers in the three academic

**Table 6.2** NSOPF 1999 mean satisfaction comparisons: part-time versus full-time

| | | Overall | pt-ft | Rewards | pt-ft | Academic Again? | pt-ft |
|---|---|---|---|---|---|---|---|
| All | | | | | | | |
| | Part-time | 3.24 | −.070 | 2.51 | −.520 | 3.22 | −.190 |
| | Full-time | 3.31 | | 3.03 | | 3.41 | |
| Arts / Humanities | | | | | | | |
| | Part-time | 3.12 | −.220 | 2.31 | −.760 | 3.30 | −.160 |
| | Full-time | 3.34 | | 3.07 | | 3.46 | |
| Social Science | | | | | | | |
| | Part-time | 3.13 | −.250 | 2.38 | −.740 | 3.30 | −.250 |
| | Full-time | 3.38 | | 3.12 | | 3.55 | |
| Hard Sciences | | | | | | | |
| | Part-time | 3.22 | −.060 | 2.47 | −.640 | 3.07 | −.430 |
| | Full-time | 3.28 | | 3.11 | | 3.50 | |
| Computer/Technology | | | | | | | |
| | Part-time | 3.39 | .070 | 2.75 | −.320 | 3.17 | −.140 |
| | Full-time | 3.32 | | 3.07 | | 3.31 | |
| Professional | | | | | | | |
| | Part-time | 3.35 | .140 | 2.62 | −.310 | 3.17 | −.200 |
| | Full-time | 3.21 | | 2.93 | | 3.37 | |
| Trades/Services | | | | | | | |
| | Part-time | 3.44 | .050 | 2.77 | −.170 | 3.14 | −.200 |
| | Full-time | 3.39 | | 2.94 | | 3.34 | |
| Low Status Pros | | | | | | | |
| | Part-time | 3.23 | −.050 | 2.61 | −.370 | 3.34 | .010 |
| | Full-time | 3.28 | | 2.98 | | 3.33 | |

*Notes*

1. All results in the table incorporate weights to model a representative sample. The number of faculty members for each group are as follows: All Part-time 2,711, All Full-time 1,572, Arts and Humanities Part-time 731, Arts and Humanities Full-time 353, Social and Behavioral Sciences Part-time 323, Social and Behavioral Sciences Full-time 161, Physical and Biological Sciences Part-time 404, Physical and Biological Sciences Full-time 241, Computing and Technology Part-time 288, Computing and Technology Full-time 129, Professional Programs Part-time 389, Professional Programs Full-time 243, Trades and Services Part-time 216, Trades and Services Full-time 165, Low Status Professionals Part-time 360, Low Status Professionals Full-time 280.
2. For each of the satisfaction variables faculty members were asked to respond on a scale of one to four: 1 = very dissatisfied, 2 = somewhat dissatisfied, 3 = somewhat satisfied, and 4 = very satisfied.
3. The "Rewards" category represents the mean of four individual satisfaction variables: satisfaction with job security, satisfaction with advancement opportunities, satisfaction with salary, and satisfaction with benefits.
4. The "Academic Again?" variable displays the results to the question: "If I had it to do over again, I would still choose an academic career." For this variable the possible responses were as follows: 1 = strongly disagree, 2 = disagree, 3 = agree, 4 = strongly agree.

groups was larger than the difference between part-timers and full-timers in the vocational groups. Furthermore, part-time faculty from all three of the vocational groups actually were more satisfied than their full-time counterparts in two of the six variables: satisfaction with the job overall and satisfaction with salary. Taken together these results show clear differences in satisfaction that appear to depend on one's status as full- or part-time and on the general group to which one belongs. That is, part-timers from the academic groups were less satisfied than part-timers in the vocational groups, but full-time faculty from the academic groups tended to be more satisfied than their counterparts from the vocational groups. Therefore, the differences among part-timers are not simply the result of uniform satisfaction differences across disciplines.

Results from our weighted least squares analysis support the general pattern indicated by the simple means. The full-time faculty groups tended to show no significant differences in their satisfaction levels, while part-time members of the arts and humanities and social and behavioral sciences groups were significantly less satisfied than all other part-time groups. In addition, members of the part-time physical and biological sciences group, while more satisfied than the other two academic groups, were less satisfied than members of the vocational groups. The mean responses for satisfaction with the job overall indicate a pattern seen in the other four demand and reward variables: there were significant differences between the part-time groups for all variables, while there were few significant differences for the full-time groups after controlling for the other independent variables. For overall job satisfaction part-timers from the three academic groups had no significant differences, while part-time members of the vocational groups were all significantly more satisfied than part-timers from the academic groups. In the full-time ranks, differences were not significant, nor were they large. The only significant difference in satisfaction for full-time groups compared to members in the arts and humanities was for members of the professional group. While part-time faculty members from the professional group were significantly more satisfied than part-time members of the arts and humanities group, the opposite applied for their full-time counterparts: the professional group was less satisfied than the arts and humanities group.

This pattern held for the other four demand and reward variables—job security, advancement opportunities, salary, and benefits. The pattern reversed itself regarding the question of whether a faculty member would be willing to pursue an academic career again. For this variable part-time faculty members from the arts and humanities group were significantly more likely to indicate a desire to pursue an academic career again. No such significant differences exist for the full-time faculty groups. Hence, even when controlling for other variables, part-timers from the academic groups, while less satisfied overall with and including other demand and reward areas, were significantly more likely to be willing to pursue an academic career again. It should be noted that gender was a significant factor in determining satisfaction, particularly for part-time faculty with regard to job security, advancement opportunities, and benefits, variables in which men were more satisfied than women.

Satisfaction data from both 1999 and 1993 demonstrate that there were significant differences between part-time and full-time faculty in general, and significant differences between the seven part-time groups in the study. These findings have proven to be robust as they are supported by both an analysis of simple group means and by weighted least square regressions.

Our data analysis reveals a number of differences in part-time faculty income, including total income and sources of income; part-time faculty perceptions of their community college position; their desire for a full-time academic position; the status and sector of their outside employment; and their satisfaction. These differences illuminate two distinct divisions in community college faculty. First, in the aggregate, compared to full-time faculty, part-time faculty in community colleges hold fewer advanced degrees, earn less income, have fewer professional development opportunities, and are less satisfied with the demands and rewards of their positions: on the whole, a bleak picture. Clearly, national data indicate that even in the aggregate part-time faculty appear to be second-class members of community colleges, and their treatment invites a myriad of problems relating to morale, instructional quality, and student outcomes.

But what of the other studies in the literature that have presented part-time faculty as a contradictory labor force? The literature presents a dichotomy about part-time faculty: are they exploited or highly trained and paid professionals? Do they bring rare and highly valued expertise and training to campuses or are they economic expedients and an easy means to efficiency? Are they excluded and marginalized on campuses or satisfied with their positions on campuses and the relative lack of demands for time their temporary positions bring?[43] The disaggregated results for the seven part-time faculty groups help unravel those contradictions. As discussed earlier, part-time labor in the New Economy can be described in two general categories: those who possess rare and highly valued skills who have numerous options for employment across numerous sectors; and those whose skills are readily available and valuable in only one specific sector. Our findings indicate that these two types of part-timers exist simultaneously on community college campuses and they can be distinguished by our disaggregation of national data sets.

The first contradiction mentioned above concerns whether part-timers are exploited or are highly paid professionals—the answer to that question depends upon which group of part-timers one examines. Part-time members of the academic transfer groups earn the lowest wages of all community college faculty and proportionately they earn less in comparison to their full-time counterparts. This group of part-timers prefers to be full-time faculty, and they earn the majority of their income from part-time academic jobs. It is also consistently reported that there is a glut of people trained for these positions. Therefore, one can view this group as exploited. Conversely, part-timers from the vocational groups are relatively well-paid with regard to total income due mostly from their high incomes from nonacademic employment and proportionately earn nearly as much as their full-time counterparts. Members of this group prefer part-time positions at colleges and tend to hold full-time positions outside of higher education. These nonacademic positions allow them to acquire training and skills, perhaps not degrees, as well as personal networks with business and industry that are rare and valued by vocational programs at community colleges. Part-time faculty from the vocational groups, then, can be described as highly trained and well-paid professionals.

The second contradiction—part-timers as highly trained professionals or economic expedients—is directly related to the first. Part-timers from the academic transfer group have few desirable employment options outside of higher education. Because of this lack of options they are willing to accept part-time positions. Colleges, therefore, are able to employ large numbers of this group to increase efficiency and flexibility. Part-time faculty from the vocational groups, while they do increase efficiency and flexibility, tend to not seek full-time employment because they have numerous employment options outside of academe, and they bring specialized training and experience to the vocational programs of colleges.

The group to which one belongs resolves the final contradiction. Part-time faculty from the academic transfer groups prefer full-time employment. That is, they seek more connection and collegiality on campuses and are unable to achieve it either because it is not offered or they have obligations at more than one school. This situation, reasonably, should create a sense of marginalization. Once again, part-time members of the vocational groups have different motivations for teaching part-time and, importantly, have opportunities for meaningful interaction outside of colleges because of their full-time careers. Thus, this group of part-timers is much less concerned about the status of their positions at community colleges.

Clearly, part-time faculty are an important labor force within community colleges and for community colleges nationally not only because of their relative size as a proportion of all faculty but also because of the tensions and contradictions they represent as a group. For our purposes, specifically, part-time faculty serve as an emblem of an institution that is enmeshed in the New Economy. The institution presents itself on the one hand as a corporation and on the other hand as a school. Part-time faculty reflect the economic competitive nature of the community college as well as the specialized training function that community colleges provide for a community or region or nation.

# 7

# Corporatism and Neo-Liberal Ideology: The Values and Meanings of Faculty Work

In this chapter, we describe the tensions between the educational values and the economic values of faculty work. Faculty perceptions and administrative perceptions are compared and combined to provide understandings of the relationships of the values and meanings of faculty work to the institution. By work, we refer to instructional roles—teaching, curriculum design and development, and advising of students—and administrative roles for full-time faculty—committee work, supervising staff and overseeing the work of part-time faculty, program maintenance (for example, supply and equipment oversight), and responding to requests from administrators (for example, attendance at college functions, providing information on programs or students). As these roles and their accompanying expectations expand, faculty work—particularly work for full-time faculty—becomes more institutional, more aligned with the needs and the demands of those who direct the institution. Community college faculty work, in short, is increasingly managed following the pattern of economic globalization, consistent with a neo-liberal ideology.

We describe the views and judgments of administrators and faculty on faculty work, including their perceptions of faculty workload, faculty use of technology, job security, faculty identity, and governance. Faculty see themselves as managed according to the ideology of neo-liberalism and corporatism,[1] not unlike Gary Rhoades' concept of "managed professionals."[2] Administrators view faculty as extensions of management and as contributors to the corporate strategies and goals of the institution. College presidents articulate a corporate ideology that connects the community college to the "new global economy."[3] Faculty are assumed to be part of the corporate workforce that contributes to institutional productivity and efficiency as well as to local economic development.

In order to identify and explain faculty behaviors and values and the connection of these to institutional actions within the community college, we began with four major questions. (1) What are faculty and administrators' perceptions of and responses to business-like and market-oriented behaviors of their institutions? (2) To what extent has managerialism occupied a central place in the community college? (3) Do faculty comprise an oppositional culture and, if so, what is the nature of their opposition? (4) Given the presence of an institutional orientation to the marketplace and the central role of managerialism, is there a new institutional context for the community college?

Using qualitative field methods for collecting and analyzing data, we relied upon interviews, observation, and document analysis for data, with interview data as the principal data source. Interviews with 171 faculty in a variety of program areas and interviews with 108 administrators (including seven board members) were conducted at seven community colleges in five legal jurisdictions for the period 1996–2003. The overwhelming majority of these interviews were carried out during 1996–98. Categories for data were developed from a framework that follows from the research questions and data within the categories were clustered.[4] One major category included data pertaining to business-like and market-oriented behaviors within the institution. A second category was named "Managerialism" and included data consistent with administrative practices that correspond to private sector rather than public sector behaviors and inculcate a homogenous value system in employees, as well as a prominent role for managers in the decision-making area normally and customarily occupied by faculty.[5] A third category used the term "Oppositional Culture" to designate those views and behaviors of a collective group of faculty that suggested resistance and even hostility to mainstream views and actions within the institution. Finally, the fourth category for data indicated a new context for the institution, reflecting new understandings and interpretations of history, mission, and culture. Table 7.1 synthesizes the views of both faculty and administrators.

Additionally, we returned to two community colleges in 2004 to interview a sample of faculty and administrators both to bring the research up-to-date and to provide a point of comparison with a large data set from the 1996–98 period. We compare these more recent data with the older data set at the conclusion of the discussion of the earlier data.

For the first question ("What are faculty and administrators' perceptions of and responses to business-like and market-oriented behaviors of their institutions?"), faculty indicate threat of job loss, institutional expectations for market behaviors and competition, and increased work, or no work, for faculty. Additionally, faculty note that government politics and money are the major forces of change and these forces affect college mission. Administrators note that fiscal reallocations and cuts have an impact on faculty morale, that private sector behaviors are ascendant, that competition within the public sector even among higher education institutions is expected, and that business-like behaviors are now customary, including the increasing reliance upon a part-time workforce. Additionally, administrators identify internal college politics and changing student demographics as major forces of change. Clearly, the pattern of behaviors within these colleges is entrepreneurial and oriented to business and to the marketplace. Indeed, faculty work to raise

**Table 7.1** Faculty and administrators' perceptions

| Clusters | Faculty's views | Administrators' views |
|---|---|---|
| Business-like and market-oriented behaviors of their institutions | Expectations for faculty to increase productivity and for institution to meet the needs of government and business | Required to compete, survive, and flourish; driven by external environmental forces such as government funding and technology |
| Managerialism occupying a central place in the community college | Management drives the institution, using economic rationales to provide education and training and as result, the mission alters and faculty become labor, with part-time faculty as a dominant instrument to achieve efficiency; loss of morale; loss of investment | Work increases and governance becomes an issue of debate; two classes of faculty—those who are willing to change and those who are reactionary—mostly old timers |
| Faculty as an oppositional culture | Rather than forming an oppositional force against management, faculty express grave misgivings about the mission alteration, the governance and the management of their institution | Administrators acknowledge institutionl alterations but view these as inevitable and beyond their control |
| New institutional context for the community college | Context of competitiveness and rapid change—largely business and job orientation<br>Mission alteration: Loss of past values and serving those in need<br>Market orientation—new educational population | Context of competitiveness and rapid change—largely business and job orientation<br>Mission alteration: Canadian colleges focus upon degrees<br>Market orientation—government funding shrinks; meet demands and needs of constituents |

money as well as assist in enrolling more students, as noted by faculty in a Washington State college:

> We are expected to solicit associations and increase enrollment in our programs . . . Faculty are getting involved in fund raising. They feel that if a program will continue to exist they need to get out in the community and raise money or solicit donations of equipment.

Performance in business-like terms has become the norm as expressed by a Nursing faculty member in an Alberta college:

> [We] are going to begin to run education more as a business—being more accountable, more concerned with key performance indicators and outcomes.

Much of the economic behaviors seem directed by those other than faculty, in that the language of those responding to interview questions suggests that the faculty are not responsible. Some other party—notably the college's administration—is propelling the college in a specific economic direction. College administrators acknowledge this shift. "The college is out at the chamber of commerce and is vigorously courting business, especially large corporations," states an administrator from the same Alberta college where the Nursing faculty member indicated that performance outcomes were the institution's concern. Even those colleges that were not formerly connected to the business community have altered their priorities, as noted by the head of public relations at a California college: "We have recently become involved in the local business community and industry, but historically this was not the case . . . [There are] increasing donations from local companies, like HP [Hewlett-Packard]."

These behaviors do not demonstrably shore up institutional morale or faculty performance. Administrators also acknowledge this perception.

> People are into survival here; people are more desperate . . . Cut here, cut there, reduce, take permanent cut. We have to make hard choices—eliminate the horse out of the pack, not one leg of each horse. (Manager of Distance Education, California college)
>
> [There are] questions of what to cut and what to allocate; questions of restructuring and reallocation. This hurts morale and meaningful participation . . . The president is deluded [in believing in participation]. Folks are frustrated, particularly Arts and Sciences faculty. (Dean of Academic Services, California college)

But, the president of this same college is not ignorant of the conditions of work and outcomes for faculty: "There is more work and fewer resources—[this] leads to fractious behaviors." At an Alberta college, the senior administrator responsible for Human Resources has a similar perception with respect to the stress placed upon faculty as a consequence of fewer resources for the same or greater levels of work: "There is an increased volume of work, [an] increase in [the] number of students and fewer support staff: [This] caused a massive increase in stress as faculty and staff work harder and longer."

The acknowledgement of these economic and business-like behaviors reflects the redefinition of mission and purposes of these colleges.

> The mission claims we are student centered but we are not student centered . . . We sell the place—almost exploitative; the opposite of student centered . . . (Counselor, British Columbia college)

> It is all expediency and a quick fix—to fit job requirements. (Environmental Science and English faculty, Washington State college)

> The push is towards more [vocational training] . . . for the new economy: fuzzy skill sets . . . Numeracy, literacy, arts—they are paid lip-service . . . We are now becoming like an institution on a pogo stick. (Union president and Science faculty, Alberta college)

> This is a free market organization: people are added or taken away. We are not preserving fields as we should . . . We have a market model—moving closer to a business. (Vice chair of Education Council, British Columbia college)

The purposes of the institution, according to these and other faculty, have shifted from education to training and to those actions that match the needs of local economic markets. Outcomes of behavior viewed by faculty to be promulgated by college managers have decidedly business-like and economic characteristics.

A group of administrators at the Dean level at an Alberta college concurs with the perceptions of faculty at their college: "The college is made to operate more like a business." This orientation is consistent with a documented pattern in higher education—from research universities to community colleges—that places institutions in a competitive marketplace.[6] In order to compete, colleges operate as businesses using economic rationales for decisions. While some higher education faculty—such as those at elite research universities—might be immune to these business-like behaviors, community college faculty are not. As an institution, the community college is firmly connected to the workforce needs of a globally competitive economy.[7]

The twin themes of productivity and efficiency and managerial control characterize managerialism at the seven community colleges examined, and indicate an answer to the second question ("To what extent has managerialism occupied a central place in the community college?"). Institutional and government documents as well as interview data from administrators and observational data corroborate faculty perceptions. The governments of several states and provinces examined—California, Washington, Alberta, and British Columbia—initiated productivity measures in their fiscal allocations to colleges. Indeed, in the province of Alberta, government required colleges to improve productivity by reducing government funding by 21 percent over a three year period in the mid-1990s and expected colleges to maintain their student enrollments at the same level or higher.[8] College planning documents and reports in all jurisdictions examined noted institutional commitment to higher levels of productivity and improved efficiency. Within the colleges, organizational behaviors are perceived by faculty as oriented toward business and the economic marketplace as colleges seek to gain favor with business and pursue additional revenues.

Actions aimed at increasing productivity and economic efficiency have educational outcomes. The department chair of Social Services at an Alberta college indicates that fiscal restraint and rescision have altered behaviors: "Cutbacks forced us to reconsider what we were doing . . . If status of departments is dependent upon revenue generation then our department is doomed." But not all faculty are opposed to the consequences of rescision, as the department chair of the Health Sciences program at a Hawaii college notes: "We will come up with budget cuts . . . We are talking about blending credit and non-credit—good idea: faster development and delivery of programs." More work for faculty, reduction of laboratory time in science courses for students, less faculty interactions with students, dropping of low enrollment courses, and a narrowing of the curriculum are all consequences of the actions that are justified by efficiency and aim to improve productivity.

But managerialism is broader than efficiency and productivity and includes control over the work of faculty, an observation we noted less strenuously in chapter 4 in our examination of collective bargaining agreements. Institutional decision making is viewed as the purview of managers, especially senior managers. This managerial control is judged as placing the faculty in a subordinate institutional role and the actions of the institution as antithetical to traditional faculty values. At some colleges, faculty participation has diminished, as claimed by Washington State faculty: "Faculty are less involved in decision-making. Faculty are supposed to be involved in the College Council but some say they don't even know what it is." At the same college, the faculty's sense of sharing in decision making under one president altered under new management: "Shared governance committees turned out not to be shared [a year later]." Indeed, managerial decisions which appear to ignore the interests, especially the financial interests, of faculty distance them from the enterprise, as indicated in the California college:

> Sometimes administration forgets what the college is all about . . . Finance people got caught because they said there was no money and denied raises. Then they found money . . . The result has been a lack of confidence.

Faculty agency is diminutive—peripheral to decision making—and for some this constitutes an erosion of past practices. Even the claim that faculty participate is presented within a context of managerial prerogative as demonstrated by the president of a Washington State college: "[The previous president] changed governance. I've changed it again. I changed it from self-governance to participatory . . . advisory." This suggests that governance of faculty work is not in the hands of faculty but instead the purview of the chief executive officer. Only in the province of British Columbia, Canada, do faculty have some semblance of a professional role in governing the institution, although this does not mean they are self-governing.[9] But, even here there is some tension over the understanding of faculty's role in governance, as expressed by a college president in 2003, reflecting upon several years of a strong role for faculty in governance: "Everybody is an expert critic; [they argue] about the co-governance model, arguing about the whole management model . . . It is not co-management; co-governance okay, but 'stay out of management. We stay out of your classroom; you stay out of our management.' But everyone is an expert here."

While governance is a complex and contentious issue for both faculty and administrators, it is the alignment of the college with private sector interests and private sector practices that typifies managerialism in the community college. The considerable market-orientation of these colleges—noted as not only tailoring programming to business interests but also modeling business behaviors—has skewed faculty work. This work is described by faculty as aligned with the needs of business and industry, with teaching as synonymous with training.

> The needs of industry influence how we do everything: we revise programs to fit their needs. (Philosophy and Composition faculty, Washington State college)
>
> There is pressure upon the institution to prepare people for jobs. (Social Science department head, British Columbia college)

Managerialism here suggests a commandeering of the institution by both external forces—such as business and industry and government, which funds and directs colleges through policy—as well as by a managerial class within the institution. The "master and commander" syndrome is clearly evident in the interview data from the President of the Alberta college and from the Chancellor of the district for the California college as well as from five other college chief executives who articulate their institutions' shifts to the economic marketplace. The president of the Alberta college, while identifying the sources of change, acknowledges the outcomes.

> In this highly competitive environment, you feel enormous pressure to be adroit, nimble, flexible, and to respond to rapidly shifting corporate, government, student demands and needs . . . We just had to operate in a far more businesslike way.

The Chancellor for the district office overseeing the California college is blunter: "If we are going to stay in business, we are going to have to be prepared to meet the challenges of a newly emerging economy."

Organizational actions are thus directed to purposes not necessarily aligned with the historical characteristics of the community college—provide access to education and training, focus upon student development, respond to the needs of the community (that is, community in all its representations), and provide a comprehensive curriculum.[10] In seven colleges in two countries, what is evident is a narrowing of both curriculum and mission, even though there are numerous claims in the literature about mission expansion.[11] The decision to orient colleges to "economic conditions" and "the needs of industry," "driven by technology," is not owned by faculty. The faculty role in institutional decision making seems to be a minor one even though faculty participate on committees, have agreements with colleges that codify working conditions, and may even numerically dominate educational bodies that make decisions. Because they are on the periphery of those decisions that determine the intended purpose of the curriculum and the allocation and management of resources, faculty serve as instruments of a managerial enterprise.

There were numerous characterizations of faculty or a group of faculty as a collective that opposed another group, and led to an answer of the third question ("Do faculty comprise an oppositional culture and, if so, what is their opposition?"). Opposition to government, administration, and other faculty was noted. Antagonism against these groups was expressed on such matters as the mission and purpose of the college, technology, and governance. The faculty's understanding of mission and institutional purpose is viewed as inconsistent with the actions of their institution. As one Biology instructor at a British Columbia college noted, "We are moving to training for slots rather than education." This concern was repeated at the other institutions, as stated by an Interior Design instructor at an Alberta college: "We are losing the heart of the college by heading for business." One contentious point is found in the use of technology, here in the form of distance education, which pits faculty against administration.

> Distance education is a point of contention between administration and faculty: we are trying to prevent a takeover of our responsibilities in curriculum and instruction. (Humanities faculty and Union copresident, Washington State college)

Disagreement between faculty and administration on the decision-making process is evident as decisions ultimately shape college mission. This point is articulated by a Business faculty member at an Alberta college: "The issue is the content of decision-making, which is poor and there is less consultation . . . Centralization is the trend of the college. Decision-making is moving to higher levels. In the long run it will hurt the mission." These expressions are antagonistic, suggesting that what the institution is doing is wrong, against what the speaker values, and deleterious to their college.

Yet, in spite of the considerable number of expressions of antagonism among the faculty at the seven colleges, there is little evidence to indicate that the like-minded faculty formed into a coalition to resist forces of power and influence, whether these are the government, administration, or other faculty. Only the faculty union serves as a resister to forces or pressures that would characterize this group as an oppositional culture to the administration, the governing board, or the government as noted by the data from union officials. These data reflect both union actions and the values of union executive members.

> We maintain the *status quo*—there is nothing innovative. The penalties are great and the rewards small. The deficit mantra stifles change. It is like a treadmill . . . The government's framework for productivity increase is bullshit: it is just put in to satisfy the public. (Faculty union president, British Columbia college)
>
> There is an increasing effort to dismantle shared governance . . . This is a state trend . . . I would not trust [the Chancellor of the district]. (Union president, California college)

> There is an incompetent administration [at] district office. They have a lack of experience with collective bargaining . . . New ways have undone shared governance: [it is] now superficial . . . The quality of teaching is [being lost]. Teaching gets lip service from administrators. Money is going to technology not to faculty support. The computer is seen as a tutor . . . [The district is looking for] a magic pill: more technology, more distance education. It is training versus classical education. The pressures from business will define the goals. Money drives . . . They are showing how faculty are no longer necessary. (Union president, California college)

> The Board of Regents [is] really out to lunch. They think we are teaching auto tech, or . . . we are a baking school. (Union Representative, Hawaii college)

> The district coordinators make decisions about curriculum . . . The district is nothing but trouble . . . There is pressure to create competitive delivery modes . . . This is a movement toward the commercialization of education. (Union copresident, Washington State college)

> Faculty are currently in negotiations regarding distance learning. Full-time faculty members want distance learning to be treated as a regular class with the same contact hours. (Union vice president, Washington State college)

> The board is an ineffectual entity, captured by administration . . . There is more pressure to be entrepreneurial . . . [The] provinc[ial government] doesn't have a handle on education. (Union president, British Columbia college)

> The college is not maintaining community college characteristics. Administration would like to concentrate on [being a] university . . . Faculty duties have increased: [There is] more counseling and more assessment of students' ability. There's also more administrative duties. (Union president, British Columbia college)

> Faculty are working hard but not recognized . . . [There is a] huge volume of work, especially for administrators. [There is] stress and unthinking acts without considering others . . . The board [has] not read their responsibilities . . . They have abdicated their responsibility. They are not knowledgeable about education. (Union president, Alberta college)

In seven colleges, union executive members articulated a general faculty view that is critical of the administration, the governing board, or the responsible government—provincial or state. The union serves a traditional role as a formal body that expresses opposition to management. None of the union officials, however, expressed antagonism toward business and industry or toward corporations, including multinationals, sources identified by scholars as the instigators of a global economy and its ills.[12]

While community college faculty are unlikely to be identified with industrial unions and their behaviors of resistance to owners and managers, their solidarity either as union members or as occupational colleagues is evident. Faculty identify with their institution and its mission and actions, even if they are opposed to some institutional actions. Catherine Casey[13] refers to these conditions as the corporatization of the self, whereby employees identify with the institution over and above occupational or associational identity. Such a condition—where employees identify with their institution and internalize the characteristics, values, and practices of the "corporation"—leads to homogeneity of views.

Homogenization of values and standardization of knowledge systems are viewed by scholars as outcomes of market competition and globalization.[14] Global competition rationalizes productivity and efficiency measures as well as organizational transformation led by a managerial class.[15] Jane Kenway in discussing education calls this a strategy of the state where stress and crisis are passed down the line in a form of centralization of authority and decentralization of responsibility, enacted by the use of accountability measures.[16] The policies, plans, and behaviors of the state are evident in the documents produced by the state—including strategic plans and funding allocations for higher education.[17] During the 1990s this placed responsibility upon community colleges for adhering to the requirements of the state.

The two views of faculty—those of faculty and those of administrators—indicate a similar view of the institution: that is, there is a changed institutional context for faculty work. The new context for community colleges is not only the local economy but also the global economy as understood by policy makers, especially governments, and leaders of business and industry. The answer to the fourth question ("Is there a new institutional context for the community college?") is in the affirmative. This new context exists in juxtaposition to the traditional context of institutional history, culture, and mission. Yet, while the traditional context is reflected in the perceptions and values of faculty, institutional actions ignore the traditional. Faculty are articulate about these alterations.

> [We] are always moving, never reflecting on projects, always go, go, go . . . There are a lot of pluses and minuses to this kind of system—a lot of pressure . . . [W]ith more computers], the faculty workload went way up . . . [There is] a new push for bigger classes. (Faculty Senate president and Outdoor Recreation faculty, California college)

> We are volume-oriented worker bees, [and] classified as government worker[s] . . . [This is the] crystallization of bureaucracy . . . The onus [here] is upon teachers to get [students] through . . . Marks have gone up . . . [This] escalation is based upon student threat[s]. (Business faculty, Alberta college)

> [We] are shifting upward and away from the low end of the mission. I don't like seeing the college [move] away from reaching the under-prepared, remedial, and working class students. (Business and Economics faculty, Alberta college)

> I still want the college to be seen as a place where adults can have a second chance at getting an education . . . I thought that a community college has a mandate to provide people . . . particularly the economically disadvantaged with an opportunity. (Social Services department chair, Alberta college)

> We are redefining the educational population. We have become more entrepreneurial and moving closer to the market. We are more conscious of the market. (Social Science chair, Hawaii college)

These perceptions suggest that the community college is an instrument of business or government or both.

> The needs of industry influence how we do everything: we revise programs to fit their needs. (Philosophy and Composition faculty, Washington State college)

> The training factor approach [leads us] to offer what is marketable. (Vice chair of Education Council, British Columbia college)
>
> Both presidents [of the two colleges are] political: they are socializing the high tech companies. Business wants training. [The college] uses technology for workforce for the local economy . . . Programs are setup for business interests. (Faculty union president, California college)
>
> I believe that if government funding was tied to repainting walls that's what we'd be doing. (Theater Arts faculty, Alberta college)
>
> I approve of the globalization initiative and the technology push in general from administration . . . A major change at the college is the increased emphasis on the market. This is a good thing . . . We need to be right in the middle of economic development . . . The college should be run like a business so it can compete and adapt quickly. You have to look like a business to please business. (Writing faculty, Alberta college)
>
> The college makes decisions based upon where [the] provincial government focuses resources. (Auto-mechanics faculty, British Columbia college)
>
> Politicians control the budget: they micro-manage the college. (Humanities chair, Hawaii college)

Governments, including political officials, along with business are viewed as steering if not directing the colleges, largely in line with economic interests that are aligned with global competitiveness.

Institutional context is also shaped by the structure of governance. In the three U.S. colleges, either a district office and its trustees—the case for a California college and a Washington State college—or a university and its board of regents—the case for a Hawaii college—served as supreme institutional authorities. The district organization for community colleges is common in the United States, particularly for urban and suburban colleges. In four Canadian colleges, the structure of a single college, a governing board, and a provincial department responsible to an elected government minister was the formal structure. This pattern is a common one in Canada.

The identified party responsible for college actions in the U.S. colleges was often the district, as noted by one faculty member at a Washington State college: "The district is nothing but trouble." At this same college, restructuring, the pressures to use distance education, as well as the managing of distance education, and fiscal decisions are all viewed as emanating from the district office. At a California college, the villainous acts of the institution are connected to the district office according to the faculty senate president. "Last year was the worst in labor relations. There was a stalemate and arbitration. The district hired a union busting law firm; custodians were fired." At a Hawaii college, the college itself, the university, and the state government were viewed as synonymous, and the college was described as a "deep bureaucracy" where "procedures stifle" because the university system is "another department of state government." Individual college managements thus react to central power structures. At this Hawaii college, the university president of the University-Community College system declared, unilaterally, that remedial course work would no longer be financed by state operating monies. Thus, the college removed its remedial program from credit offerings, and provided remedial course work through its noncredit operation, a cost-recovery venture that removed both curriculum and faculty from the collective bargaining agreement as well as from college curricular and instructional policies.

While the union tradition is more robust in Canada, at the Alberta college, a similar movement of remedial education from credit to noncredit occurred but with a different rationale. There was no central edict from a district office, but rather a strategy of management to generate revenue, according to both faculty and administrators. Moving remedial from credit to noncredit permitted the institution to charge higher tuition fees for instruction, and remedial education became a profit center, an action confirmed by both administrators and by college financial reports. This action also permitted management to circumvent collective agreements and curricular and instructional policies. Thus, remedial education and the program, English as a Second Language, were removed from institutional policies and labor agreements that governed credit curriculum and instruction. If authority for curriculum and instruction has customarily been identified as synonymous with faculty, these actions in two countries demote that authority role to observer role.

The predominant expression of faculty values is at odds with the economic behaviors of the institution. Although faculty are the agents of many of these behaviors—for example, they develop and teach the curriculum that serves both government priorities and business interests—they articulate their opposition to the serving of these interests by their college. As agents of the institution, faculty are compromised. As institutional participants, faculty consent to the choices and reasoning, and indeed domination, of administrators, governments, and private businesses—those who have power over the meaning of work in the community college.[18] Faculty's work as educators—teaching, the development of curriculum, counseling and advising of students, and committee service—is configured or framed within an economic and competitive context, even though their values may be based upon other principles and other goals, such as personal and cognitive development of students or the social advancement of their society. Faculty frame this tension as a conflict between education and training, between traditional institutional goals, such as student-centered, and economic interests, such as business and industry-centered, and between centralized, hierarchical decision making and decentralized, democratic or shared decision making. Yet, these tensions do not result in a condition of overt cultural conflict between faculty and faculty, faculty and administration, or faculty and external influencers including government and business. In this sense, faculty, with the exception of the faculty unions, could be considered to be situated at the periphery of both institutional decision making and institutional influence on matters of institutional action related to purpose, even though faculty work—curriculum and teaching—is the core of institutional action.

Although faculty claim that they are central to both institutional functioning and institutional purpose, and they certainly participate in the administration of work at the community college, their aspirations for the institution are unrealized because the institution's economic goals—including training for a competitive global economy—and policies as well as accountability measures from governments are pursued as priorities. The press for greater productivity and efficiency by governments and other external influencers, such as business and industry, coupled with a managerial model of institutional decision making has called into question the professional identity of faculty and skewed their work as educators. Unless faculty can extricate themselves and their identity from the globalized community college or change institutional actions and the underlying corporate culture, this new environment of employee compliance with institutional purposes of a high productivity and market-oriented institution may constitute a more lasting norm for the community college. We argued in chapter 2 that the professional identity of faculty is predicated upon the institution's identity and that faculty engagement, and not disengagement, in the development of the community college is imperative. Based upon our research, on the trajectory of the community college as a corporatized, neo-liberal institution, the choice for faculty is weighted in favor of disengagement. This suggests that faculty in community colleges may have to forge an identity separate from that of their institution.

In 2004, we returned to two of the colleges and their faculty. One was a California college; the other was a college in the Canadian province of Alberta. We interviewed twenty-three faculty and administrators, including a sample of part-time faculty. Almost all the faculty we interviewed in 2004 were not interviewed previously for our research; approximately half of the administrators were interviewed previously.

In both colleges, there is increasing evidence that the institution has evolved a corporate identity. The mission of each college is firmly entrenched in both the rhetoric and practices of organizational members. For the California college, student access is a paramount value, with the concept of diversity—such as student identity, difference in the content of curriculum, and institutional social and cultural events—as the emblematic characteristic of discourse. Coupled with these values are the self-proclaimed behaviors of organizational members' performance: fast-paced, high intensity, and innovative.

Such behaviors lead to faculty expectations of activities that are beyond the norm of expectations for community college faculty.

> People are now coming into a highly competitive environment, in terms of that skill set, and so we do have many more faculty with doctorates than you might find at community colleges, [with] the kind of publication record that our faculty might have . . . Many of our faculty hold offices in their professional organizations. We're very proud of that, and I think it has upped the ante in terms of what we're looking for from the faculty. That has provided pressures with our collective bargaining agreement as well. (College president)

These pressures along with the budget problems of the day, which reportedly led to increased workload for faculty as classes were cut and instructors took on more students in their classes, suggest that time was the preeminent commodity for faculty.

> I would say that as an instructor there is so much time required for both teaching classes and doing these extra-curricular activities and professional development, and just an atmosphere of sharing in a collegial way the aspects of teaching and learning. I think that's what everyone wants. At least that is what I hear from a lot of my faculty, that we don't take a step back from all this busy stuff to better ourselves as individuals or just exchange information that is useful in the classroom. There is just not enough time for that. . . . Part of it is the culture here and that this is a busy place. There are a lot of things going on; people just don't stop. (Academic dean)

A consequence of the pressures of a high performance culture is on the one hand a loss of personal relationships within the institution.

> People now have far-ranging interests and we're much more diverse, so you don't have that same type of collegiality that we had before. I hear this from a lot of the old-timers. I'm not quite sure what they're saying all the time. Sometimes I think they say that a lot of these other people are just not like me, that it's hard to get close to them. Others are saying it's just harder for them to get involved with other people because there are so many demands on their time. (Academic dean)

On the other hand, what is lost in an environment of productivity and competition is what some view as the integrity of higher education, a critique apt for all of higher education, not just community colleges.

> Now, you have Business schools operating separately, Law operating separately, and Medicine operating separately, and within the Humanities and Social Sciences all the specialization shows up as a cluster, a constellation of institutes. They no longer have contact with the core of general education. So, the student comes in and the programs that offer the degrees say, "We're not getting prepared students." Well, most of everything is being farmed off to temporary, contingent faculty who aren't part of the system, can't do the kind of collegial governance work that is needed to develop an integrated structure, and it's all basically becoming remedial. You're starting to get the lower divisions separated off, whatever the program. Even though you see 20% of the students move down to the community colleges, even the others that come in are being taught primarily by teaching assistants and grad students who are no longer being mentored by their full-time faculty. They're just teaching a class. That whole idea that this is a teaching tool is gone. I think it's a disaster. I don't see the saving grace. The community college is the goal, the ideal, the image of a democratized higher education that would provide the humanized possibility for citizens in a highly technical, democratic society, but that is being co-opted by job training. Even if it's in the area of Humanities and Social Sciences, it's still being forced to be preparatory work to some line of career development or direction. The focus disappears from the educational experience. (Part-time faculty)

Furthermore, faculty use of electronic technology and the growth of distance education at the college comprised additions to not only faculty workload but also performance pressures. Ironically, full-time faculty continued to teach overloads, similar to their behaviors of the mid-1990s,[19] sustaining these workload pressures, not because of love of teaching but because of the costs of living in this high performance area of California.

Overall, faculty values at the California college are consistent with traditional community college purposes—teaching students.[20]

> Although I think we do a pretty good job of it, I think we need to keep reminding ourselves that the bottom line of everything we do here is student outcome. Sometimes we get focused on "the budget" or "the hire" or "the computer" and we may or may not consider why we are buying that computer or doing that hire. (Chair of Faculty Senate)
>
> I've always believed in community colleges because I think the focus is on teaching. You're catching a lot of students and getting them in those first two years thinking right and disciplined, and then they move on to universities. I don't think there's a better program going than the 2 + 2 program. I wouldn't want to be anywhere but a community college. (Science faculty)

Budget shortfalls—reductions from state and provincial governments and increased costs for instruction and other operations—are common in 2004 to both the California college and the Alberta college. Pressures on faculty productivity—and in both cases this played out as increasing class sizes—expanded faculty work and indicate that both colleges' faculty are highly industrious and focus upon achievement, as both groups emphasized faculty concern with educational quality and student learning. Although mission is a central feature of daily life at the Alberta college, the mission, unlike that at the California college, has less in common with traditional understandings of the community college.

The orientation and a large set of organizational behaviors of the Alberta college, beginning in the 1990s—promulgated largely by the senior administrative group—concern university status. The goal of the Alberta community college is to become an undergraduate university that focuses upon teaching. While this goal was nascent in the mid-1990s, by 2004 it was entrenched within the institution.

> We're moving to become a university . . . Our plan is to become a university. We still have some diplomas [for two-year programs], but many of the diplomas are post-degree diplomas. There are a few undergraduate diplomas left, but they are the ones that generally lead to applied degrees, as people need better credentials. The idea is to mainly do university degrees, change the applied degrees because the legislation in what colleges can do, our applied degrees will change into something more. (Academic dean)

Accompanying this determination, not only by administrators and the governing board but also by large numbers of faculty, to make the alteration from community college to university, there is conflict within the institution over both institutional designation change and mission alteration.

> [Faculty] are pretty divisive. 50% see it as an opportunity and 50% feel threatened. The ones who feel threatened are those who teach in the diploma programs . . . People have been pretty frank around here. While they've said we're not getting rid of diplomas, if you ask people where we're going to be in 20 years, if you ask if they see diplomas in this institution, they say, "No. That's not going to be the case." There might be another institution in the city, one called Valley College. That would probably fit, in terms of the system and where students would access different credentials. They would be the diploma granting institution in the city most likely, if we were to become an undergraduate university. So, they feel threatened, [faculty in] those diploma areas . . . because it just doesn't fit with where we're headed. They're worried. It goes up and down when we hear there's a chance the mandate is going to change, but then we hear "no." We get different messages, and it must be difficult for the faculty, because they're on a roller coaster. (Associate dean, Career Programs)
>
> The arts faculty is all for becoming a university, and they're poised and ready to go. The applied degrees are doing fine. They still have a lot of work. The problem is we didn't pause long enough to get those applied degree programs really solid. Some of them are still coming on stream. There will be some faculty, especially those who like the idea of becoming a professor, who say, "Yes, it's great." Those who like research, great. Those who still teach in some of the diploma programs, like in social work and child care, don't think it's necessary to become a university. Of course they don't. Where are they going to go? What's going to happen to them? How will they fit in if they're not teaching university courses? What about pay levels and all of those things. They're not particularly keen, although they're not objecting. Nobody is objecting—that's what blows my mind. They're talking, but they're not standing up and telling our president, "We don't want to be a university." I might have to do that. (Faculty coordinator)

On one level, then, the conflict revolves around job security. On another, the transformation is about the mission and purpose of the institution.

> People are thinking selfishly and not thinking about [our city] and what kind of education students need in [our city]. We've got a university. We're big enough to have two universities, but we used to provide two-year diplomas that filled a huge educational need. What's going to happen to them? They're gone! Well, the applied degrees soared. I think we're caught in this prestige thing and we're not paying attention to the educational needs of [people in this city]. (Faculty coordinator)

There are additional pressures upon faculty work—electronic technology, new student populations, new rhetoric and assumptions about student learning, and of course the need for increased productivity in order to meet enrollment targets and fiscal conditions and parameters. One former faculty member who is now an administrator described the outcomes of these pressures as a redefinition of the role of faculty. She uses the term "unbundling" to characterize a loss of the professional identity as an autonomous expert.

> What I've seen is that in the last three or four years, we've had what is called the unbundling of the faculty role. I think that has happened quite dramatically here . . . Once more, it seemed like a slow process, and then it really accelerated over the last two years. I think it's going on even faster, at least from my perspective . . . I can see this happening a lot faster than a lot of people know. Instead of one person being prepared to teach a course, we have a lot of online work now where two or three people work as a team, who never taught the course and never will, preparing the curriculum for online delivery. I think you're going to see lots more of that on this campus. The link between faculty member and curriculum has broken down, so you have curriculum that exists independently, or in bits and pieces, from community work and latest research, then you have people who come in to teach, some of them part-time. I see that as unbundling. I think faculty are very concerned about that, understandably so.

Notwithstanding the expressions of faculty devotion to students and to student learning—whether in the form of student-centered learning environments or outcomes-based learning—the role of faculty as autonomous professional is compromised in the corporate college. Budget problems pressure faculty to accept more students in classes, in spite of pedagogical objections; funding limitations are justifications for the hiring of more and more part-time, contingent faculty, so that the college mission of access can be fulfilled; and competition for resources makes colleges dependent upon resource providers including the state, business and industry, and students so that curriculum and instruction are tailored, modified, and arguably corrupted to satisfy the "customers" as well as the political and economic agendas of external influencers.

# 8

# In Their Own Words

In counterpoint to what we have developed thus far, some practitioners and scholars may take issue with our analysis. One such argument is from a senior administrator at a California community college who communicated with us several times on his view of community college faculty. His observations are both engaging and direct.

> As I look at most full-time faculty . . . I see many of them, especially the "academic faculty," who are still almost completely buffered from these [economic and globalization] effects. Most of them engage in traditional instruction for 12 to 15 hours a week, make $65–138K a year for a 175 day contract, do some office hours and then pursue either their day jobs or whatever their bliss happens to be. Most do not have any contact with local business and very few contacts within the community as community college professionals. Most "academic" faculty in California do not live in the world they describe. Few have any sustained contact with business or community. Most continue the abysmal teaching patterns described by Grubb. (California community college vice president, January 2005)

We will call this vice president "George" to give him some measure of anonymity. George was a faculty member in a community college for decades and in the past several years he has occupied a senior administrative position at a substantial California community college where he has managed the academic/instructional divisions of the entire college. Essentially his view is that the economic and political forces that we have expressed as neo-liberalism, new capitalism, and globalization have bypassed academic faculty, at least from his experiences at his institutions. Of course it needs to be pointed out that George is talking about full-time faculty and academic faculty. Based upon our calculations using national data on community college faculty that suggest academic faculty constitute 47 percent of all faculty, a conservative estimate is that full-time academic faculty comprise 30 percent of community college faculty, nationally. We rely upon national data that report part-time faculty constitute 64 percent of all community college faculty.[1]

George is certainly talking about faculty from the perspective of administrators and managers.

> The colleges are increasingly market driven. Administrators feel intense pressure to be highly efficient managers and good "businessmen." While we are

> forcing faculty to be more productive and they do have to do more of their own "grunt work" on the desk-top, the academic faculty continue to do pretty much what they have already done. Some find they can cut corners . . . expecting less of the students and remaining buffered behind Senates, unions, and the managerial bureaucracy. (California community college vice president, February 2005)

Following from George's perspective, and from what we assume will be that of those who may not be convinced of our views, we offer the narratives of faculty themselves, both full-time and part-time and both academic faculty and those faculty from other program areas such as professional and vocational. We think that George's views both misconstrue the work of faculty and the compensation for that work and underestimate the professional challenges that face these faculty. Furthermore, because George's articulated conception of faculty is limited to "academic faculty" and to full-time faculty he wrongly generalizes their characteristics and behaviors.

First we present the narrative of Jack, a full-time faculty member in the Music program at Suburban Valley Community College in California[2] and the new president of the Academic Senate at his institution. Jack is not a typical faculty member; rather we view him as a faculty leader. He might be thought of as an exceptional case, given his workload and responsibilities, although in our experiences he is fairly typical of those faculty who serve in leadership roles. His perspective, we suggest, permits him to offer a portrait of faculty and faculty perceptions at his institution that serves to illuminate a general condition.

> My background is as a musician, since my field here as a faculty member is Music, electronic music originally through Music Theory and Composition. At one time I was a trombone player. I have done some professional performing though I really don't do that anymore. I'm a teacher these days. One of the things that I think is true about me is that if you think about the spectrum of faculty types, there is the type that is very centered on one sort of discipline or a sub-discipline. That becomes their life. I'm a little broader than that; I actually have a number of interests besides music. I won't detail all those, but there are some others that are not necessarily part of my job here.
>
> . . . [M]y history as a teacher is that I was a part-timer for ten years here . . . before I was hired here as a full-time faculty member in 1989. I've been a community college faculty member for twenty-five years, fifteen of those as a full-time faculty member. Community colleges are the only place where I've taught.
>
> In terms of teaching I have kind of an interesting combination in that I teach two different subjects. I teach electronic music and I teach General Ed courses. A typical survey course that folks take as a lower division Humanities requirement is Intro to Music. I get a lot of general Ed students; they're about half my load, so I interact with all of the kinds of students on campus, maybe not so much the vocational folks or those doing some lifelong learning things. I also interact with folks who are not only focused on the discipline of music, but are more focused on electronic music itself which is a pretty small piece of that.

Another part of it is that partly by nature and partly by my training in electronic music is that I have used computer technology and electronic technology since about 1970 in college. I've been an early adopter of a lot of technology stuff for teaching and learning. It'll sound like I'm blowing my own horn here, but just to let you know I was the first person to do an online class that was based on some kind of internet tool. Originally it was an e-mail list and website. I did the first college website here in 1985. So, I've been co-chair of the campus technology planning team and I've done training. We also had a project last year in which we got about 200 faculty members to create faculty websites in a matter of about six to eight months, so that's another piece of what I do.

In regular faculty work, I teach four classes when I'm doing a regular schedule. Now I have a lot of release time so I have a reduced schedule. I teach a couple of General Education classes. For me there are two traditional four day a week, one hour a day classes teaching music, and then I normally would have two electronic music classes in the mid-afternoon, one on Monday/Wednesday, the other on Tuesday/Thursday. I also have office hours which are normally on Wednesdays, and I teach overload normally which is an electronic music class on Fridays. So, I'm here every day, which is probably not typical. Probably the majority of faculty are not here five days a week.

What my schedule plays out as now is that I teach an 8:30 class four times a week. Currently I get two-thirds release time. It was three-quarters release time, but we agreed to a temporary reduction because of the budget problem. The difference is that normally I would teach one class per quarter, and now I have to teach one additional class in one of those quarters . . . I go to an unbelievable number of meetings, both at the college and at the district. Half the day on Monday is spent preparing for the Senate meetings. The officers get together for an hour or two to go over our agenda and how we're going to present things. We like to be clear about our individual perspectives on particular issues so that in the meeting if we're going to contradict one another we know that ahead of time. It's not like we're trying to pull a fast one on anybody. We try to think of a strategy for moving the Senate toward a particular goal. That meeting is usually a couple of hours long, and then I usually need about an hour afterwards to decompress to digest what happened and what I need to do about it. We also have a planning meeting on Wednesdays to put together the agenda for the following Monday.

Some of the other major things that I'm involved in are the Chancellor's Advisory Committee which meets every two weeks. That is a shared governance group with representatives from just about any constituency you can imagine; it's a pretty big group. Then, there is what is called the Joint Development Group which is essentially a Chancellor's group to focus on those areas, in California law, of primary reliance where the faculty has legal authority to set the path, on things like programs and curriculum. Anything that is going down those roads, before it goes to the Board of Trustees, will go through the Joint Development Group. That meets every other week.

I sit on the campus and district budget committees. Those can be weekly or every other week depending on how bad things are going, or how serious things are. I attend the Board meetings every other Monday night. Mondays are interesting. I arrive at 7:20 in the morning, and on the Mondays with a Board meeting, I go home after the Board meeting which could be 10:00 or 11:30. That's a long day.

The major hiring committees—I try to stay off the faculty position and the classified position hiring committees that I typically would have been on in the past. So I'm on the President Search Committee, and if we had a VP position it's pretty likely that I would be on it, or one of the Senate officers would be on it if not me. And then there is some informal stuff that goes on. As Senate President you get pulled into issues where you have to stand up and say, "Hey! You can't do that. That's an area of faculty authority. Stop! You're overstepping your bounds." I've got one or two of those going on right now where I may have some phone calls with faculty or meetings with the Dean. I work a lot with the VP of Instruction. We sometimes also have some inter-faculty conflicts that come up where a couple of people within a department can be at odds about something. We try to make those issues things that the faculty will resolve rather than going to administration. We have a process for that, both an informal way of dealing with it, and then a Professional Relations Committee that we can take those issues to; it's a committee of the Senate. I'm spending a lot of time on those lately.

The kinds of things that happen, a lot of them actually get into academic freedom or curriculum areas where you're talking about something that is really within faculty authority. For example, text book selection, or an issue of revising curriculum, where the question is—I'm not saying who is right or wrong on these issues; as Academic Senate President I have to be careful—but the question we have to ask is, are the faculty acting ethically and responsibly in this area? Or, do we have to look at whether a Dean is assuming authority over something that is really a faculty area. For example, telling people what textbook to use, or telling a group of them they will all use the same textbook. Those are the kinds of issues, and we have some issues around the textbook selection, that we're dealing with right now in the Senate. We're dealing with policy around textbook issues.

In fairness, being a dean is a difficult thing. We're one of those colleges where the dean position is really a mid-level administrative position, but a lot of times those people come out of the faculty [ranks]. They have faculty perspective and experience, and I think if I moved into that position I would think maybe I had an even more well-rounded and authoritative perspective on faculty issues than the faculty do . . . So sometimes I think it's difficult for them to figure out which areas they had authority over as faculty and still allow their faculty to retain authority in those areas. That leads to tension often enough that it's an ongoing issue. I'm sure there are two perspectives on that; either they're a terrible faculty member who can't get their act together, or the dean is overstepping [his] bounds. So, we deal with those kinds of things.

You can imagine a college president or vice president coming in and trying to make a decision about something that's in an area of faculty authority or about a person and their continued employment or their schedule. I don't see that currently happening, though that kind of stuff—scheduling—can be an area of conflict between deans and faculty. By the way, when it comes to scheduling the Faculty Association, the Union, also has a big role in that. That's an interesting thing that happens here: there are some areas where faculty have to figure out if it's a union issue or if it's a senate issue . . . For example, there have been some issues with curriculum where a change in curriculum might lead to a change in someone's job, the types of courses they teach, or their schedule. It's a Faculty Association issue, but if it's curriculum it's also a senate issue.

We actually work that out pretty well. The Senate and the Union meet regularly and we have a similar perspective on the principles of that, so at least this year we haven't gotten into any conflicts that we couldn't resolve where the authority would lie. The Union is really leery about getting into, for example, arguments between faculty members. If it's a curriculum issue it comes to us. If it's a scheduling issue or a working condition thing, it's a union issue. We can speak together when necessary and do our independent parts.

As a faculty member, there are probably a few [major pressures or forces that are affecting . . . work]. One, obviously in California and probably nationwide, is how we respond to the budgetary problems. Those pressures come in several forms. One primary one is the whole issue of productivity: . . . how many hours do you serve per faculty person? There are different ways that ends up playing out. One can [have] an obsession with class size. An obsession with class size can play out as if you don't get a class size of X then that class will be cancelled. There is a lot of pressure on people about that. "I got 19 but they'll cancel it [below] 20." That's true even if it's not that simple. Sometimes there is a sense that some administrators, particularly at the dean level, . . . may use that as pressure on faculty. So if they have 19 they have to go out and try to find other people.

There is also pressure to shift your curriculum towards the classes that are large, which is definitely an issue of Senate interest. That's a tricky thing . . . In my own area, music for example, there are some courses that are pretty big, like those General Ed courses. In Creative Arts in general that is probably true; we have a lot of Art History classes and they generate big productivity numbers for us. At the same time, there [are] some classes that can't be that big, like Beginning Singing where you may only want five students.

Here, the[ere is] distance learning online class pressure—actually I think that has decreased lately. But a few years ago—again you're talking to one of the first people to do that here so I'm not against it at all though I do have a perspective that's evolved over about ten years—there was a time when a lot of people, and those people are still out there, who believe that the future of community college education would all be on-line. I don't think that has panned out nor will it pan out because for a certain number of students it's a great way to learn, but for most students that is not the ideal way to learn. It may be a viable second choice if they can't be here for the better way. For most of them it's better to be in some kind of place where they have face-to-face interaction. There was some concern that people were pushed into adopting online stuff because it is high-tech, because it also can generate some of those big numbers. We tried to put the brakes on that one; I think we've backed off a little bit on that right now.

What we do see a lot of, the place where the action is really happening with technology in teaching, is not in the online sphere. We have a distance learning program, but it's really happening in the classroom where people are finding ways to incorporate various tools and resources. That's really where the evolution is happening. People are having students write stuff on the web, and they're bringing web-based materials into class or making materials available to their students off the web. So I think we've seen change in that, and that has been the source of some pressure in the past.

There is a threshold level above which you're really pushing people to do things that aren't good for them. I also think there are a lot of faculty who see some value in using some technology resources in their teaching, but don't see that the only place to do that is by teaching an online course. They see that they can do that in their class. Most of the students do have internet access. If they don't have access at home they can access it at the lab. We can now incorporate some of those things in class and assume that most people will be able to do them.

There is one other issue that people have been talking about more recently, kind of a political issue that I think is interesting, that is related to the funding issues: calls for increased fees. I guess I'm talking more now as Senate President. It's the idea that people should pay more [of] their own way for community college. Especially in California that is contradictory to our nearly five decades' old master plan for higher education, and so the thought is—and people have been articulating this a little more clearly and more publicly—that one of the problems has been that we've talked so much about individual benefits of higher education. For example, "if you go to college, you will have a better job; you will buy a house; and you will have a good car." If that's the goal, then why shouldn't someone pay more, that basically they should make their own down payment on what they're going to get later on. We've de-emphasized the public benefit and the public good, and consequently we've lost some ground in making the argument to keep the fees low.

The other part of it that is really interesting is that as that's happened, you'll hear people, politicians particularly, talk about the failings of public education. So, we've got to try something new to fix those problems. In California, I like to say that we've conducted an experiment for forty-five years with a three-tier system of higher education with access to the UC [University of California] system for all the students who qualify and access to the CSU [California State University] system for all students who qualify, and a low-cost community college system. The result was a massive migration to California and California having this huge economy, with all this technology stuff that's happened here, the entertainment industry—all of those things. The experiment was conducted and the outcome can be measured, and now we're trying something different which has all kinds of problems. I think we need to get attention both about that, the issue of public versus individual, and the fact that we're not talking about something that has a history of failure; it has a history of success that we're moving away from, and that is problematic.

I think a lot of the [college's] goals are not actually new. I know our chancellor likes to talk about equity, access, and excellence. I like those three words. Access is important. This is the place where those who may not get access to higher education, or vocational education, or transfer courses, can get those. It's a really high goal for us to make sure that happens. And then equity once they're here so that they don't just get in the door, but once here they have an equal chance of getting out the door. We have some fairly objective goals about that. In terms of equity we have a goal that says if we look at different demographic groups that we won't see more than a five point difference in terms of success rates. I actually can't tell you where we are in terms of meeting that goal, but I think it's a great goal. Excellence—once you get people here and try to create this environment where they have equitable ability to use the resources and come out meeting their goals, that you do it in a way that the folks who come out are coming out with a really high quality community college education. I think we're pretty successful on that. Personally I think that's a great goal; so I'm in synch with that.

I always like to look at the other ones too. So what are some of the goals that maybe I'm not so in synch with? Sometimes we get into a little bit of confusion about who we're here for in two ways. The more minor of those, it's kind of traditional, is between transfer and vocational kinds of students. I think we're pretty good; I don't think that's a big issue, but it is something we have to pay attention to. Sometime we get, in my view, a little bit off-track when we use terms like "global." Global can mean, to some people, that we're trying to be a community college for the entire world, and we may focus on, say if we're talking about a distance learning program, people who are way outside of what I would normally consider our service area, even international in some cases. My own perspective asks why we're doing that, unless we've exhausted our ability to serve folks in our local area. The reasons for doing that, you could say, are to enhance what happens on your own campus, and it can also enhance your budget. That can be a place, occasionally, where I'm not in synch with all of the thinking. It's not a real big issue here.

One of the things I look at is other colleges in other districts in California. If you live in your own little world you see the problems and you think this is just how it is. Going to the State Academic Senate and actually having colleagues on other campuses that I talk to from time to time, when I compare the way, for example, that we dealt with our budget problems this year versus the way that a number of other colleges in districts have dealt with it, I would have to say that it's been a pretty good model of how people can work so that you can accommodate the interests of the bargaining units and the staff and the faculty and the students and the administrators. We had our conflicts and our disagreements, quite often out in the open at meetings where people would challenge someone's numbers and people would come back and talk about the numbers. As the year went on I think we all had kind of figured out where this was going to go, and there were no mass layoffs as we've seen in some other districts in California. I don't know if you're familiar with the Contra Costa Community College District situation, but they gave layoff notices to the entire faculty—that kind of adversarial stuff.

Part-time faculty don't have a very big voice . . . On the faculty side, I go way back on that. When I was a part-timer here, it was at a time when our faculty association was very resistant to part-time representation. I and two other part-time faculty members decided we were going to start a part-time faculty subcommittee of the faculty association and publish a part-time faculty newsletter. We had to fight tooth and nail with our own union to get that to happen. Compared to those days, things have changed in that part-time faculty members are represented on the Union's governing body, and we have part-time representatives specifically on [the] Senate, and we have no issue with a division sending part-time faculty as their representatives on [the] Senate as well . . .

I'm sure you're aware of this, but another issue with part-timers is that they have different levels of desire to be part of the activities of the college. I first found this out back in the days of starting the newsletter when we decided one of the things we were going to do was survey part-time faculty. My goal, at that time, was to become a full-time faculty member, and I assumed that is what everyone wanted to do. One of the survey questions essentially got at, "If offered, would you be interested in full-time?" I was shocked that there were a percentage of people who just wanted to teach one class because they were working somewhere else and this was augmenting their income. There were a percentage of people who wanted to teach a couple of classes but they didn't really want full-time because they didn't want to work full-time. And then, there were maybe a third or more who really wanted to be full-time faculty. Among one part of those people, you find folks who really like to be involved with the institution, and another part that just want to teach their class and go.

There are probably two reasons for having part-time faculty. There is the valid reason and then there is the unfortunate reason. The valid reason is that we need people with expertise in certain areas that we don't have in the full-time faculty, so we like to bring them in and have flexibility with those people. The unfortunate reason is that we've built into our assumptions in the state, in terms of budgeting, that half the faculty will be paid at this level that is half the cost. So, part-time faculty, particularly those who really want to be full-time faculty, probably begin by regarding part-time teaching partially as the way they're going to get the experience and connections to get to full-time. Then, they come to feel that because they are part-time faculty they're regarded as second-class faculty, and they end up being less likely to be hired. In fact, sometimes it works to your advantage, and you may be more likely to get hired by your local campus. Sometimes it works to your disadvantage because they know everything about you, the good and the bad, and then some outsider applies and you only see the good.

There is reasonable movement of folks from part-time to full-time. The main impediment to that is that we still have so many part-timers and not enough full-time positions. I remember this conflict myself—if you're a part-timer here and someone says, "Let's decrease the number of part-time faculty and increase the number of full-time faculty." It was actually the result of something like that that I got my job here. That's a double-edged sword. If you increase the number of full-time positions, and in response decrease the number of part-time positions, some of the part-timers may be the ones who benefit from those full-time positions. But, then again, the part-timer may lose their position; they may find that their class is no longer there to teach. I think part-timers can be conflicted about that one. Some will argue for keeping some kind of part-time status that is maybe better paid. My view is that the real place to go is to have a greater percentage of full-time faculty statewide so that qualified part-timers can diffuse into those positions around the state. Then the responsibilities of being a full-time faculty member are shared by a larger number of people. I think the short-term fear for part-timers is that they'll lose their classes. For me, when I went from part-time to full-time, the alternatives were that either I was going to get the position, or I was going to lose half of my teaching. Part-timers don't always speak with one voice about how to deal with that.

There are probably two things [I like about my work here], and one is institutional in that I actually like the way this place works. The quality of the work people do here is fine, and there are opportunities for people to do things outside of the one thing they're here to do. If you're interested in something, particularly at Suburban Valley, you can try something in developing programs. You may not get support for it, but at least you can try. That plays into my own personal preference which is not to be just an electronic music teacher. I like to be involved in a lot of different things and for me there are lots of opportunities to do that.

Although I think we do a pretty good job of it, I think we need to keep reminding ourselves that the bottom line of everything we do here is student

> outcome. Sometimes we get focused on "the budget" or "the hire" or "the computer" and we may or may not consider why we are buying that computer or doing that hire. That can be an issue occasionally. From the faculty side, I think we have some stuff to pay attention to here about what my colleagues like to refer to as "Faculty Rights and Responsibilities." That gets to that intersection I talked about earlier between mid-level management work, the Dean level, and faculty. We've had examples of this in this past year of places where we thought maybe authority was being assumed, but then again we weren't being clear with what our authority was. So, both sides have responsibilities in that area. I'll stop there. (May, 2004)

There is obvious complexity and nuance in Jack's narrative.[3] On the one hand he shows us that faculty are closely attached to the actions of their institutions and that the identity of faculty is intimately connected to organizational identity. On the other hand he demonstrates one of our recurring points: that faculty are complicit in and mutually responsible for what we have called *nouveau* college—an institution adapted to the New Economy and its neo-liberal ideology as well as an institution where the moral sentiment is expressed as access and education for students. Jack is a seasoned faculty member who has both internalized the earlier values of the traditional community college and embraced the more formal arrangements between labor and management that have accrued since the 1980s. Indeed, illustrative of the multiple views and roles of faculty is the twin bodies of the Senate and the Union. While on numerous issues, there is clarity on what is senate business and what is union business, on other matters, such as curriculum and workload, the boundaries are less clear. Jack manages to bridge these separate spheres through asserting solidarity with faculty generally, in relation to administrators, whose interests he suggests are not always those of the faculty.

From Jack's perspective, faculty through either the Senate or the Faculty Association (union) have considerable responsibility and authority in the functioning of Suburban Valley Community College. His narrative suggests that the serious and contentious issues facing the college are addressed by the senate and the union or by their interactions with the administration.

But if Jack's perspective is that of a faculty leader, as well as reflective of the views of a full-time faculty member, do those who are less influential and whose occupational status as part-time have another understanding of faculty work? Dolores is a part-time instructor in the Computer Science program at the same institution as Jack—Suburban Valley Community College in California. While Dolores is unlikely to represent all part-time faculty, she does shed light upon that large group of part-time faculty who are economic instruments of community colleges: a flexible and efficient labor force for the institution.

> I started teaching back in 1978 at the high school level. I taught Mathematics for a year in the central valley of California. From there I decided to leave teaching to go into industry where I could make some money. I moved back to [this] area because I had a job offer working for a research company doing database

design work. I worked for them for a while, got laid off, and went to work for an electronics company, which downsized. During the time I worked for the electronics company I decided to pursue my Master's degree in Information Systems, and went for my MBA at [private, comprehensive] University. I did that while working full-time. It took me six years to complete.

During the time I was doing my MBA I did some consulting work. I went to the city of [Metro] on some projects . . . I worked at a corporation as a systems administrator. I worked at the [major city newspaper] as a systems analyst. Then, two things happened: my daughter was in school at the time and the [newspaper] wanted me to work an increased number of hours for the same salary. At the time, my husband was also working [in] high-tech. We couldn't both put in 60 hour work weeks and have any quality of life, so I decided to do consulting work for the school district. They had just installed new computers and needed somebody to come in and install software and train teachers to use the new software. So I did that as a consultant for a couple of years. Once they got set up and trained . . . Suburban Valley Community College offered me a part-time teaching position for one class. For a couple of years I was doing both.

In 1998, what started out to be one class [at Suburban Valley] of thirty students grew to two classes of ninety very quickly during the boom of the dot com times. I had more than enough work to keep me on. Plus, our sister college put me on as adjunct faculty teaching web design during the summer times or whenever a teacher took a quarter leave. I held a 60 percent load during those times.

One of the issues, for me as part-time faculty, is that I would love to have a three-quarter position, 75 percent load. But, I don't see that as a reality at this point in time. You're likely to work sixty hours a week, or they give you one class, not anything in between because of the drop [in] enrollment for computer science students, and the drop of budget funds from the state of California. We've got two things happening right now: one is that the dot com boom is now bust, and people are no longer able to get the same job offers they were a few years ago. In addition to that, with the budget cuts to the community colleges they've dropped courses. A lot of students have come to me and said they wished they could get all the courses they need to finish in a short period of time, but they've cut so many classes here that people are kind of stuck.

It's happening at the high school level too. My daughter is in high school, in special education, and it's hard for her to get all the classes she needs in order to graduate. She may be attending community colleges, but I've told her she'll have the same problem at community college that you have in your high school. She may not be able to get the courses she needs to graduate on time. That is an issue in secondary education as well as the college level.

Students from the UCs and Cal State colleges are saying that they can't get the courses they need so they're coming here to take them. People are scrambling to get classes, and they're full. I went from two classes down to one, and I have to turn students away. I can't take more than forty students and still provide . . . quality . . . education . . .

Typically I teach four days per week. Right now I have one class that meets from 9:30–10:20. I will typically get up around 7:00 in the morning, read my e-mail, respond to student requests, then come up here and teach. I travel about forty-five minutes a day to teach a forty-five minute class.

I spend as much time driving as I do teaching. In addition to that I'm taking a course here at Suburban in VV.net to expand my skills. That meets at 12:30. So typically between 10:30 and 12:30 I'll go to the lab and do some work, take a lunch break, and then go to class. It meets five days a week. From there I pick up my teenage daughter and chauffeur her for the next few hours to her activities. Then I come home, cook dinner, and prepare for the next day's class. So, even though I'm only teaching one class and taking one class, I have a pretty busy schedule.

The number one challenge I'm facing right now is financial survival. I'm mortgaging my house to pay my bills. My goal is to financially survive until my daughter finishes high school, and then bail out of this area. It is too expensive to live here on what we make. My husband has not had a job raise in three years. The cost of our benefits has gone up 20 percent this year. As far as a future career path, I would love to be able to teach more courses here or at our sister college, although right now, unless someone leaves . . . They offered golden handshakes to some instructors who meet certain criteria based on age and the number of years teaching, so as some of the more senior people leave, perhaps it will open up more part-time positions. That's basically what I'm hanging in for, to see if in the fall they open up more part-time faculty positions. In addition to teaching Computer Science, I can teach Business because I have an MBA. I've approached the Dean of the Business School. If someone accepts the golden handshake, there is a possibility that I can take on a business course and teach it.

So, the biggest challenge I'm facing right now is how to survive economically . . . teaching one class with my husband working in a high tech job. We're in a deficit of about $1,500 per month.

A part-time faculty member cannot teach [legally] more than 60 percent of what a full-time faculty member can teach. And, there are two pay scales. Part-time people make, on the average, 40 percent of what a full-timer makes.

If you teach more than 50 percent load you get insurance fully paid for you and your dependents; you get six days of sick leave; and you have a choice of retirement plans. You can either choose a cash balance plan or the state retirement system. If you drop below 50 percent load, you can pay half the cost of the medical insurance, which in my case is $500 a month, and keep the other benefits. In addition to that, we get one hour per week of office hour pay.

Basically, my car is my office. I carry a backpack on wheels. My house looks like a warehouse. I have an office at home that looks like a library . . . I can use a phone in the lab, and I have voice mail here. They do not provide me with a computer or printer or software, but I can use the facilities here. Those are things that are provided to full-time faculty that I have to bear the cost . . . myself.

Besides the money situation, it's the not knowing if I'm going to get laid off, if I'm going to have a job. At the California Part-time Faculty Association that was an issue. They asked if I would consider having a one-year contract, and I said "yes." Then, you would know for a year you wouldn't have to worry about being laid off. Even if they could only offer you one class, you'd know you at least have that. Right now, we go quarter-to-quarter, and if your classes don't meet enrollment, you're laid off. My husband has to worry about that too. High-tech companies have lay offs every week.

I see the college as trying to balance their budget and maintain quality of education as much as they can. However, they've increased class sizes, and there is encouragement for faculty members to take more students than what their contract specifies. I have done that in the past to the detriment to the quality of the course I offered, so now I refuse to take more than the seat count.

If my class has a forty seat count, I'll take forty-five students at the beginning knowing that I'm probably going to lose a few. I probably end up with thirty-five students at the end of the course. When you talk about attrition or retention of students, we have a pretty high retention rate, but part of that is because instructors will take more than what their seat count specifies. Some instructors will do online courses because then there is not a limitation to the number of students they can take. But then suppose you've got a forty seat count class, and you're trying to deliver the same instructional materials but now you've got fifty students. They're contact hours. They are not in class teaching, but they have to e-mail and voice mail and contact all of those students individually, so the workload becomes heavier. I see that as being another thing that Suburban Valley is encouraging, distance learning, because then they get more bang for their buck.

They get more students per class, fifty instead of forty, and you get offered an online course and there is no additional money for taking those additional ten students. They say you're not teaching face-to-face and it's not the same kind of contact hours as you do when you're teaching a stand up class.

We [part-time faculty] have representatives on the Academic Senate here, and on the Faculty Association which is like our bargaining unit, as well as in Sacramento. Our advocate there is really strong in supporting part-time faculty issues. There are some senate bills in Congress right now that are addressing this saying they want to keep line items for part-time office pay, for equity pay, and for benefits for part-time faculty. They're trying to get that to be a statewide thing rather than being district-by-district. They haven't achieved it.

I do think we have a decent voice at least in my division. Our dean listens to what we have to say. My department chair is an ex-part-time faculty member so she's really responsive as far as part-time issues [are concerned] and in trying to help us with being able to teach and get the courses we need.

I've applied to companies as well. I'm actively seeking whatever is going to pay my bills. I really don't want to be stuck working sixty hours a week again because I still have a child who needs a chauffeur in the afternoons. It's not just the chauffeur thing; it's about spending quality time with your kids. Most of her friends are from divorced families, and the parents are spread so thin they have no time for their kids. The kids all come to our house. We have the computers, DSL, the latest software. The kids form study groups and they all come to our house. If I were not there, the kids could still meet, that's not an issue, but it's nice to have a parent in the home. People have a higher comfort level knowing there is a parent around than if it were just a bunch of teenagers hanging out together. There is that issue of quality time as well, so ideally if I could have a three-quarter load or teach another course at a college nearby. I don't want to be a freeway flyer. I'm already a freeway flyer.

I guess I could . . . substitute at the high school level. I have a teaching credential, so that would be an option. It's really not what I want to do. I'd rather stay at the community college. I like teaching at the community college because you're not forced to publish the way you are at the PhD level, and you have a better quality of student overall than you do at the high school. They're here because they want to be here and they're paying for it, so you get the best of both worlds. It's that in-between. It also serves the community. We have a lot of people who come here to learn and train for new careers. In the course I take in the afternoon the average age is probably forty. (May, 2004)

Dolores' narrative addresses both the political economy as well as her place within that economy. Her story concerns her working conditions and her occupational status. She extends her situation to those of others—to part-time faculty, to students in public schools, colleges, and universities, and to the working poor. From an organizational perspective, she and those like her, are clearly economic instruments used to meet institutional goals within a condition of limited resources. From a phenomenological perspective, she is without autonomy in her personal and professional life. As an integral part of the labor force of the community college, Dolores' plight must be addressed if community college faculty are to attain professional status. Because part-time faculty constitute such a large proportion of all faculty—64 percent nationally—their working conditions and compensation reflect a workforce that is not only contingent but also similar to itinerant farm workers or traveling salespeople of another era.

Although we have not discussed gender as an issue in the work of faculty, Dolores reminds us that as a woman and mother she has a social role with considerable onus for domestic and family duties and responsibilities, including child-rearing and the oversight of adolescents. These responsibilities not only add to her workload but also help to frame how she views her professional identity. If we are to understand faculty work more comprehensively, we should also consider such matters as gender and race/ethnicity, among other variables.

Finally, we present the narrative of Jeff Jackson, who teaches in the Adult Basic Education, Adult High School, and GED program at a rural college in North Carolina. Jeff expresses a sentiment about teaching students, especially those with weak academic backgrounds, that contradicts the views of both George, Vice President of a college in California and the general findings of Norton Grubb in his examination of community college teaching.[4]

I started [at the college part-time] with my one class and then that grew into more and more and more and then I fell in love with the program and I began to feel like that I had a place that I felt that I could make some contributions to . . . I taught here for six years part-time without any benefits, on contract month-to-month basis, class to class basis. And then with a new president, we became more organized and I was teaching day and night. I was teaching like thirty-nine hours per week. And then they suddenly realized that that was not a legal thing to do and so they made me full-time with benefits and now I'm teaching more than ever.

I wear two hats. I mean, most of my classes are in the adult high school, which is a program I really believe in, but at the same time, this past year I started teaching one class a week of ABE too. And those are students who come in and take the placement test and they miss either in reading or language or math, they miss the scores, the required scores by one or two points. And so they come into my class and work with me, and we pinpoint their problems and correct it and I move them on. They either go into the high school program or go into the GED. It's an effective program because once you know a person's weakness you can correct those and if a student's never been taught fractions or if a student's never been taught verb tenses then now this is their chance to learn it, so teach it to them. And then send them on. Let them make progress.

I have friends who think I'm absolutely crazy and stupid because I'm at a community college. I mean, they use the term community college [in a] very, derogatory [way] . . . They think it's rather pedestrian, you know, that kind of tone. But I don't. I mean I grew up here. I was born here, and I grew up here, and I know the community . . . But I really believe, I really believe in our program. And when I get through with the students in the English classes and send them over there [to more advanced courses], they're ready. Well, most of them are. But I teach them the traditional, like for example, traditional research procedures. And they know how to write a research paper. They know how to write an essay, hopefully. I try. And I use the old [approach]: I use the old traditional method of making them do rough drafts and giving them back . . . You know, reading them again and making corrections and learning from their mistakes and that kind of thing. It's not all what some of my friends call it: fantasy education, where you talk about it and you pretend that they absorb it and don't make the same mistakes again.

Our students are as diverse as the phone book. There are times when as an instructor and as a human being I want to do everything on earth for them. There are other times when I would like to strangle them and make them completely disappear. Most of them have had challenges all of their life. Most of them have no encouragement at home. A lot, a lot have been told all their lives that they're nobody and nothing and they will never amount to anything. So they've been put down. I try to be honest with my students. I tell them exactly like it is. They appreciate that. If they have done well, I tell them that but I don't sugar coat it. I don't make them think that they . . . have gone beyond the limits. But I try to be very realistic with them. Sometimes, we always like to think about the good ones. I worry about the ones that fall between the cracks. I always worry about the ones that drop out. They come for a while and then they drop out and we never hear from them again. I often wonder what happens to them. Sometimes they come back. And then sometimes they never do. And that's, in a class of twenty, when you start out with a class of 24 and when you turn in, at the end of the semester when you turn in all your final grades and your reports and everything and your attendance and you have only like fourteen or fifteen and you wonder if you did something wrong or just what happened in that process.

And then some of the women have babies [during the course] . . . Some of the guys might have a criminal record. They may have done something and gotten in trouble and had to drop out of school. But, I never want to know all that. I try not to. I don't want to be privy to any of that information. I take them; when they walk in that door they're all equal and they are all my students and so I treat them [alike]. I don't want to know anything about them.

Sometimes I feel, when I get up in the morning and I have my class to look forward to and I'm happy and I'm upbeat and I come to work, sometimes I think about if I were in their shoes, that in some of their shoes, I probably would not even bother. Because they don't have that much to really look

> forward to or, you know, they don't have that much encouragement. A couple of years ago I had this young guy in my class. He was so shy and I remember in English 3, . . . junior English, I kept saying you have to write this essay. And I would try to help him and one day he started shaking. He said "Mr. Jackson, all through school I was told I could not write," and he said, "I'm afraid to try to write because I don't want to disappoint you." I said, "oh just forget about that." I said, "just take this topic and think about it and you go home tonight and you write an essay and I'll help you with it." I said, "no matter what you do, it'll be a start. We'll take what you've got and we'll work on it." He came back the next day; he had written one of the best essays I had read in years. But all through school he'd been told that he couldn't write . . . There are a lot of little things that we have to [do] sometimes. I think at the end of the day that I've been walking, because I'm an active teacher, I don't sit at a desk and give commands. Because I'm all over the classroom and at any time I know what just about everybody's doing. But sometimes I feel like I've been walking around eggs and eggshells all day. Because you have to with all of their backgrounds and all the diverse experiences they've had, you have to be very acute. If a student comes in and they're sitting there and they're not participating and you just have a feeling, you just have to know to leave them alone that day because you don't know what's happened in their environment that's causing them to be that way, or if they forgot to take their Ritalin or just what happened. It can be tense at times.
>
> . . . The one thing I've learned, I never take them [students] for granted. They always will surprise me. They keep me on my toes. My ABE class makes me a better teacher because they come right out, they're very honest. They say "Mr. Jackson, I've never understood what fractions are in my whole life, I slept through school when we were doing fractions and I've never been able to do them. Would you please explain it?" So we start. And then they have innocent questions very often that turn into good discussions in class, which helps everybody I think. And of course we're always proud of the ones that . . . have gone on, military, college, whatever. They're always coming by to say "hello," and that says something I think. That's when we get paid. You know, they walk in and you think, "oh, I can't believe what a difference [education has made]." (May, 2003)

Clearly this is a personal testimony from a faculty member who views himself as a teacher first and foremost. He defines teaching as a relationship with his students, as if they are his patients and he is trying to make them well or he is their guardian and he ministers to their educational needs. This is indeed an "old" approach, an idealized image of teacher, and surely not "fantasy education" as Jeff's friends refer to community college teaching.

Jeff's work has little evident connection to the New Economy, save that his students are the likely outcomes of that economy. But Jeff's art is untouched by managerial interference, by technology, or by his noninstructional roles and responsibilities. Although he acknowledges that as a part-time faculty member he did not have job security or reasonable compensation and working conditions, his focus is not on himself as an economic entity but on his students and his relationships with them. His full-time status provides him with security and confidence, as well as what is no doubt a professional identity. Even in the face of considerable obstacles and with derision from friends, Jeff is both committed to his work which to him is a cause, and a noble one at that.

Is this then an idealized image of community college faculty? Or, instead, is Jeff an exemplary model, reflecting what is at the heart of the matter for faculty at community colleges? In our final chapter, we pursue the problem of the professional identity of community college faculty.

# 9

# The Professional Identity of Community College Faculty

In this final chapter we reflect, within the context of what we call *nouveau* college, on the professional role and status of community college faculty. Community college faculty are educators as well as corporate workers employed within an organization that encompasses cultural, economic, educational, and social missions. Community colleges have not only multiple missions[1] but also various purposes and functions.[2] These multiple missions have been cast within neo-liberal practices including economic competition which have corporatized faculty work and left professionals questioning, as does a part-time faculty member at Suburban Valley Community College in California: "How do we move back and reconstruct the profession? Economically and structurally we can't just jump back. It's got to be a process." Or perhaps, for many community college faculty, the question is not whether or how to move back and reconstruct, but rather how to move forward and create their professional role in the New Economy.

This chapter brings together the interrelated themes of our book and moves beyond the glum prospect of faculty as instruments of neo-liberal ideology to generate a view of community college faculty as professionals, agents of knowledge dissemination and participants in a socially and personally transformative process, and as workers, facilitators of postindustrial production. Indeed, community college faculty in the New Economy are well positioned to engage in the social construction of their roles as professionals. They continue to be the core workforce within the community college; student numbers are increasing; and the need of employers for an educated workforce proceeds unabated. Additionally, pressures on higher education for the production of baccalaureate degree students suggest that community colleges are a logical choice to fulfill these needs whether as transfer institutions or as stand-alone baccalaureate degree granting institutions. Community college faculty are significant components in all of these endeavors and possess considerable potential power both because of their numbers and criticality.

On a personal level through both our practice and our research, we have witnessed promising stories in different environments of community college faculty, who shape their roles as professionals. We suggest the opportunity exists, given the infancy of *nouveau* college, for faculty to chart incremental change[3] in redefining their role and status as professionals. We forecast the opportunity for full-time faculty as well as part-time faculty to reframe their professional identity within and beyond the boundaries of disciplines, programs, and individual colleges, in institutional and state or provincial governance decisions, in the development and implementation of institutional mission, and in the use of technology within their disciplines, programs, and colleges. We appeal to faculty to assess their environmental conditions and define a path for the development of professional identity appropriate to a new context. Although the neo-liberal state offers a glum prospect for faculty, we propose avenues for faculty to pursue within the context of new organizational and market-based definitions of professional work.[4]

However, before embarking on a discussion of the professionalization of faculty in *nouveau* college, we must outline some of the major products and outcomes of the community college over the past two decades, during which time managerial preferences that encompass technological advancement, neo-liberal values, and private sector business behaviors have played out in individual institutions and within the policy community. It is here that we explain the larger but "real world context" of faculty at work in the New Economy, using the framework of Roland Scholz and Olaf Tietje[5] for the embedded case study.

In understanding, conceptualizing, and explaining community college faculty, we need to delve into the present condition of the community college. Community colleges have now situated themselves within the New Economy. While the vestiges of the old community college with its mission of access and individual opportunity remain, another institution rises, as we noted in chapter 2.[6] *Nouveau* college has emerged as part transfer institution, economic development engine, social welfare agency, entrepreneurial institute, and baccalaureate and post-baccalaureate college. The discourse of the New Economy and the role of the community college within that context is extolled by constituencies external to the institution. These constituencies include business and industry who depend on community colleges to provide a trained workforce and governmental and political entities who depend on the colleges to address not only economic development agendas but also changing social and cultural imperatives, such as accommodating new and diverse student populations. The discourse is also embraced by practitioners, especially executives, professional analysts, and policy makers.

This embrace is manifest in the economic and instrumental role fashioned for community colleges, characterized by appellations such as "the learning college,"[7] "the entrepreneurial community college,"[8] and "the globalized community college."[9] But to what end? The reform of the community college's form and function is, if not complete, certainly advanced. What, then, has been accomplished through this project of new managerialism? What has been achieved beyond the disheartening change to organizational regimes and cultures, what Rosemary Deem sees as "the adoption by public sector organizations of organizational forms, technologies, management practices and values more commonly found in the private business sector"[10] and the alteration of the "values of public sector employees to more closely resemble those found in the private 'for profit' sector"[11]? Is there a parallel here between the outcomes for community colleges and those for nations under corporate globalization, outcomes which critics refer to as "socially and politically suicidal"?[12]

We have identified those changes of most saliency for community colleges during the project we call new managerialism, initiated in the 1980s, spurred on by educational, social, and economic forces and articulated in a neo-liberal ideology. These include the following:

- Resource dependency which is externally focused,
- Increasing enrollments and changing demographics,
- Growth in the contingent labor force, and
- Technological integration and the advancement of distributed learning.

While not an exhaustive list, these conditions and trends have coalesced to shape the development of *nouveau* college, and in conjunction with global social and economic forces have begun to reshape the traditional ideal of professionalism and probably brought an end to facets of that tradition. According to Steven Brint,[13] professionalism based on social purposes and knowledge-based authority is eroding in a market-based environment. The convergence of these conditions and trends that shape *nouveau* college, combined with the changing nature of professionalism, generally, has affected faculty work in profound ways.

As we have noted, community colleges have increasingly focused their mission on outcomes influenced by external entities—businesses, governments, and multinational corporations. Through this orientation, one which is arguably motivated by the need to acquire resources as a consequence of diminishing state support, faculty have lamented the loss of institutional purpose that was directed to the education of citizens. A part-time faculty member at Suburban Valley Community College captures this lament: "the community college is the goal, the ideal, the image of a democratized higher education that would provide the humanized possibility for citizens in a highly technical democratic society, but that is being co-opted by job training." Not only has the erosion of a once prominent mission stemmed from the focus upon instrumental education—training for business and industry—but also the access mission has notably shifted toward the economic development mission, and the necessity to acquire revenue streams to accommodate increasing student numbers and an expansion of institutional activities.

We observe, as have others,[14] that public higher education institutions, including community colleges, have over the past two decades increased their dependence upon the private sector for financing their operations. Community colleges in particular are dependent upon students as fee payers, including international students who pay considerably more than local students, on business and industry through training contracts, on individual donors for equipment and money, and even on corporate sponsors who advertise their interests within the institution. Additionally, government funding behaviors for community colleges imitate business practices as colleges are required to compete for funding when in the past such funding was a component of base funding.

In addition to a competitive resources focus, there has been considerable growth in the number of credit students in community colleges, from almost five million (4.9) in 1990 to five million seven hundred thousand (5.7) by 2000, with a change in the percentage of minority student enrollment from 19.9 percent of the total to 34.4 percent.[15] By the fall of 2001, this growth trend continued, with close to six million (5.9) in enrollment and 36.5 percent categorized as minority students.[16] To accomplish funding this increase in student enrollments, community colleges have resorted to a contingent labor force—part-time faculty—that is now 64 percent of the teaching workforce nationally.[17] State and provincial funding for community colleges has not kept pace with enrollment growth and with increases in students who have needs and requirements different from that of traditional students.[18]

Not surprisingly, another significant change for community college faculty over the past twenty years has been the integration of technology throughout instruction. Information technologies have by all appearances and reports become not just instruments for administrative and instructional work at community colleges but essential components as well as expected elements of the curriculum and its delivery. Distance or on-line education is among those "innovations" that promoters view as a panacea for the community college's limited resources—to extend access and accommodate increasing numbers of students. But, while increased productivity was realized, questions of learning outcomes have surfaced, noted in chapter 8 by the faculty leader at Suburban Valley Community College. In those colleges where on-line instruction has been adopted and where faculty are becoming more accepting of the practice as recently as 2004, there continue to be both claims about pressures to use technology as well as critiques of the use of on-line teaching and learning. At North Mountain College in Alberta, where the use of instructional technology is becoming the norm, a Nursing faculty member indicates that there is considerable pressure from management and students to increase such use.

> When I'm talking about pressures I'm talking from administration down. There also are pressures from students. They want websites; they're really onto them now. They want Blackboard. They want the class notes on Blackboard. I've really found in recent years students are becoming more demanding as to what they want in clinical placements . . . There really is more consumerism from the students. They want things. They want feedback. They want it quickly. So there are pressures coming from different directions.

From the same institution, a faculty member who teaches History notes the limitations of instruction that relies primarily upon information technologies.

> The on-line course is text-based, so they're getting that chronological narrative history. The whole thing I teach in survey courses is that history isn't chronological; it's not narrative. It doesn't have to be. It's more analytical. You really can't get them there on their own when they're sitting in their den with their bunny slippers on. I can do a multiple choice test at the end—that's what they did in high school—but that's what's killing history. That's not what the history process is about. You need the different analytical constructs, like how you apply class or gender or sexuality to understand an issue. I can give them that kind of reading, but without some guidance they're not going to get it. They're not even going to get the thesis out of it. They're just going to be frustrated.

While not a comprehensive list, the conditions of resource dependency, increasing demand, and technological change have undoubtedly influenced the development of *nouveau* college and reconceptualized for faculty the traditional nature of their professional work.

In addition to external forces and trends affecting the professional role of faculty, there are internal conditions which enable or impede faculty professionalism. In examining faculty work, we look to the prescribed role of faculty in shaping institutional missions. We examined their role in governance over time. Both the rhetoric of employee participation as well as the formal requirements for and reported behaviors of faculty in institutional governance suggest that there is more sharing in institutional decision making than in the past, when the community college was viewed as bureaucratic and even autocratic in decision making. But the activity of faculty participation masks the substantive nature of this participation: relegated to areas that do not and cannot affect the significant institutional outcomes of who is served and the substance of education and training, faculty are de-professionalized, cogs in the corporate educational wheel or gear. Program establishment and disestablishment as well as fiscal allocations for programs, for example, are the purview of managers, governing boards, and state government, not the faculty—not even formally requiring faculty advice in almost every jurisdiction. In decisions of substance, the faculty lack a significant role in the formation and decisions pertinent to institutional mission and direction, including resource allocation.

> Because of [budget] pressures, they [administration] bought into the idea of corporatizing the structure of administrative processes and governance. That process, when it comes into community colleges, reinforces the fragmentations that are already there. It breaks down the shared governance process. (Part-time faculty member at Suburban Valley Community college)

What are the consequences of, on the one hand, claiming that the institution practices participatory governance, or at least values faculty participation in decision making, and on the other hand bypassing the faculty in critical decisions, such as program establishment and resource allocations? Our evidence indicates that while faculty are a much more visible component of the institution than in the recent past, they are a diminishing influence on matters that count: their expertise and professional judgment are discounted. This pattern is consistent with the views of other scholars on higher education faculty generally but notably university faculty.[19]

Moreover, we question the outcomes for students through the practices of community colleges in the New Economy. Is teaching, then, in the community college better in the present than in the past with the rise of new managerialism? Not according to an extensive investigation which finds little to recommend in institutional instructional performance in the late 1990s.[20] Are all students better served than in the past in accessing programs and further education as a consequence of a more entrepreneurial and market-oriented approach promoted by governments and institutional leaders? Not according to several examinations of under-served students.[21]

Evidently, the project of the reform of the community college, involving new managerial practices, valorization of both economic competition and private sector behaviors, increasing programmatic orientation to the requirements of business and industry, and attention to specific kinds of outcomes, including a narrow and economically rationalized view of learning behaviors, has not yielded results or ends that further the mission of community colleges. The wisdom in continuing such projects is also under question. While the institution is productive and perhaps efficient, there is no evidence to suggest effectiveness as a consequence. Indeed, effectiveness is largely concerned with economic goals. Even numerical outcomes, such as student transfer rates from community college to university, have not improved over the past several decades. And even if community colleges have become more productive in serving more students with relatively fewer resources or through rising offerings in distance education, to what end?

Nonetheless, community college faculty now reside in the context of the New Economy with emphasis on efficiency in the guise of innovation. And while we decry the condition of the faculty, suggesting that they are "worker bees," cogs in the neo-liberal organization that we call *nouveau* college, we assert that they have academic status as professionals. While the traditional definition of professionals is evolving, so are the faculty. We support Brint's characterization of professionals as individuals who display "a strong commitment to education and meritocracy as principles of advancement; are sensitive to issues involving autonomy and self-direction; and find congenial efforts to synthesize and balance opposed political and value positions."[22] We see a spectrum in the professional role of faculty which varies contextually by institution, geographical location and organizational structure. In our examination, this contextual variation includes among other features, nations—the United States versus Canada—and locations—for example, rural versus urban—as well as institutional history and mission. In suggesting the incremental social construction of the professional role of faculty in *nouveau* college, we offer examples which may inform and indeed empower faculty in similar contexts.

At one end of the spectrum of professionalism, faculty at North Mountain College in Alberta are increasingly required to have doctoral degrees as a condition of employment as the institution is in the process of becoming a baccalaureate degree-granting institution. Faculty described an environment of increased autonomy and an emphasis on changing work to include scholarly research. An administrator at North Mountain College told us that if "the credentials that we are requiring of the faculty coming in are going to change, then presumably the work that they are doing will change as well." Another administrator reported an institutional goal of increasing the percentage of faculty with doctoral degrees. "Our goal is that 70% of our faculty will have PhDs . . . That is our target—70%. Right now we're at about 50%." While affecting individual hiring decisions and faculty workload, there are broader implications as a result of changing the institutional mission to include the provision of baccalaureate degree programs and degrees. Organizational changes for institutions that implement baccalaureate degree programs include advanced degree requirements for faculty, with implications for professional development funding, the potential for an evaluative requirement for scholarly research and publications, and the establishment of a bicameral governance system, where there is either divided or equal authority involving faculty and administrators or governing boards.[23] Such a change fits well with Burton Clark's view of increasing the professional status of community college faculty. He noted over eighteen years ago that the lack of involvement in disciplines and in scholarship is the "Achilles heel" of community college faculty.[24] But as Gary Rhoades has noted, status also diminishes with increasing numbers of contingent labor as part of the profession.[25]

Equity for the contingent labor market within institutions is another example of the development of a professional role for faculty as part-time professional employees in Washington State begin to move in from the periphery. Of twenty-one contracts we reviewed for governance decisions in Washington State included in the 1995–96 Higher Education Contract Analysis System (HECAS), fifteen covered part-time faculty as well (NEA, 1995–96). In the Spring 2003 HECAS database, of the twenty-six faculty contracts we reviewed, twenty-two cover both full-time and part-time faculty. In addition to greater inclusion, part-time faculty have made inroads in securing budgetary resources in institutions such as Whatcom Community College, where the 1995–97 contract states that "areas, accordingly, will hold regular meetings with all full-time and as many part-time faculty as is appropriate and possible. Because part-time faculty input is important and valued, part-time faculty who are so approved will be paid subject to budgetary considerations" (NEA, 1998–99, Article X, B).

Another example of the improved conditions and equity for part-time faculty is evident in Napa Valley Community College in California, which has developed a step system for part-time faculty pay. Faculty have the opportunity to improve their professional role and integrate a large contingent labor force by accepting policies and practices through collective bargaining, or working conditions' requests in nonunionized environments. The development of a professional role for faculty is likely dependent on fair treatment and support for part-time faculty as members of a faculty profession within the organization. It is worth noting that the Academic Senate for California Community Colleges in its report on part-time faculty argues that the professional stature of full-time faculty is dependent on the equitable treatment of part-time faculty.[26] We note as well that part-time faculty in several Canadian jurisdictions are given prorated pay and benefits, a considerable improvement over the norm in the United States jurisdictions where payment for credit courses can be as low as $1000 for a fifteen-week course of three to four hours a week of instruction, with no benefits accruing to the instructor. Payment for some Adult Education and English as a Second Language courses, especially where they are not categorized as credit, can be lower. Many of these deficiencies stem from government funding.

There is little doubt that community colleges are governed within a state or provincial legal framework. Almost all state and provincial government legislation limits the role of faculty in governance. The province of British Columbia in Canada is the sole example we found where faculty in that jurisdiction's colleges where given legal authority in institutional decision making. Indeed, faculty were not only represented on college governing boards but they were also major authorities on educational decisions, from student admissions to curriculum, within their institutions. In order for this professional role to be realized, legislative change was imperative.[27]

Furthermore, faculty in community colleges can be more deliberate in negotiating or consenting to their working conditions and responsibilities so that these are aligned with their professional responsibilities. We note through the examination of collective agreements that faculty may not have exercised their legal status as partners with management in deciding upon their responsibilities in the management of their colleges. While they may have agreed to participate in decision making, they have not done so uniformly, with well over 50 percent of colleges nationwide formally excluding faculty from decisions in numerous areas of critical importance to the professional roles of faculty—such as the hiring of peers and the curricular change of programs. The claim of faculty expertise in teaching and curriculum is certainly one characteristic that can be put forward as an argument for faculty to achieve greater organizational power and enhance their professional identity.[28]

The use of information technology is another domain where faculty professional status is challenged. The use of technology in the classroom changes the role of the faculty from delivering instruction to facilitating learning. A faculty member at North Mountain College in Alberta told us with enthusiasm that instead of just instructing students, with alternative delivery methods she now brings students along with her in the learning process. She acknowledged that the use of technology enhanced her role as a professional. Technology has broadened the opportunities for faculty to define their roles in the workforce. While prudent use of electronic technology can allow students to be engaged and socially integrated into the institution through increased interaction with faculty, the challenge for faculty as professionals will be to ensure that technology supports the learning process (as well as the faculty) instead of inhibiting the learning process and dictating faculty work. As we noted in chapter 5, technology will continue to unbundle the role of faculty, creating a hierarchy of work, from curriculum design to delivery. It will behoove faculty not only to use technology but also to guide it and not abdicate responsibility to managers and technicians charged with increasing the efficiency of the institution.

In redefining the role of the professional, we suggest that student learning and thus teaching remains the core function of the community college. Faculty are the gatekeepers of knowledge, whatever the characteristics and orientation of the institutional environment—entrepreneurial, traditional academic, or workforce development. Faculty have the rights and responsibilities to mediate student learning. As such, they need to position themselves more aggressively as the intermediaries between student learning and institutional mission. They need to move to the core of the institution, a core that includes the fashioning as well as the implementation of mission. But the move will not be easy, nor will it be without challenges.

As community colleges move to awarding baccalaureate degrees, as has occurred, or is reported as about to occur, for several states (Arizona, Arkansas, Hawaii, Florida, Nevada, Utah, Washington State) and three Canadian provinces (Alberta, British Columbia, and Ontario),[29] faculty will be challenged further in their status, professional development, and work. As a faculty member at an institution that grants baccalaureate degrees noted, the bar will be raised: raised on degree requirements for faculty where a terminal degree will be expected; and raised on research and scholarly writing requirements where a new level of knowledge production not limited to knowledge dissemination will be expected. Faculty need to consider how these alterations will affect faculty evaluative and tenure processes. Will the offerings of baccalaureate degrees create another level of hierarchy within institutions, even among and within disciplines and programs?[30]

Another challenge for faculty in *nouveau* college will be the economic development dilemma. Are faculty to be instruments of business and industry or student advocates? Are these mutually exclusive due to resource dependency, or can faculty serve both employers and students well? Faculty, as educators, have a responsibility for engaging students in learning beyond skills that students require for their employment. For the training of students, faculty need to forecast required technical skills and knowledge and work with business and industry in curricular development and design in order to prepare students for the labor market as well as to enhance student learning, in both specialized skills and general education.

Increasingly, faculty will be asked to do more with less, serve students across a widening spectrum—educationally, from adult basic education to individuals with doctoral degrees interested in changing careers; and demographically, from students with diverse ethnic backgrounds with multitudes of cultural nuances which may affect learning, to traditional aged students whose numbers are also growing at community colleges. Faculty will need to be more active in defining the curriculum and the needs of these various student groups.

Our observations of opportunities for faculty to redefine their profession do not suggest a one-size fits-all-description of how community college faculty need to become professionalized. We are not advocating a radical change, but pointing out that the current path of managerialism and administrative direction of institutional mission is problematic. We see community college faculty as *nouveau* professionals, as agents of knowledge creation and dissemination and as facilitators of postindustrial production. Community college faculty are expected to be experts in student learning and they need to secure that position as experts. As such, they will fit well within Brint's view of the reconstituted professional, who functions "ever more exclusively on the basis of applied formal knowledge or expertise."[31]

We have endeavored to theorize community college faculty through both their work and the potential of their role. We have implied if not stated that the professional identity of community college faculty is bound to the identity of the community college. Unlike faculty at research universities and faculty at elite four-year colleges who possess a professional identity distinct from their institution, largely as a consequence of their scholarly prominence or research productivity, or both, community college faculty are tied to their institution. And as such, they must take a more central role in both fashioning and directing the institution to enhance their professional identity as faculty.

# Notes

## Preface

1. Simon Marginson, "Response to Burton Clark" (Paper presented at the Annual Meeting of the Association for the Study of Higher Education, Kansas City, MO, November 3, 2004).
2. Henry Mintzberg, *Power in and Around Organizations* (Englewood Cliffs, NJ: Prentice Hall, Inc., 1983), Henry Mintzberg, "The Professional Bureaucracy," in *Organization and Governance in Higher Education*, ed. Marvin Peterson (Needham Heights, MA: Simon & Schuster, 1991).
3. Steven Brint, *In an Age of Experts: The Changing Role of Professionals in Politics and Public Life* (Princeton: Princeton University Press, 1994), Gary Rhoades, *Managed Professionals: Unionized Faculty and Restructuring Academic Labor* (Albany: State University of New York Press, 1998).

## 1 Themes and Overview

1. Michael Apple, "Comparing Neo-Liberal Projects and Inequality in Education," *Comparative Education* 37, no. 4 (2001): 409–423, Martin Carnoy, *Sustaining the New Economy: Work, Family, and Community in the Information Age* (New York: Russell Sage Foundation, 2000), James Paul Gee, Glynda Hull, and Colin Lankshear, *The New Work Order: Behind the Language of the New Capitalism* (Boulder, CO: Westview Press, 1996), Nelly P. Stromquist, *Education in a Globalized World: The Connectivity of Economic Power, Technology, and Knowledge* (Lanham, MD: Rowman & Littlefield, 2002).
2. John Levin et al., "Not Professionals?: Community College Faculty in the New Economy" (Symposium for the Annual Meeting of the American Educational Research Association, Chicago, April 2003).
3. Catherine Casey, *Work, Society and Self: After Industrialism* (New York: Routledge, 1995).
4. Ibid., p. 139.
5. Vicki Smith, *Crossing the Great Divide: Worker Risk and Opportunity in the New Economy* (New York: Cornell University Press, 2001).
6. Kent Phillippe and Madeline Patton, *National Profile of Community Colleges: Trends and Statistics*, 3rd ed. (Washington, DC: Community College Press, American Association of Community Colleges, 2000). We use the 1999 national figures although in the May 2005 update from the National Center for Educational Statistics, *2004 National Study of Postsecondary Faculty (NSOPF: 04): Report on Faculty and Instructional Staff in Fall 2003* (Washington, DC: U.S. Department of Education, 2005) the figure for part-time faculty has risen to 66.7%.

7. W. Norton Grubb, *Honored but Invisible: An Inside Look at Teaching in Community Colleges* (New York: Routledge, 1999), George Vaughan, "The Big Squeeze at Community Colleges," *The News & Observer*, March 24, 2002, 29a.
8. W. Norton Grubb et al., *Workforce, Economic and Community Development: The Changing Landscape of the Entrepreneurial Community College* (Berkeley: National Center for Research in Vocational Education, The University of California, 1997), John Levin, *Globalizing the Community College: Strategies for Change in the Twenty-First Century* (New York: Palgrave, 2001).
9. Levin et al., "Not Professionals?: Community College Faculty in the New Economy."
10. Cristie Roe, "Effects of Information Technology on Community College Faculty" (Paper presentation, American Education Research Association, Chicago, April 2003).
11. Gary Rhoades, *Managed Professionals: Unionized Faculty and Restructuring Academic Labor* (Albany: State University of New York Press, 1998).
12. Phillippe and Patton, *National Profile of Community Colleges: Trends and Statistics.*
13. Earl Seidman, *In the Words of the Faculty* (San Francisco: Jossey-Bass Publishers, 1985).
14. Grubb, *Honored but Invisible: An Inside Look at Teaching in Community Colleges.*
15. Rosemary Deem, " 'New Managerialism' and Higher Education: The Management of Performances and Cultures in Universities in the United Kingdom," *International Studies in Sociology of Education* 8, no. 1 (1998): 47–70, Cynthia Hardy, *The Politics of Collegiality: Retrenchment Strategies in Canadian Universities* (Buffalo: McGill-Queen's University Press, 1996), John Levin, "Neo-Liberalism, Higher Education, and the Challenge for Faculty, Administrators, and Trustees" (Paper presented at the Moore Chair Lecture, North Carolina State University, Raleigh, NC, November 19, 2003), Rhoades, *Managed Professionals: Unionized Faculty and Restructuring Academic Labor.*
16. Hardy, *The Politics of Collegiality: Retrenchment Strategies in Canadian Universities.*
17. Casey, *Work, Society and Self: After Industrialism*, Jane Kenway, "Fast Capitalism, Fast Feminism, and Some Fast Food for Thought" (Paper presented at the Annual Meeting of the American Educational Research Association, San Diego, April 1998), John Ralston Saul, *The Unconscious Civilization* (Concord, Ontario: House of Anansi Press, 1995).
18. Hardy, *The Politics of Collegiality: Retrenchment Strategies in Canadian Universities.*
19. Deem, " 'New Managerialism' and Higher Education: The Management of Performances and Cultures in Universities in the United Kingdom."
20. Casey, *Work, Society and Self: After Industrialism.*
21. Simon Marginson and Mark Considine, *The Enterprise University: Power, Governance and Reinvention in Australia* (New York: Cambridge University Press, 2000), Sheila Slaughter and Larry Leslie, *Academic Capitalism, Politics, Policies, and the Entrepreneurial University* (Baltimore: The Johns Hopkins University Press, 1997), Sheila Slaughter and Gary Rhoades, *Academic Capitalism and the New Economy: Markets, State, and Higher Education* (Baltimore: The Johns Hopkins University Press, 2004), Sheila Slaughter and Gary Rhoades, "The Neo-Liberal University," New Labor Forum (2000, Spring/Summer): 73–79.

22. Casey, *Work, Society and Self: After Industrialism.*
23. Jan Currie and Janice Newson, *Universities and Globalization* (Thousand Oaks, CA: Sage Publications, 1998), Marginson and Considine, *The Enterprise University: Power, Governance and Reinvention in Australia*, Slaughter and Rhoades, *Academic Capitalism and the New Economy: Markets, State, and Higher Education.*
24. Rhoades, *Managed Professionals: Unionized Faculty and Restructuring Academic Labor.*
25. W. Richard Scott, *Institutions and Organizations* (Thousand Oaks, CA: Sage Publications, 1995).
26. Steven Brint, *In an Age of Experts: The Changing Role of Professionals in Politics and Public Life* (Princeton: Princeton University Press, 1994).
27. Marginson and Considine, *The Enterprise University: Power, Governance and Reinvention in Australia*, Slaughter and Leslie, *Academic Capitalism, Politics, Policies, and the Entrepreneurial University.*
28. Arthur Cohen and Florence Brawer, *The American Community College* (San Francisco: Jossey-Bass, 2003).
29. Ibid.; Grubb, *Honored but Invisible: An Inside Look at Teaching in Community Colleges.*
30. Arthur Cohen and Charles Outcalt, "A Profile of the Community College Professoriate" (A report submitted to the small research grant program of the Spencer Foundation. Center for the Study of Community Colleges, Los Angeles, CA, June 2001), Charles Outcalt, *A Profile of the Community College Professoriate, 1975–2000* (New York: Routledge Falmer, 2002).
31. Stromquist, *Education in a Globalized World: The Connectivity of Economic Power, Technology, and Knowledge.*
32. Apple, "Comparing Neo-liberal Projects and Inequality in Education," John Campbell and Ove Pedersen, "Introduction: The Rise of Neoliberalism and Institutional Analysis," in *The Rise of Neoliberalism and Institutional Analysis*, ed. John Campbell and Ove Pedersen (Princeton: Princeton University Press, 2001), 2–23, Noam Chomsky, *Profit Over People: Neoliberalism and Global Order* (New York: Seven Stories Press, 1999), George DeMartino, *Global Economy, Global Justice: Theoretical Objections and Policy Alternatives to Neoliberalism* (New York: Routledge, 2000), Catherine Kingfisher, *Western Welfare in Decline: Globalization and Women's Poverty* (Philadelphia: University of Pennsylvania Press, 2002), Mark Olssen, *The Neo-liberal Appropriation of Tertiary Education Policy: Accountability, Research and Academic Freedom* (2000 [cited May 2004]); available from http://www.surrey.ac.uk/Education/profiles/olssen/neo-2000.htm, Stromquist, *Education in a Globalized World: The Connectivity of Economic Power, Technology, and Knowledge*, Anthony P. Welch, "Globalisation, Post-Modernity and the State: Comparative Education Facing the Third Millennium," *Comparative Education* 37, no. 4 (2000): 475–492.
33. Campbell and Pedersen, "Introduction: The Rise of Neoliberalism and Institutional Analysis."
34. Derek Bok, *Universities in the Marketplace: The Commercialization of Higher Education* (Princeton: Princeton University Press, 2003), Marginson and Considine, *The Enterprise University: Power, Governance and Reinvention in Australia*, Slaughter and Leslie, *Academic Capitalism, Politics, Policies, and the Entrepreneurial University.*

35. Slaughter and Rhoades, *Academic Capitalism and the New Economy: Markets, State, and Higher Education,* Slaughter and Rhoades, "The Neo-liberal University."
36. John Levin, "The Revised Institution: The Community College Mission at the End of the 20th Century," *Community College Review* 28, no. 2 (2000): 1–25.
37. Levin, *Globalizing the Community College: Strategies for Change in the Twenty-First Century.*
38. Casey, *Work, Society and Self: After Industrialism.*
39. David Held et al., *Global Transformations: Politics, Economics and Culture* (Stanford, CA: Stanford University Press, 1999), Levin, *Globalizing the Community College: Strategies for Change in the Twenty-First Century*, Roland Robertson, *Globalization: Social Theory and Global Culture* (London: Sage Publications, 1992), Malcolm Waters, *Globalization* (New York: Routledge, 1996).
40. Apple, "Comparing Neo-liberal Projects and Inequality in Education," Martin Carnoy, *Sustaining the New Economy: Work, Family, and Community in the Information Age* (New York: Russell Sage Foundation, 2000), DeMartino, *Global Economy, Global Justice: Theoretical Objections and Policy Alternatives to Neoliberalism*, Eric Gould, *The University in a Corporate Culture* (New Haven: Yale University Press, 2003), Kingfisher, *Western Welfare in Decline: Globalization and Women's Poverty*, Olssen, *The Neo-Liberal Appropriation of Tertiary Education Policy: Accountability, Research and Academic Freedom* ([cited]), Adriana Puiggrós, *Neoliberalism and Education in the Americas* (Boulder, CO: Westview Press, 1999), Stromquist, *Education in a Globalized World: The Connectivity of Economic Power, Technology, and Knowledge*, Carlos A. Torres and Daniel Schugurensky, "The Political Economy of Higher Education in the Era of Neoliberal Globalization: Latin America in Comparative Perspective," *Higher Education* 43 (2002): 429–455.
41. John Dennison and Paul Gallagher, *Canada's Community Colleges* (Vancouver: University of British Columbia Press, 1986).
42. John Levin, "The Community College as a Baccalaureate-Granting Institution," The Review of Higher Education 28, no. 1 (2004): 1–22, John S. Levin, "*The Higher Credential*" (Tucson, Arizona: The Canadian Embassy in Washington, DC, 2001).
43. Roland W. Scholz and Olaf Tietje, *Embedded Case Study Methods: Integrating Quantitative and Qualitative Knowledge* (Thousand Oaks, CA: Sage Publications, 2002).
44. Levin, "The Revised Institution: The Community College Mission at the End of the 20th Century."
45. John Levin, "The Community College as a Baccalaureate-Granting Institution," *The Review of Higher Education* 28, no. 1 (2004): 1–22.
46. Levin, *Globalizing the Community College: Strategies for Change in the Twenty-First Century.*
47. Cohen and Brawer, *The American Community College*, Levin, *Globalizing the Community College: Strategies for Change in the Twenty-First Century.*
48. Kevin Dougherty, *The Contradictory College* (Albany, NY: State University of New York Press, 1994), Dennis McGrath and Martin Spear, *The Academic Crisis of the Community College* (Albany, NY: State University of New York Press, 1991), Richard Richardson, Elizabeth Fisk, and Morris Okun, *Literacy in the Open-Access College* (San Francisco: Jossey-Bass Publishers, 1983), Kathleen

Shaw, "Defining the Self: Construction of Identity in Community College Students," in *Community Colleges as Cultural Texts*, ed. Kathleen Shaw, James Valadez, and Robert Rhoads (Buffalo: State University of New York Press, 1999), 153–171.

49. John Frye, "Educational Paradigms in the Professional Literature of the Community College," in *Higher Education: Handbook of Theory and Research*, ed. John Smart (New York: Agathon Press, 1994), 181–224, Grubb, *Honored but Invisible: An Inside Look at Teaching in Community Colleges.*
50. Dougherty, *The Contradictory College*, David F. Labaree, *How to Succeed in School Without Really Learning* (New Haven: Yale University Press, 1997).
51. Burton Clark, "Small Worlds, Different Worlds: The Uniqueness and Troubles of American Academic Professions," *Daedalus* 126, no. 1 (1997, Fall): 21–42, McGrath and Spear, *The Academic Crisis of the Community College.*
52. Cynthia Hardy, "Configuration and Strategy Making in Universities: Broadening the Scope," *Journal of Higher Education* 62, no. 4 (1991): 363–393.
53. John Levin, "What's the Impediment? Structural and Legal Constraints to Shared Governance in the Community College," *The Canadian Journal of Higher Education* XXX, no. 2 (2000): 87–122.
54. Susan Kater, "Shared Governance in the Community College: The Rights, Roles, and Responsibilities of Unionized Community College Faculty" (Unpublished Doctoral Dissertation, Tucson, AZ: The University of Arizona, 2003).
55. Levin, *Globalizing the Community College: Strategies for Change in the Twenty-First Century*, John Levin, "Is The Management of Distance Education Transforming Instruction in Colleges?" *The Quarterly Review of Distance Education* 2, no. 2 (2001): 105–117, Rhoades, *Managed Professionals: Unionized Faculty and Restructuring Academic Labor.*
56. John Levin, "In Education and Work: The Globalized Community College," *The Canadian Journal of Higher Education* XXXII, no. 2 (2002): 47–78.
57. Rhoades, *Managed Professionals: Unionized Faculty and Restructuring Academic Labor*, Steven Peter Vallas, *Power in the Workplace: The Politics of Production at AT&T* (Albany: State University of New York, 1993).
58. Everett Rogers, *Diffusion of Innovations*, 3rd ed. (New York: The Free Press, 1983).
59. Langdon Winner, *The Whale and the Reactor: Searching for Limits in an Age of High Technology* (Chicago: University of Chicago Press, 1986).
60. Levin, *Globalizing the Community College: Strategies for Change in the Twenty-First Century.*
61. Cheryl Bullock and John Ory, "Evaluating Instructional Technology Implementation in a Higher Education Environment," *American Journal of Evaluation* 21, no. 3 (2000): 315–328, Donald P. Ely, "Conditions that Facilitate the Implementation of Educational Technology Innovations," *Journal of Research on Computing in Education* 23, no. 2 (1990): 298–305, P. Rups, "Training Instructors in New Technologies," *T.H.E. Journal* 26, no. 8 (1999): 66–69.
62. Ananda Mitra, Timothy Steffensmeier, and Stefne Lenzmeier, "Changes in Attitudes Toward Computers and Use of Computers by University Faculty," *Journal of Research on Computing in Education* 32, no. 1 (1999): 189–202.
63. Winner, *The Whale and the Reactor: Searching for Limits in an Age of High Technology.*
64. Levin, *Globalizing the Community College: Strategies for Change in the Twenty-First Century*, Cristie E. Roe, "Effects of Informational Technology on

Community College Faculty" (The University of Arizona, 2002), Slaughter and Rhoades, *Academic Capitalism and the New Economy: Markets, State, and Higher Education.*

65. Levin, *Globalizing the Community College: Strategies for Change in the Twenty-First Century*, Roe, "Effects of Information Technology on Community College Faculty."
66. Katrina Meyer, "Quality in Distance Education: Focus on Online Learning," in *ASHE-ERIC Higher Education Reports* (2002).
67. Steven Gilbert, *Punished for Success* (Washington, DC: The TLT Group, American Association for Higher Education, 1998), Lawrence Gladieux and Watson Swail, *The Virtual University and Educational Issues of Equity and Access for the Next Generation* (Washington, DC: The College Board, 1999).
68. We use part-time faculty to refer to a group of faculty also called adjunct, sessional, and temporary.
69. Gareth Morgan, *Images of Organization* (Thousand Oaks, CA: Sage Publications, 1997).
70. Rhoades, *Managed Professionals: Unionized Faculty and Restructuring Academic Labor.*
71. Levin, *Globalizing the Community College: Strategies for Change in the Twenty-First Century.*
72. Carnoy, *Sustaining the New Economy: Work, Family, and Community in the Information Age*, Manuel Castells, *The Rise of the Network Society*, 2nd ed. (Malden, MA: Blackwell, 2000), Paul Osterman et al., *Working in America: A Blueprint for the New Labor Market* (Cambridge, MA: MIT Press, 2001), Smith, *Crossing the Great Divide: Worker Risk and Opportunity in the New Economy.*
73. Deem, " 'New Managerialism' and Higher Education: The Management of Performances and Cultures in Universities in the United Kingdom."
74. Levin, "In Education and Work: The Globalized Community College."
75. Casey, *Work, Society and Self: After Industrialism.*
76. Carnoy, *Sustaining the New Economy: Work, Family, and Community in the Information Age*, Levin, *Globalizing the Community College: Strategies for Change in the Twenty-First Century.*
77. John Dennison, "*Comment*," ed. John Levin (Vancouver, Canada: 2004).˙
78. Scholz and Tietje, *Embedded Case Study Methods: Integrating Quantitative and Qualitative Knowledge.*

## 2 From Comprehensive Community College to *Nouveau* College

1. Stanley Aronowitz and William Di Fazio, *The Jobless Future: Sci-tech and the Dogma of Work* (Minneapolis: University of Minnesota Press, 1994), Catherine Casey, *Work, Society and Self: After Industrialism* (New York: Routledge, 1995), Jeremy Rifkin, *The End of Work: The Decline of the Global Labor Force and the Dawn of the Post-Market Era* (New York: G.P. Putnam's Sons, 1995), George Ritzer, *The McDonaldization Thesis: Explorations and Extensions* (Thousand Oaks, CA: Sage Publications, 1998), Richard Sennett, *The Corrosion of Character: The Personal Consequences of Work in the New Capitalism* (New York: W.W. Norton & Company, 1998).
2. K. Patricia Cross, "Community Colleges on the Plateau," *The Journal of Higher Education* 52, no. 2 (1981): 113–123.

3. K. Patricia Cross, "Determining Missions and Priorities for the Fifth Generation," in *Renewing the American Community College*, ed. William Deegan, Dale Tillery, and Associates (San Francisco: Jossey-Bass Publishers, 1985), 34–50, William Deegan, Dale Tillery, and Associates, eds., *Renewing the American Community College* (San Francisco: Jossey-Bass, 1985).
4. Arthur Cohen, *Dateline '79: Heretical Concepts for the Community College* (Beverly Hills: Glencoe Press, 1969).
5. Steven Brint, "Few Remaining Dreams: Community Colleges since 1985," *The Annals of the American Academy of Political and Social Sciences* (2003, March): 16–37, W. Norton Grubb, *Honored but Invisible: An Inside Look at Teaching in Community Colleges* (New York: Routledge, 1999), Robert Rhoads and James Valadez, *Democracy, Multiculturalism, and the Community College* (New York: Garland Publishing, 1996), Kathleen Shaw, Robert Rhoads, and James Valadez, eds., *Community Colleges as Cultural Texts* (Albany: State University of New York Press, 1999), George Vaughan, "The Big Squeeze at Community Colleges," *The News & Observer*, March 24, 2002.
6. Melanie Griffith and Ann Connor, *Democracy's Open Door: The Community College in America's Future* (Portsmouth, NH: Boynton/Cook Publishers, 1994), Dennis McGrath and Martin Spear, *The Academic Crisis of the Community College* (Albany, NY: State University of New York Press, 1991), Lynn Taber, "Chapter and Verse: How We Came to Be Where We Are," in *The Company We Keep: Collaboration in the Community College*, ed. John Roueche, Lynn Taber, and Suanne Roueche (Washington, DC: American Association of Community Colleges, 1995), 25–37.
7. Steven Brint and Jerome Karabel, *The Diverted Dream: Community Colleges and the Promise of Educational Opportunity in America*, 1900–1985 (New York: Oxford University Press, 1989), Arthur Cohen and Florence Brawer, *The American Community College* (San Francisco: Jossey-Bass, 1982), John Dennison and Paul Gallagher, *Canada's Community Colleges* (Vancouver: University of British Columbia Press, 1986), Richard Richardson and Louis Bender, *Fostering Minority Access and Achievement in Higher Education* (San Francisco: Jossey-Bass Publishers, 1987), Richard Richardson, Elizabeth Fisk, and Morris Okun, *Literacy in the Open-Access College* (San Francisco: Jossey-Bass Publishers, 1983), John Roueche and George A. Baker, III, *Access and Excellence* (Washington, DC: The Community College Press, 1987).
8. John Frye, "Educational Paradigms in the Professional Literature of the Community College," in *Higher Education: Handbook of Theory and Research*, ed. John Smart (New York: Agathon Press, 1994), 181–224.
9. Kevin Dougherty, *The Contradictory College* (Albany: State University of New York Press, 1994).
10. Roueche and Baker, Access and Excellence, John Roueche and Suanne Roueche, *Between a Rock and a Hard Place* (Washington, DC: Community College Press, 1993).
11. Grubb, *Honored but Invisible: An Inside Look at Teaching in Community Colleges*, Rhoads and Valadez, *Democracy, Multiculturalism, and the Community College*.
12. Lois Weis, *Between two Worlds: Black Students in an Urban Community College* (Boston: Routledge and Keegan Paul, 1985).
13. John Levin, *Globalizing the Community College: Strategies for Change in the Twenty-First Century* (New York: Palgrave, 2001).

14. James Paul Gee, Glynda Hull, and Colin Lankshear, *The New Work Order: Behind the Language of the New Capitalism* (Boulder, CO: Westview Press, 1996).
15. Robert Barr and John Tagg, "From Teaching to Learning: A New Paradigm for Undergraduate Education," *Change* (1995, November/December): 13–25.
16. Gee, Hull, and Lankshear, *The New Work Order: Behind the Language of the New Capitalism.*
17. John Tagg, *The Learning Paradigm College* (Bolton, MA: Anker Publishing Company, 2003).
18. Gee, Hull and Lankshear, *The New Work Order: Behind the Language of the New Capitalism.*
19. Thomas R. Bailey and Vanessa Smith Morest, "The Organizational Efficiency of Multiple Missions for Community Colleges" (New York: Teachers College, Columbia University, 2004), John Levin, "The Community College as a Baccalaureate-Granting Institution," *The Review of Higher Education* 28, no. 1 (2004): 1–22.
20. Anne-Marie McCartan, "The Community College Mission: Present Challenges and Future Visions," *The Journal of Higher Education* 54, no. 6 (1983): 676–692, Richardson, Fisk, and Okun, *Literacy in the Open-Access College.*
21. Fred Pincus, "Contradictory Effects of Customized Contract Training in Community Colleges," *Critical Sociology* 16, no. 1 (1989): 77–93.
22. Kevin Dougherty and Marianne Bakia, "Community Colleges and Contract Training: Content, Origins, and Impact," *Teachers College Record* 102, no. 1 (2000): 197–243, Kevin J. Dougherty and Marianne Bakia, "The New Economic Role of the Community College: Origins and Prospects," (Occasional Paper, Community College Research Center, Teachers College, New York, June: 1998).
23. John Dennison, "Community College Development in Canada since 1985," in *Challenge and Opportunity*, ed. John Dennison (Vancouver: The University of British Columbia Press, 1995), 13–104.
24. Frye, "Educational Paradigms in the Professional Literature of the Community College."
25. Ken Meier, "The Community College Mission: History and Theory" (Bakersfield, CA: 2004).
26. Levin, *Globalizing the Community College: Strategies for Change in the Twenty-First Century*, John Levin, "In Education and Work: The Globalized Community College," *The Canadian Journal of Higher Education* XXXII, no. 2 (2002): 47–78.
27. Levin, "In Education and Work: The Globalized Community College."
28. Arthur Cohen and Florence Brawer, *The American Community College* (San Francisco: Jossey-Bass, 2003), Terry O'Banion, *The Learning College for the 21st Century* (Phoenix, AZ: American Council on Education and the Oryx Press, 1997), Polly S. Owen and Ada Demb, "Change Dynamics and Leadership in Technology Implementation," *The Journal of Higher Education* 75, no. 6 (2004): 636–666.
29. Manuel Castells, *The Rise of the Network Society* (Cambridge, MA: Blackwell Publishers, 1996).
30. Levin, *Globalizing the Community College: Strategies for Change in the Twenty-First Century.*
31. Thomas R. Bailey and Irina E. Averianova, "Multiple Missions of Community Colleges: Conflicting or Complementary" (Occasional Paper, Community

College Research Center, Teachers College, New York: 1998), Bailey and Morest, "The Organizational Efficiency of Multiple Missions for Community Colleges," Dougherty, *The Contradictory College*, David F. Labaree, *How to Succeed in School Without Really Learning* (New Haven: Yale University Press, 1997), John Levin, "The Community College as a Baccalaureate-Granting Institution," *The Review of Higher Education* 28, no. 1 (2004): 1–22, Kathleen Shaw, Robert Rhoads, and James Valadez, "Community Colleges as Cultural Texts: A Conceptual Overview," in *Community Colleges as Cultural Texts*, ed. Kathleen Shaw, James Valadez, and Robert Rhoads (Albany: State University of New York Press, 1999).

32. Dougherty, "State Policies and the Community College's Role in Workforce Preparation," Dougherty and Bakia, "The New Economic Role of the Community College: Origins and Prospects," W. Norton Grubb et al. *Workforce, Economic and Community Development: The Changing Landscape of the Entrepreneurial Community College* (Berkeley: National Center for Research in Vocational Education, The University of California, 1997), Jacobs and Winslow, "Welfare Reform and Enrollment in Postsecondary Education," Shaw and Rab, "Market Rhetoric versus Reality in Policy and Practice: The Workforce Investment Act and Access to Community College Education and Training."
33. The League for Innovation in the Community College, Web site (2005 [cited March 2005]); available from http://www.league.org.
34. D. Franklin Ayers, "Neoliberal Ideology in Community College Mission Statements: A Critical Discourse Analaysis." *The Review of Higher Education*, 28, no. 4 (2005): 545.
35. Gary Rhoades, *Managed Professionals: Unionized Faculty and Restructuring Academic Labor* (Albany: State University of New York Press, 1998).
36. Casey, *Work, Society and Self: After Industralism.*

## 3 The Scholarly Literature, The Theoretical Bases, and Research Methods

1. John Levin, *Globalizing the Community College: Strategies for Change in the Twenty-first Century* (New York: Palgrave, 2001), John Levin, "In Education and Work: The Globalized Community College," *The Canadian Journal of Higher Education* XXXII, no. 2 (2002): 47–78, John Levin, "Two British Columbia University Colleges and the Process of Economic Globalization," *The Canadian Journal of Higher Education* XXXIII, no. 1 (2003): 59–86.
2. Jan Currie and Janice Newson, *Universities and Globalization* (Thousand Oaks, CA: Sage Publications, 1998), Simon Marginson and Mark Considine, *The Enterprise University: Power, Governance and Reinvention in Australia* (New York: Cambridge University Press, 2000), Gary Rhoades, *Managed Professionals: Unionized Faculty and Restructuring Academic Labor* (Albany: State University of New York Press, 1998), Michael Skolnik, "The Virtual University and the Professoriate," in *The University in Transformation: Global Perspective on the Futures of the University*, ed. Sohail Inayatullah and Jennifer Gidley (Westport, CT: Bergin & Garvey, 2000), 55–67, Sheila Slaughter and Larry Leslie, *Academic Capitalism, Politics, Policies, and the Entrepreneurial University* (Baltimore: The Johns Hopkins University Press, 1997), Sheila Slaughter and Gary Rhoades, *Academic Capitalism and the New Economy: Markets, State, and Higher Education* (Baltimore: The Johns Hopkins University Press, 2004).

3. Slaughter and Rhoades, *Academic Capitalism and the New Economy: Markets, State, and Higher Education.*
4. Harris M. Cooper, "The Integrative Research Review: A Systematic Approach," in *Applied Social Research Methods Series*, v. 2 (Beverly Hills, CA: Sage, 1984).
5. Malcolm Waters, *Globalization* (New York: Routledge, 1996).
6. Roland Robertson, *Globalization: Social Theory and Global Culture* (London: Sage Publications, 1992).
7. Ibid., p. 27.
8. Ibid., p. 175.
9. Scott Davies and Neil Guppy, "Globalization and Educational Reforms in Anglo-American Democracies," *Comparative Education Review* 41, no. 4 (1997): 435–459.
10. Mauro Guillén, "Is Globalization Civilizing, Destructive, or Feeble? A Critique of Five Key Debates in the Social Science Literature," *Annual Review of Sociology* 27 (2001): 235–260.
11. Catherine Kingfisher, *Western Welfare in Decline: Globalization and Women's Poverty* (Philadelphia: University of Pennsylvania Press, 2002).
12. Rosemary Deem, " 'New Managerialism' and Higher Education: The Management of Performances and Cultures in Universities in the United Kingdom," *International Studies in Sociology of Education* 8, no. 1 (1998): 47–70.
13. William Sites, *Remaking New York: Primitive Globalization and the Politics of Urban Community* (Minneapolis, MN: University of Minnesota Press, 2003).
14. Gary Teeple, *Globalization and the Rise of Social Reform* (New Jersey: Humanities Press, 1995).
15. Peter Scott, "The Death of Mass Higher Education and the Birth of Lifelong Learning," in *Lifelong Learning. Education Across the Lifespan*, ed. Mal Geicester (London: Routledge Falmer, 2000), 29–42.
16. Geoffrey Alderman, "The Globalization of Higher Education: Some Observations Regarding the Free Market and the National Interest," *Higher Education in Europe* 26, no. 1 (2001): 47–52.
17. Marek Kwiek, "Globalization and Higher Education," *Higher Education in Europe* 26, no. 1 (2001): 27–38.
18. Majia Holmer Nadesan, " 'Fortune' on Globalization and the New Economy: Manifest Destiny in a Technological Age," *Management Communication Quarterly* 14, no. 3 (2001): 498–506.
19. Grant McBurnie, "Leveraging Globalization as a Policy Paradigm for Higher Education," *Higher Education in Europe* 26, no. 1 (2001): 11–26.
20. John Levin, "Public Policy, Community Colleges, and the Path to Globalization," *Higher Education* 42, no. 2 (2001): 237–262.
21. Noam Chomsky, *Profit Over People: Neoliberalism and Global Order* (New York: Seven Stories Press, 1999).
22. Michael Apple, "Comparing Neo-liberal Projects and Inequality in Education," *Comparative Education* 37, no. 4 (2001): 409–423.
23. George DeMartino, *Global Economy, Global Justice: Theoretical Objections and Policy Alternatives to Neoliberalism* (New York: Routledge, 2000).
24. Richard Sennett, "A Flawed Philosophy," *Guardian Weekly* (2002, June 20–26): 15.
25. John Campbell and Ove Pedersen, "Introduction: The Rise of Neoliberalism and Institutional Analysis," in *The Rise of Neoliberalism and Institutional Analysis*, ed. John Campbell and Ove Pedersen (Princeton: Princeton University Press, 2001), 2–23, DeMartino, *Global Economy, Global Justice: Theoretical Objections and Policy Alternatives to Neoliberalism.*

26. Henry Giroux, "The War on the Young," in *Growing up Postmodern: Neoliberalism and the War on the Young*, ed. Ronald Strickland (Lanham, MD: Rowman & Littlefield, 2002).
27. Adriana Puiggrós, *Neoliberalism and Education in the Americas* (Boulder, CO: Westview Press, 1999), Nelly P. Stromquist, *Education in a Globalized World: The Connectivity of Economic Power, Technology, and Knowledge* (Lanham, MD: Rowman & Littlefield, 2002).
28. D. Franklin Ayers, "Neoliberal Ideology in Community College Mission Statements: A Critical Discourse Analysis." *The Review of Higher Education*, 28, no. 4 (2005): 527–549, Marginson and Considine, *The Enterprise University: Power, Governance and Reinvention in Australia*, Slaughter and Rhoades, *Academic Capitalism and the New Economy: Markets, State, and Higher Education.*
29. Richard Barnet and John Cavanagh, *Global Dreams: Imperial Corporations and the New World Order* (New York: Simon & Schuster, 1994).
30. John Ralston Saul, *The Unconscious Civilization* (Concord, ON: House of Anansi Press, 1995).
31. Catherine Casey, *Work, Society and Self: After Industrialism* (New York: Routledge, 1995).
32. Derek Bok, *Universities in the Marketplace: The Commercialization of Higher Education* (Princeton: Princeton University Press, 2003), Eric Gould, *The University in a Corporate Culture* (New Haven: Yale University Press, 2003), Slaughter and Rhoades, *Academic Capitalism and the New Economy: Markets, State, and Higher Education.*
33. Bill Readings, *The University in Ruins* (Cambridge, MA: Harvard University Press, 1997).
34. Sheila Slaughter and Gary Rhoades, "The Neo-liberal University," *New Labor Forum* (2000, Spring/Summer): 73–79.
35. Levin, "In Education and Work: The Globalized Community College."
36. Jeremy Rifkin, *The End of Work: The Decline of the Global Labor Force and the Dawn of the Post-Market era* (New York: G.P. Putnam's Sons, 1995).
37. Casey, *Work, Society and Self: After Industrialism.*
38. Manuel Castells, *The Rise of the Network Society* (Cambridge, MA: Blackwell Publishers, 1996).
39. Ibid., p. 476.
40. Simon Marginson, "Response to Burton Clark" (Paper presented at the Annual meeting of the Association for the Study of Higher Education, Kansas City, MO, November 3, 2004).
41. Richard Sennett, *The Corrosion of Character: The Personal Consequences of Work in the New Capitalism* (New York: W.W. Norton & Company, 1998).
42. Martin Carnoy, *Sustaining the New Economy: Work, Family, and Community in the Information Age* (New York: Russell Sage Foundation, 2000).
43. Slaughter and Leslie, *Academic Capitalism, Politics, Policies, and the Entrepreneurial University.*
44. Jeffrey Pfeffer and Gerald Salancik, *The External Control of Organizations: A Resource Dependence Perspective* (New York: Harper and Row, 1978).
45. Ibid., p. 40.
46. David Held et al., *Global Transformations: Politics, Economics and Culture* (Stanford, CA: Stanford University Press, 1999), Levin, *Globalizing the Community College: Strategies for Change in the Twenty-First Century*, Waters, *Globalization.*

47. Slaughter and Leslie, *Academic Capitalism, Politics, Policies, and the Entrepreneurial University.*
48. Linda C. Strauss, "Addressing the Discourse on the Future of Post-secondary Education: The Relationship Between Mission and Funding in Community Colleges," in *Eric Clearinghouse for Community Colleges* (Los Angeles, CA: 2001).
49. James C. Palmer, "Funding the Multipurpose Community College in an Era of Consolidation," in *A Struggle to Survive: Funding Higher Education in the Next Century.* 17th Annual Yearbook of the American Educational Finance Association, ed. Kathleen C. Westbrook (Thousand Oaks, CA: Corwin, 1996).
50. Richard Fonte, "Community College Funding: Presidential Perceptions of State Plans," *Community/Junior College Quarterly of Research and Practice* 16, no. 2 (1992): 123–132.
51. Chris Lubienski, "The Relationship of Competition and Choice to Innovation in Education Markets: A Review of Research on Four Cases" (Paper presented at the Annual Meeting of the American Educational Research Association, Seattle, WA, 2001).
52. Robin Marris, "Higher Education and the Mixed Economy: The Concept of Competition," *Studies in Higher Education* 11, no. 2. (1986): 131–154.
53. Marginson and Considine, *The Enterprise University: Power, Governance and Reinvention in Australia.*
54. Slaughter and Leslie, *Academic Capitalism, Politics, Policies, and the Entrepreneurial University.*
55. Marginson and Considine, *The Enterprise University: Power, Governance and Reinvention in Australia.*
56. W. Norton Grubb et al., *Workforce, Economic and Community Development: The Changing Landscape of the Entrepreneurial Community College* (Berkeley: National Center for Research in Vocational Education, The University of California, 1997).
57. Michael M. Roche and Lawrence D. Berg, "Market Metaphors, Neo-liberalism and the Construction of Academic Landscapes in Aotearora/New Zealand," *Journal of Geography in Higher Education* 21, no. 2 (1997): 147–161.
58. Heinz-Dieter Meyer, "Universal, Entrepreneurial, and Soulless? The New University as a Contested Institution," *Comparative Education Review* 46, no. 3 (2002): 339–347.
59. Cynthia Hardy, *The Politics of Collegiality: Retrenchment Strategies in Canadian Universities* (Buffalo: McGill-Queen's University Press, 1996).
60. Edward S. Mason, "The Apologetics of Managerialism," *Journal of Business* 31, no. 6 (1958): 1–11.
61. Levin, *Globalizing the Community College: Strategies for Change in the Twenty-First Century.*
62. John Robst, "Cost Efficiency in Public Higher Education Institutions," *The Journal of Higher Education* 72, no. 6 (2001): 730–750.
63. Slaughter and Leslie, *Academic Capitalism, Politics, Policies, and the Entrepreneurial University.*
64. Deem, " 'New Managerialism' and Higher Education: The Management of Performances and Cultures in Universities in the United Kingdom."
65. Tim Simkins, "Education Reform and Managerialism: Comparing the Experience of Schools and Colleges," *Journal of Education Policy* 15, no. 3 (2000): 317–332.

66. Marginson and Considine, *The Enterprise University: Power, Governance and Reinvention in Australia.*
67. Halil Dundar and Darrell R. Lewis, "Determinants of Research Productivity in Higher Education" *Research in Higher Education* 39, no. 6 (1998): 607–637.
68. William F. Massy, "Improving Productivity in Higher Education Microform: Administration and Support Costs" (U.S. Dept. of Education OERI, ERIC: 1991).
69. William F. Massy and Robert Zemsky, *Using Information Technology to Enhance Academic Productivity* (Washington, DC: Educom, 1995).
70. William F. Massy and Andrea K. Wilger, "Technology's Contribution to Higher Education Productivity," *New Directions for Higher Education* 26, no. 3 (1998): 49–59.
71. Mary Renck Jalongo, "Faculty Productivity in Higher Education," *Educational Forum* 49, no. 2 (1985): 171–182.
72. Jon J. Denton, Chiou-Yueh Tsai, and Connie Cloud, "Productivity of Faculty in Higher Education Institutions," *Journal of Teacher Education* 37, no. 5 (1986): 12–16.
73. Beatrice Baldwin, "Linking Instructional Productivity Measures and Fiscal Policy: Accountability in Higher Education" (Paper presented at the Annual Meeting of the American Educational Research Association, Chicago, IL, March 24–28, 1997).
74. David A. Shupe, "Productivity, Quality, and Accountability in Higher Education," *Journal of Continuing Higher Education* 47, no. 1 (1999): 2–13.
75. James M. Ferris, "Competition and Regulation in Higher Education: A Comparison of the Netherlands and the United States," *Higher Education* 22, no. 1 (1991): 93–108.
76. Ida R. Hoos, "The Costs of Efficiency: Implications of Educational Technology," *The Journal of Higher Education* 46, no. 2 (1975): 141–160.
77. John Cowan, "Effectiveness and Efficiency in Higher Education," *Higher Education* 14, no. 3 (1985): 235–239.
78. Robert Birnbaum, *Management Fads in Higher Education: Where They Come From, What They Do, Why They Fail* (San Francisco: Jossey-Bass, 2000), David Noble, Digital Diploma Mills: The Automation of Higher Education [Web site] (1998 [cited); available from http://www.firstmonday.dk/issues/issue3_1/noble/, Slaughter and Rhoades, *Academic Capitalism and the New Economy: Markets, State, and Higher Education.*
79. Davies and Guppy, "*Globalization and Educational Reforms in Anglo-American Democracies.*"
80. Christopher Mazzeo, Sara Y. Rab, and Julian L. Alssid, *Building Bridges to College and Careers: Contextualized Basic Skills Programs at Community Colleges* (Brooklyn, NY: Workforce Strategy Center, 2003).
81. John T. Dever and Robert G. Templin, Jr., "Assuming Leadership: Community Colleges, Curriculum Reform, and Teaching," *Educational Record* 75, no. 1 (1994): 32–34.
82. Debra D. Bragg and James D. Layton, "The Role of the Urban Community College in Educational Reform," *Education and Urban Society* 27, no. 3 (1995): 294–312.
83. Albert L. Lorenzo and Nancy A. LeCroy, "A Framework for Fundamental Change in the Community College," *Community College Journal* 64, no. 4 (1994): 14–19.

84. Julie Sturgeon, "Coping with the Crunch," *College Planning and Management* 3, no. 3 (2000): 22–24.
85. John S. Nixon and Sara Lundquist, "The Partnership Paradigm: Collaboration and the Community College," *New Directions for Community Colleges* 103 (1998): 43–50.
86. David W. Sink, Jr. and Karen Luke Jackson, "Successful Community College Campus-based Partnerships," *Community College Journal of Research and Practice* 26, no. 1 (2002): 35–46.
87. Larry Johnson, ed., *Common Ground: Exemplary Community College and Corporate Partnerships* (Mission Viejo, CA: League for Innovation in the Community College, 1996).
88. Lynn A. DeNoia and John L. Swearingen, "Linking Administrative and IT Productivity in Higher Education," *Cause/Effect* 15, no. 3 (1992): 34–41.
89. Cheryl Bullock and John Ory, "Evaluating Instructional Technology Implementation in a Higher Education Environment," *American Journal of Evaluation* 21, no. 3 (2000): 315–328.
90. Donald P. Ely, "Conditions that Facilitate the Implementation of Educational Technology Innovations," *Journal of Research on Computing In Education* 23, no. 2 (1990): 298–305.
91. Kenneth C. Green, "2002 Campus Computing Report. The 2002 National Survey of Information Technology in U.S. Higher Education" (Encino, CA: Campus Computing, 2002).
92. Ananda Mitra, Timothy Steffensmeier, and Stefne Lenzmeier, "Changes in Attitudes Toward Computers and Use of Computers by University Faculty," *Journal of Research on Computing in Education* 32, no. 1 (1999): 189–202.
93. Anthony P. Carnevale, "Community Colleges and Career Qualifications." *New Expeditions Issue Paper Series* 11 (Washington, DC: Community College Press, 2000).
94. James March and Michael Cohen, *Leadership and Ambiguity: The American College President* (New York: McGraw-Hill Book Company, 1974).
95. Everett Rogers, *Diffusion of Innovations*, 3rd ed. (New York: The Free Press, 1983).
96. Steven Peter Vallas, *Power in the Workplace: The Politics of Production at AT&T* (Albany: State University of New York, 1993).
97. Langdon Winner, *The Whale and the Reactor: Searching for Limits in an Age of High Technology* (Chicago: University of Chicago Press, 1986).
98. Cristie Roe, "Effects of Information Technology on Community College Faculty" (Paper presentation, American Education Research Association, Chicago, April: 2003).
99. Don Tapscott, *The Digital Economy: Promise and Peril in the Age of Networked Intelligence* (New York: McGraw Hill, 1996).
100. George Baker and Associates, *Cultural Leadership: Inside America's Community Colleges* (Washington, DC: The Community College Press, 1992).
101. Kathleen Shaw, Robert Rhoads, and James Valadez, eds., *Community Colleges as Cultural Texts* (Albany: State University of New York Press, 1999).
102. Melanie Griffith and Ann Connor, *Democracy's Open Door: The Community College in America's Future* (Portsmouth, NH: Boynton/Cook Publishers, 1994).
103. Kevin Dougherty, *The Contradictory College* (Albany: State University of New York Press, 1994).

104. Penelope. E. Herideen, *Policy, Pedagogy, and Social Inequality: Community College Student Realities in Post-Industrial America* (Westport, CT: Bergin & Garvey, 1998).
105. James Valadez, "Cultural Capital and its Impact on the Aspirations of Nontraditional Community College Students," *Community College Review* 21, no. 3 (1996): 30–44.
106. Joshua L. Smith and Fayyaz A. Vellani, "Urban America and the Community College Imperative: The Importance of Open Access and Opportunity," *New Directions for Community Colleges* 27, no. 3 (1999): 5–13.
107. John Levin, "Non-Traditional Students and Community Colleges: The Conflict of Justice and Neo-liberalism. An Overview" (Paper presented at the American Educational Research Association, Montreal, April 2005).
108. We use the term community college faculty rather than two-year college faculty for several reasons, even though a considerable portion of the literature and national data refer to two-year college faculty. We consider the term two-year faculty both limiting and erroneous. First, community colleges are not two-year institutions, neither currently nor historically. Rather, legal language has framed these institutions as colleges that offer two-year programs or place limits on the length of programming to two years. Second, with programs such as Nursing which are *de facto* three-year programs and baccalaureate degree programs, which are four year programs, the term two-year is anachronistic.
109. Charles Outcalt, *A Profile of the Community College Professoriate, 1975–2000* (New York: Routledge Falmer, 2002), James Palmer and L. Zimbler, "*Instructional Faculty and Staff in Public Two-Year Colleges*" (Washington, DC: U.S. Department of Education, Office of Educational Research and Improvement, 2000), Tronie Rifkin, "Differences Between the Professional Attitudes of Full-and Part-Time Community College Faculty" (Paper presented at the American Association of Community Colleges, Miami, April 1998).
110. W. Norton Grubb, *Honored but Invisible: An Inside Look at Teaching in Community Colleges* (New York: Routledge, 1999).
111. Steven Brint and Jerome Karabel, *The Diverted Dream: Community Colleges and the Promise of Educational Opportunity in America*, 1900–1985 (New York: Oxford University Press, 1989).
112. Robert Rhoads and James Valadez, *Democracy, Multiculturalism, and the Community College* (New York: Garland Publishing, 1996), Shaw, Rhoads, and Valadez, eds., *Community Colleges as Cultural Texts.*
113. Richard Wagoner, "Community College Faculty Satisfaction Across Missions and over Time: A Quantitative Analysis" (Paper presented at the Annual Meeting of the Association for the Study of Higher Education, Portland, November 2003).
114. Linda S. Moxley, "Job Satisfaction of Faculty Teaching Higher Education. An Examination of Herzberg's Dual-Factor Theory and Porter's Need Satisfaction Research," in *Education Eric Document No. ED. 139–349*, 1977.
115. Blannie Bowen and Rama B. Radhakrishna, "Job Satisfaction of Agricultural Education Faculty: A Constant Phenomena," *Journal of Agricultural Education* 32, no. 2 (1991): 16–22.
116. Faye D. Plascak-Craig and John P. Bean, "Education Faculty Job Satisfaction in Major Research Universities" (Paper presented at the Annual Meeting of the Association for the Study of Higher Education, Atlanta, GA, November 2–5: 1989).

117. Martin J. Finkelstein, Robert Seal, and Jack H. Schuster, "New Entrants to the Full-Time Faculty of Higher Education Institutions." 1993 National Study of Postsecondary Faculty (NSOPF-93). Statistical Analysis Report (Washington, DC: National Center for Education Statistics, 1998).
118. James R. Valadez and James Soto Antony, "Job Satisfaction and Commitment of Two-year College Part-Time Faculty," *Community College Journal of Research and Practice* 25, no. 2 (2001): 97–108.
119. Wagoner, "Community College Faculty Satisfaction Across Missions and Over Time: A Quantitative Analysis."
120. Bowen and Radhakrishna, "Job Satisfaction of Agricultural Education Faculty: A Constant Phenomena," Finkelstein, Seal, and Schuster, "New Entrants to the Full-Time Faculty of Higher Education Institutions. 1993 National Study of Postsecondary Faculty (NSOPF-93). Statistical Analysis Report," Plascak-Craig and Bean, "Education Faculty Job Satisfaction in Major Research Universities."
121. Elizabeth A. Pollicino, "Faculty Satisfaction with Institutional Support as a Complex Concept: Collegiality, Workload, Autonomy" (Paper presented at the Annual Meeting of the American Educational Research Association, New York, NY, April 8–13, 1996).
122. F. Felicia Ferrara, "Faculty Management: Maximizing Autonomy and Job Satisfaction Under Economic, Administrative and Technological Changes" (Paper presented at the Annual Meeting of the Popular Culture Association and the Annual Conference of the American Culture Association, Orlando, FL, April 8–11, 1998).
123. Mark Nickerson and Sue Schaefer, "Autonomy and Anonymity: Characteristics of Branch Campus Faculty," Metropolitan Universities: *An International Forum* 12, no. 2 (2001): 49–59.
124. Andrew Joseph Mazzoli, "Faculty Perceptions of Influences on the Curriculum in Higher Education," in *Eric Clearinghouse*, No: HE034523 (2000).
125. John Nixon, "Professional Identity and the Restructuring of Higher Education," *Studies in Higher Education* 21, no. 1 (1996): 5–16.
126. Ferrara, "Faculty Management: Maximizing Autonomy and Job Satisfaction Under Economic, Administrative and Technological Changes."
127. Vallas, *Power in the Workplace: The Politics of Production at AT&T.*
128. Rhoades, *Managed Professionals: Unionized Faculty and Restructuring Academic Labor.*
129. Gary Rhoades, "*The Production Politics of Teaching and Technology: Deskilling, Enskilling, and Managerial Extension*" (Unpublished manuscript: 1996).
130. Helen Connole, "Cyborgs and Knowledge Workers? Gendered Constructions of Workers in Vocational Education and Training," *Studies in Continuing Education* 18, no. 2 (1996): 122–134.
131. Andrea Berger et al., "A Profile of Part-Time Faculty: Fall 1998" (National Center for Educational Statistics, 2002).
132. Judith M. Gappa, and David. W. Leslie, *The Invisible Faculty: Improving the Status of Part-Timers in Higher Education* (San Francisco: Jossey-Bass, 1993).
133. Ibid.
134. Ernest Benjamin, "Variations in the Characteristics of Part-Time Faculty by General Fields of Instruction and Research," in *The Growing Use of Part-Time Faculty: Understanding Causes and Effects*, ed. David. W. Leslie, New Directions for Higher Education (San Francisco: Jossey-Bass, 1998), 45–60.

135. Rhoades, "The Production Politics of Teaching and Technology: Deskilling, Enskilling, and Managerial Extension."
136. Gareth Morgan, *Images of Organization* (Thousand Oaks, CA: Sage Publications, 1997).
137. Victoria Smith, "Teamwork vs. Tempwork: Managers and the Dualisms of Workplace Restructuring," in *Working in Restructured Workplaces: New Directions for the Sociology of Work.*, ed. Holly McCammon (Thousand Oaks, CA: Sage, 2001), 7–28.
138. John Roueche, Suanne Roueche, and Mark Milliron, *Strangers in Their Own Land: Part-Time Faculty in American Community Colleges* (Washington, DC: Community College Press, 1995).
139. Carol Lucey, "Civic Engagement, Shared Governance, and Community Colleges," *Academe* 88, no. 4 (2002): 27–31.
140. Sue Kater and John Levin, "Shared Governance in Community Colleges in the Global Economy," *Community College Journal of Research and Practice* 29, no. 1 (2005): 1–24.
141. Cheryl Lovell and C. Trought, "State Governance Patterns for Community Colleges," *New Directions for Community Colleges* 117 (2002): 91–100.
142. John Levin, "What's the Impediment? Structural and Legal Constraints to Shared Governance in the Community College," *The Canadian Journal of Higher Education* XXX, no. 2 (2000): 87–122.
143. Martin J. Finkelstein, Robert K. Seal, and Jack K. Schuster, *The New Academic Generation* (Baltimore: The Johns Hopkins University Press, 1998).
144. Joanne Martin and Debra Meyerson, "Organizational Cultures and the Denial, Channeling and Acknowledgment of Ambiguity," in *Managing Ambiguity and Change*, ed. Lewis R. Pondy, Richard J. Boland, and Howard Thomas (New York: John Wiley & Sons, 1988), 93–125, Linda Smircich, "Concepts of Culture and Organizational Analysis," *Administrative Science Quarterly* 28 (1983): 339–358.
145. William Tierney, "Organizational Culture in Higher Education: Defining the Essentials," in *Organization and Governance in Higher Education*, ed. Marvin Peterson (Needham Heights, MA: Simon & Schuster, 1991), 126–139.
146. Levin, *Globalizing the Community College: Strategies for Change in the Twenty-First Century.*
147. Ken Kempner, "Understanding Cultural Conflict," in *Culture and Ideology in Higher Education*, ed. William. G. Tierney (New York: Praeger, 1991), 129–150.
148. Thomas R. Bailey and Vanessa Smith Morest, "The Organizational Efficiency of Multiple Missions for Community Colleges" (New York: Teachers College, Columbia University, 2004), Dougherty, *The Contradictory College*, Ken Kempner, "The Community College as a Marginalized Institution" (Unpublished paper presented at annual meeting of Association of the Study of Higher Education, Boston, 1991), Shaw, Rhoads, and Valadez, eds., *Community Colleges as Cultural Texts.*
149. Arthur Cohen and Florence Brawer, *The American Community College* (San Francisco: Jossey-Bass, 2003).
150. Grubb, *Honored but Invisible: An Inside Look at Teaching in Community Colleges.*
151. Cohen and Brawer, *The American Community College.*
152. Howard London, *The Culture of a Community College* (New York: Praeger Publishers, 1978).

153. John Frye, "Educational Paradigms in the Professional Literature of the Community College," in *Higher Education: Handbook of Theory and Research*, ed. John Smart (New York: Agathon Press, 1994), 181–224.
154. Ibid.
155. Dennis McGrath and Martin Spear, *The Academic Crisis of the Community College* (Albany, NY: State University of New York Press, 1991).
156. John Levin, "The Community College as a Baccalaureate-Granting Institution," *The Review of Higher Education* 28, no. 1 (2004): 1–22, Levin, "Public Policy, Community Colleges, and the Path to Globalization."
157. Bailey and Morest, "The Organizational Efficiency of Multiple Missions for Community Colleges."
158. Roland W. Scholz and Olaf Tietje, *Embedded Case Study Methods: Integrating Quantitative and Qualitative Knowledge* (Thousand Oaks, CA: Sage Publications, 2002).
159. Kathleen Eisenhardt, "Building Theories From Case Study Research," *Academy of Management Review* 14, no. 4 (1989): 532–550.
160. Michael Dubson, *Ghosts in the Classroom: Stories of College Adjunct Faculty and the Price We All Pay* (Boston: Camels Back Books, 2001).
161. Benjamin, "Variations in the Characteristics of Part-Time Faculty by General Fields of Instruction and Research."
162. Chao-Ying Joanne Peng et al., "The Use and Interpretation of Logistic Regression in Higher Education Journals: 1988–1999," *Research In Higher Education* 43, no. 4 (1999): 259–293.
163. William H. Rogers, "Regression Standard Errors in Clustered Samples," *State Technical Bulletin* 13 (1993): 19–23.
164. Levin, "What's the Impediment? Structural and Legal Constraints to Shared Governance in the Community College."
165. Jennifer Mason, *Qualitative Researching* (Thousand Oaks, CA: Sage Publications, 1996).
166. Robert Burgess, *In the Field: An Introduction to Field Research* (London: George Allen and Unwin, 1984), Frederick Erickson, "Qualitative Methods in Research on Teaching," in *Handbook of Research on Teaching*, ed. Marvin Wittrock (New York: Macmillan Publishing Company, 1986), 119–161, Catherine Marshall and Gretchen Rossman, *Designing Qualitative Research*, 3rd ed. (Thousand Oaks, CA: Sage Publications, 1999), Mason, *Qualitative Researching*, Matthew Miles and A. Michael Huberman, *Qualitative Data Analysis* (Thousand Oaks, CA: Sage Publications, 1994), Michael Patton, *Qualitative Evaluation Methods* (Newbury Park, CA: Sage Publications, 1990), Catherine Riessman, "Analysis of Personal Narratives," in *Handbook of Interview Research: Context and Method*, ed. Jaber F. Gubrium and James A. Holstein (Thousand Oaks, CA: Sage Publications, 2002), 695–710, Robert Yin, *Case Study Research: Design and Methods* (Thousand Oaks, CA: Sage Publications, 1994).

## 4 Faculty and Institutional Management and Governance

1. Edward Hines, "The Governance of Higher Education," in *Higher Education: Handbook of Theory and Research*, XV, ed. John Smart and William Tierney (New York: Agathon Press, 2000), 105–155.

2. John Levin, *Globalizing the Community College: Strategies for Change in the Twenty-First Century* (New York: Palgrave, 2001), Simon Marginson and Mark Considine, *The Enterprise University: Power, Governance and Reinvention in Australia* (New York: Cambridge University Press, 2000), Sheila Slaughter and Gary Rhoades, *Academic Capitalism and the New Economy: Markets, State, and Higher Education* (Baltimore: The Johns Hopkins University Press, 2004), William Tierney, ed., *Competing Conceptions of Academic Governance: Negotiating the Perfect Storm* (Baltimore: The Johns Hopkins University Press, 2004).
3. Levin, *Globalizing the Community College: Strategies for Change in the Twenty-First Century.*
4. John Levin, "The Business Culture of the Community College: Students as Consumers; Students as Commodities," in *Arenas of Entrepreneurship: Where Nonprofit and For Profit Institutions Compete. New Directions for Higher Education*, ed. Brian Pusser (San Francisco: Jossey-Bass Publishers, 2005): 11–26.
5. We use pseudonyms for colleges where we interviewed college members so that we could maintain the anonymity of our sources. While we refer to locations—states and provinces—or to colleges in a state or province, such as "an Alberta college," we only give the actual name of institutions when we refer to public documents. In this chapter those documents are colleges' collective bargaining agreements.
6. Levin, *Globalizing the Community College: Strategies for Change in the Twenty-First Century.*
7. Joseph Gilmour, Jr., "Participative Governance Bodies in Higher Education: Report of a National Study," *New Directions for Higher Education* 75 (1991): 27–39, Hines, "The Governance of Higher Education," Levin, *Globalizing the Community College: Strategies for Change in the Twenty-First Century*, John Levin, "Public Policy, Community Colleges, and the Path to Globalization," *Higher Education* 42, no. 2 (2001): 237–262, John Levin, "What's the Impediment? Structural and Legal Constraints to Shared Governance in the Community College," *The Canadian Journal of Higher Education* XXX, no. 2 (2000): 87–122.
8. William Tierney, "Organizational Culture in Higher Education: Defining the Essentials," in *Organization and Governance in Higher Education*, ed. Marvin Peterson (Needham Heights, MA: Simon & Schuster, 1991), 126–139.
9. Levin, "What's the Impediment? Structural and Legal Constraints to Shared Governance in the Community College," Tierney, ed., *Competing Conceptions of Academic Governance: Negotiating the Perfect Storm.*
10. Rosemary Deem, " 'New Managerialism' and Higher Education: The Management of Performances and Cultures in Universities in the United Kingdom," *International Studies in Sociology of Education* 8, no. 1 (1998): 47–70, Cynthia Hardy, *The Politics of Collegiality: Retrenchment Strategies in Canadian Universities* (Buffalo: McGill-Queen's University Press, 1996), John Levin et al., "Not Professionals?: Community College Faculty in the New Economy" (Symposium for the Annual Meeting of the American Educational Research Association, Chicago, April, 2003), Gary Rhoades, *Managed Professionals: Unionized Faculty and Restructuring Academic Labor* (Albany: State University of New York Press, 1998).
11. Deem, " 'New Managerialism' and Higher Education: The Management of Performances and Cultures in Universities in the United Kingdom."
12. John Levin, "In Education and Work: The Globalized Community College," *The Canadian Journal of Higher Education* XXXII, no. 2 (2002): 47–78, Marginson

and Considine, *The Enterprise University: Power, Governance and Reinvention in Australia*, Sheila Slaughter and Larry Leslie, *Academic Capitalism, Politics, Policies, and the Entrepreneurial University* (Baltimore: The Johns Hopkins University Press, 1997).

13. Levin, "The Business Culture of the Community College: Students as Consumers; Students as Commodities," Levin, *Globalizing the Community College: Strategies for Change in the Twenty-First Century.*
14. Steven Brint, *In an Age of Experts: The Changing Role of Professionals in Politics and Public Life* (Princeton: Princeton University Press, 1994).
15. Catherine Casey, *Work, Society and Self: After Industrialism* (New York: Routledge, 1995).
16. Cynthia Hardy, "Configuration and Strategy Making in Universities: Broadening the Scope," *The Journal of Higher Education* 62, no. 4 (1991): 363–393, Henry Mintzberg, "The Professional Bureaucracy," in *Organization and Governance in Higher Education*, ed. Marvin Peterson (Needham Heights, MA: Simon & Schuster, 1991).
17. John Corson, *Governance of Colleges and Universities* (New York: McGraw Hill, 1960).
18. Hines, "The Governance of Higher Education."
19. Gordon B. Arnold, *The Politics of Faculty Unionization: The Experience of Three New England Universities* (Westport, CT: Bergin & Garvey, 2000), Susan Kater, "Shared Governance in the Community College: The Rights, Roles, and Responsibilities of Unionized Community College Faculty" (Unpublished doctoral dissertation. Tucson, AZ: The University of Arizona, 2003).
20. Levin, *Globalizing the Community College: Strategies for Change in the Twenty-first Century*, Marginson and Considine, *The Enterprise University: Power, Governance and Reinvention in Australia*, Rhoades, *Managed Professionals: Unionized Faculty and Restructuring Academic Labor*, Slaughter and Leslie, *Academic Capitalism, Politics, Policies, and the Entrepreneurial University.*
21. William Kaplin and Barbara Lee, *The Law of Higher Education: A Comprehensive Guide to Legal Implications of Administrative Decision-Making*, 3rd ed. (San Francisco, CA: Jossey-Bass, 1995), Levin, *Globalizing the Community College: Strategies for Change in the Twenty-First Century*, Christopher Morphew, "Challenges Facing Shared Governance Within the College," *New Directions for Higher Education* 105 (1999): 71–79, Gary L. Riley and Victor J. Baldridge, eds., *Governing Academic Organizations: New Problems New Perspectives* (Berkeley, CA: McCutchan Publishing, 1977), Slaughter and Leslie, *Academic Capitalism, Politics, Policies, and the Entrepreneurial University.*
22. Levin et al., "Not Professionals?: Community College Faculty in the New Economy," Susan Twombly and Barbara Townsend, "Conclusion: The Future of Community Policy in the 21st Century," in *Community Colleges: Policy in the Future Context*, ed. Barbara Townsend and Susan Twombly (Westport, CT: Ablex, 2001), 283–298.
23. Rhoades, *Managed Professionals: Unionized Faculty and Restructuring Academic Labor.*
24. Kaplin and Lee, *The Law of Higher Education: A Comprehensive Guide to Legal Implications of Administrative Decision-Making.*
25. Ibid., p. 153.
26. We analyzed collective bargaining agreements between full-Time faculty and public community colleges in twenty-two states and three Canadian provinces.

Collective agreements between faculty unions and community colleges codify behaviors, giving actions legal authority within the context of state and federal legislation. While the language or text of these agreements may constitute legitimate evidence of behaviors one needs to be cautious in this assumption. See Jennifer Mason, *Qualitative Researching* (Thousand Oaks, CA: Sage Publications, 1996). Contract language is promissory: it constitutes an intention and a prescription; it is not evidence of actual behaviors. Conditions specified in collective agreements, however, "are primary factors establishing the legal parameters of managerial direction and of professional autonomy, involvement, and constraint in the academic work place." See Rhoades, *Managed Professionals: Unionized Faculty and Restructuring Academic Labor*, p. 19. Our research utilizes three primary data sources for document analysis: the 1995–96, 1998–99, and the Spring 2003 Higher Education Contract Analysis System (HECAS) CD-ROMs created by the NEA (1995–96; 1998–99; 2003). The Higher Education Contract Analysis System (NEA 1995–96; 1998–99; 2003) is a collection of bargaining agreements from both NEA member institutions and non-NEA bargaining units. The entire accessible population of full-time faculty contracts for community colleges in California, Hawaii, Illinois, Oregon and Washington were analyzed from the 1995–96 HECAS CD-ROM (NEA, 1995–96) utilizing Levin's analytical framework for shared governance, and the entire accessible population of full-time faculty contracts for community colleges in Florida, Iowa, Kansas, Maine, Maryland, Massachusetts, Michigan, Minnesota, Missouri, Montana, Nebraska, New Jersey, New York, Ohio, Oregon, Pennsylvania and Rhode Island were analyzed from the 1998–99 HECAS CD-ROM (NEA, 1998–99) and coded, completing the database available for the identified states between the 1995–96 and 1998–99 HECAS CD ROMs. Different HECAS databases were utilized (NEA, 1995–96, 1998–99) due to the time frame in which the contract analysis took place. The states analyzed from the 1995–96 database were part of Levin's study of shared governance in the United States and Canada. See Levin, "What's the Impediment? Structural and Legal Constraints to Shared Governance in the Community College." The line of inquiry into shared governance was initiated again in 1999, and the 1998–99 HECAS (NEA) database was utilized for states not reviewed in Levin's study. Additional comparisons were made between accessible contracts from the late 1980s to early 2000s using the HECAS 2003 database. The Higher Education Contract Analysis System contains a number of search parameters and functions that allow for ease of access and retrieval of the data. These tools supported the reliability of the information coding, but did not take the place of detailed reading of the contracts. Each contract was printed and reviewed. Validity checking of samples of contract coding took place throughout the process, by both the researcher and an expert consultant. Three additional contracts from colleges in the study states were reviewed as they were obtained in the course of the research, contracts representing Miami-Dade Community College, Foothill-De Anza Community College District, and Des Moines Area Community College District. The additional contracts were not purposefully sampled. They represented institutions in states which were already included in the study population. Sixteen governance areas were identified for coding including (1) budget, (2) calendar, (3) curriculum, (4) discipline, (5) evaluation, (6) faculty hiring, (7) general problems, (8) grievance, (9) management hiring, (10) new positions, (11) professional development, (12) program changes, (13) retrenchment,

(14) sabbatical, and (15) tenure. These, according to Levin (2000), were the major content areas of collective bargaining that pertain to decision making in community colleges. Coding was open to the emergence of other governance areas during document analysis. Discrete governance areas were then aggregated to traditional areas of shared governance, nontraditional areas of shared governance, and ancillary areas for overall analysis.

27. Arthur Cohen and Florence Brawer, *The American Community College*, 3rd ed. (San Francisco: Jossey-Bass, 1996; San Francisco: Jossey-Bass, 2003).
28. Levin, "*What's the Impediment? Structural and Legal Constraints to Shared Governance in the Community College.*"
29. Mason, *Qualitative Researching.*
30. Kaplin and Lee, *The Law of Higher Education: A Comprehensive Guide to Legal Implications of Administrative Decision-Making*, p. 150.
31. J. Victor Baldridge et al., "Assessing the Impact of Faculty Collective Bargaining" (Washington, DC: AAHE-ERIC/Higher Education Research Report No. 8/The George Washington University, 1981), Cohen and Brawer, *The American Community College,* Levin, *"What's the Impediment? Structural and Legal Constraints to Shared Governance in the Community College,"* Richard C. Richardson Jr., Clyde E. Blocker, and Louis W. Bender, *Governance for the Two-Year College* (Englewood Cliffs, NJ: Prentice-Hall, 1972).
32. Jan W. Henkel and Norman J. Wood, "Legislative Power to Veto Collective Bargaining Agreements by Faculty Unions: An Overlooked Reality?" *Journal of Law and Education* 11, no. 1 (1982): 79–95.
33. Richardson Jr., Blocker, and Bender, *Governance for the Two-Year College*, p. 69.
34. Arnold, *The Politics of Faculty Unionization: The Experience of Three New England Universities.*
35. Warner Woodworth and Christopher Meek, *Creating Labor-Management Partnerships* (Reading, MA: Addison-Wesley, 1995).
36. Gwen B. Williams and Perry A. Zirkel, "Academic Penetration into Faculty Collective Bargaining Contracts in Higher Education," *Research in Higher Education* 28, no. 1 (1988): 76–95.
37. Cohen and Brawer, *The American Community College*, Hardy, Configuration and Strategy Making in Universities: Broadening the Scope.
38. Hardy, "Configuration and Strategy Making in Universities: Broadening the Scope."
39. Ibid.
40. Levin, *Globalizing the Community College: Strategies for Change in the Twenty-first Century.*
41. "Hardy, Configuration and Strategy Making in Universities: Broadening the Scope," Levin, *Globalizing the Community College: Strategies for Change in the Twenty-First Century.*
42. Patricia Gumport, "The Contested Terrain of Academic Program Reduction," *The Journal of Higher Education* 64, no. 3 (1993): 283–311.
43. Rhoades, *Managed Professionals: Unionized Faculty and Restructuring Academic Labor.*
44. Robert Birnbaum, *How Colleges Work* (San Francisco: Jossey-Bass Publishers, 1988).
45. Douglas Toma, Personal communication on review of earlier draft of the research (New Orleans: 2001).
46. Kenneth Mortimer and Thomas Raymond McConnell, *Sharing Authority Effectively*, 1st ed. (San Francisco: Jossey-Bass, 1978).

47. Ibid.
48. Richard Hurd, Jennifer Bloom, and Beth Hillman Johnson, "Directory of Faculty Contracts and Bargaining Agents in Institutions of Higher Education" (Baruch College, The City University of New York: The National Center for the Study of Collective Bargaining in Higher Education and the Professions, 1998).
49. Paul DiMaggio and Walter Powell, "The Iron Cage Revisited: Institutional Isomorphism and Collective Rationality in Organizational Fields," *American Sociological Review* 48 (1983): 147–160.
50. Kenneth White, "Shared Governance in California," *New Directions for Community Colleges* 102 (1998): 19–29.
51. Levin, "What's the Impediment? Structural and Legal Constraints to Shared Governance in the Community College."
52. John Dennison, "Characteristics of the University College in British Columbia: Governance and Administration" (Paper for an international conference on new developments in higher education. Bermuda, October: 2000), John Levin, "Organizational Paradigm Shift and the University Colleges of British Columbia," *Higher Education* 46, no. 4 (2003): 447–467, John Levin, "Two British Columbia University Colleges and the Process of Economic Globalization," *The Canadian Journal of Higher Education* XXXIII, no. 1 (2003): 59–86.
53. Levin, *Globalizing the Community College: Strategies for Change in the Twenty-First Century.*
54. Hines, "The Governance of Higher Education."
55. Richard Alfred and Patricia Carter, "New Colleges for a New Century: Organizational Change and Development in Community Colleges," in *Higher Education: Handbook of Theory and Research*, ed. John C. Smart and William G. Tierney (New York: Agathon Press, 1999), 240–283, Frank Annunziato, "From Conflict to Accord: Collective Bargaining at the Academy," *New Directions for Higher Education* 92 (1995): 51–57, Gilmour, "Participative Governance Bodies in Higher Education: Report of a National Study," Hines, "The Governance of Higher Education," Henry C. Katz and Thomas A. Kochan, *An Introduction to Collective Bargaining and Industrial Relations* (Boston: Irwin McGraw-Hill, 2000), Levin, *Globalizing the Community College: Strategies for Change in the Twenty-First Century*, Levin, "Public Policy, Community Colleges, and the Path to Globalization," Levin, "What's the Impediment? Structural and Legal Constraints to Shared Governance in the Community College," Woodworth and Meek, *Creating Labor–Management Partnerships.*
56. Rhoades, *Managed Professionals: Unionized Faculty and Restructuring Academic Labor.*

## 5 Faculty Use of Instructional Technology and Distributed Learning

1. Michael G. Moore, "Recent Contributions to the Theory of Distance Education," *Open Learning* 5, no. 3 (1990): 10–13.
2. Kenneth C. Green and Steven Gilbert, "Great Expectations: Content, Communications, Productivity, and the Role of Information Technology in Higher Education," *Change* 27, no. 2 (1995): 8–18.
3. Charlie Tuller and Diana Oblinger, "Information Technology as a Transformation Agent," *Cause and Effect* 20, no. 4 (1998): 33–45.

4. Cristie E. Roe, "Effects of Informational Technology on Community College Faculty," Unpublished doctoral dissertation, Tucson, AZ: The University of Arizona, 2002.
5. William Baumol, "Macroeconomics of Unbalanced Growth: The Anatomy of Urban Crisis," *American Economic Review* 57, no. 3 (1967): 415–426, William Baumol and Sue Blackman, "How to Think about Rising Colleges Costs," *Planning for Higher Education* 23, no. 4 (1995): 1–7, William Bowen, *The Economics of Major Private Research Universities* (Berkeley, CA: Carnegie Commission on Higher Education, 1967).
6. Baumol, "Macroeconomics of Unbalanced Growth: The Anatomy of Urban Crisis," Baumol and Blackman, "How to Think about Rising Colleges Costs," Bowen, *The Economics of Major Private Research Universities.*
7. Veronica Diaz, "The Digitization and Control of Intellectual Property: Institutional Patterns of Distributed Learning Behavior and the Organizational Policy Response," Unpublished doctoral dissertation, Tucson, AZ: The University of Arizona, 2004.
8. Helen Dixon, "The Effects of Policy on Practice: An Analysis of Teachers' Perceptions of School Based Assessment Practice" (Palmerston, NZ., Massey University, 1999).
9. Diaz, "The Digitization and Control of Intellectual Property: Institutional Patterns of Distributed Learning Behavior and the Organizational Policy Response," Sheila Slaughter and Gary Rhoades, *Academic Capitalism and the New Economy: Markets, State, and Higher Education* (Baltimore, MD: The Johns Hopkins University Press, 2004).
10. Diaz, "The Digitization and Control of Intellectual Property: Institutional Patterns of Distributed Learning Behavior and the Organizational Policy Response."
11. Dan Carnevale, "More Professors Teach by Using Other College's Online Courses," *Chronicle of Higher Education*, October 15, 2004, A28–A29.
12. Ibid.
13. David H. Autor, Lawrence F. Katz, and Alan B. Kreuger, "Computing Inequality: Have Computers Changed the Labor Market?," *Quarterly Journal of Economics* 113, no. 4 (1998): 1169–1213.
14. Manuel Castells, *The Rise of the Network Society*, 2nd ed. (Oxford: Blackwell Publishers, 2000).
15. John Levin, "The Business Culture of the Community College: Students as Consumers; Students as Commodities," in *Arenas of Entrepreneurship: Where Nonprofit and For Profit Institutions Compete. New Directions for Higher Education*, ed. Brian Pusser (San Francisco: Jossey-Bass Publishers, 2005): 11–26, John Levin, *Globalizing the Community College: Strategies for Change in the Twenty-First Century* (New York: Palgrave, 2001), John Levin, "In Education and Work: The Globalized Community College," *The Canadian Journal of Higher Education* XXXII, no. 2 (2002): 47–78.
16. Castells, *The Rise of the Network Society*, p. 100.
17. Levin, *Globalizing the Community College: Strategies for Change in the Twenty-First Century.*
18. John Levin, "The Revised Institution: The Community College Mission at the End of the 20th Century," *Community College Review* 28, no. 2 (2000): 1–25.
19. Levin, *Globalizing the Community College: Strategies for Change in the Twenty-First Century.*

20. Ibid.
21. Roe, "Effects of Informational Technology on Community College Faculty."
22. Ann Deden and Vicki K. Carter, "Using Technology to Enhance Students' Skills," in *Preparing Competent College Graduates: Setting New and Higher Expectations for Student Learning*, ed. Elizabeth A. Jones, *New Directions for Higher Education* (San Francisco: Jossey-Bass Publishers, 1996), 81–92.
23. Autor, Katz, and Kreuger, "*Computing Inequality: Have Computers Changed the Labor Market?*" W. Norton Grubb, *Honored but Invisible: An Inside Look at Teaching in Community Colleges* (New York: Routledge, 1999).
24. Levin, *Globalizing the Community College: Strategies for Change in the Twenty-First Century.*
25. Roe, "Effects of Informational Technology on Community College Faculty".
26. Levin, *Globalizing the Community College: Strategies for Change in the Twenty-First Century.*
27. Sarah Hebel, "No Room in the Class: As Student Populations Explode in Some States, Public Colleges Struggle to Find Enough Places—Even for High Achievers," *Chronicle of Higher Education* (July 2, 2004), 19.
28. Roe, "Effects of Informational Technology on Community College Faculty".
29. Levin, *Globalizing the Community College: Strategies for Change in the Twenty-First Century.*
30. Levin, "The Business Culture of the Community College: Students as Consumers; Students as Commodities," Levin, *Globalizing the Community College: Strategies for Change in the Twenty-First Century.*
31. Levin, *Globalizing the Community College: Strategies for Change in the Twenty-First Century.*
32. Sheila Slaughter, "Federal Policy and Supply-Side Institutional Resource Allocation at Public Research Universities," *The Review of Higher Education* 21, no. 3 (1998): 209–244, Slaughter and Rhoades, *Academic Capitalism and the New Economy: Markets, State, and Higher Education.*
33. Kenneth C. Green, "The Campus Computing Project." The 12th National Survey of Computing and Information Technology in Higher Education, (2001).
34. Molly A. McGill and Sally M. Johnstone, "Distance Education: An Opportunity for Cooperation and Resource Sharing," in *Distance Education Strategies and Tools*, ed. Barry Willis (Englewood Cliffs, NJ: Educational Technology Publications, 1994), 265–276.
35. Levin, *Globalizing the Community College: Strategies for Change in the Twenty-First Century.*
36. Gary Rhoades, *Managed Professionals: Unionized Faculty and Restructuring Academic Labor* (Albany: State University of New York Press, 1998).
37. Karen Paulson, "Reconfiguring Faculty Roles for Virtual Settings," *Journal of Higher Education* 73, no. 1 (2002): 123–140.
38. Ibid.
39. Levin, *Globalizing the Community College: Strategies for Change in the Twenty-First Century.*
40. John Levin, "Two British Columbia University Colleges and the Process of Economic Globalization," *The Canadian Journal of Higher Education* XXXIII, no. 1 (2003): 59–86.
41. John Roueche, Suanne Roueche, and Mark Milliron, *Strangers in Their Own Land: Part-Time Faculty in American Community Colleges* (Washington, DC: Community College Press, 1995), Richard Wagoner, "The Contradictory

Faculty: Part-Time Faculty at Community Colleges," (Unpublished doctoral dissertation, Tucson, AZ: The University of Arizona, 2004).

42. Robert Barr and John Tagg, "From Teaching to Learning: A New Paradigm for Undergraduate Education," *Change* (1995, November/December): 13–25, Dixon, "The Effects of Policy on Practice: An Analysis of Teachers' Perceptions of School Based Assessment Practice," Don Quick and Timothy Gray Davies, "Community College Faculty Development: Bringing Technology into Instruction," *Community College Journal of Research and Practice* 23, no. 7 (1999): 641–653.
43. Barr and Tagg, "From Teaching to Learning: A New Paradigm for Undergraduate Education," James L. Cooper, Pamela Robinson, and Molly McKinney, "Cooperative Learning in the Classroom," in *Changing College Classrooms*, ed. Diane Halpern and Associates (San Francisco: Jossey-Bass, 1994), 74–92, James Davis, Interdisciplinary courses and Team Teaching: New Arrangements for Learning (Phoenix: American Council on Education and Oryx Press, 1995), PsychSim 4.0: Interactive Graphic Simulations for Psychology, Worth, New York.
44. Roe, "Effects of Informational Technology on Community College Faculty."
45. Ibid.
46. Rhoades, *Managed Professionals: Unionized Faculty and Restructuring Academic Labor*, Steven Peter Vallas, *Power in the Workplace: The Politics of Production at AT&T* (Albany: State University of New York, 1993).
47. Roe, "Effects of Informational Technology on Community College Faculty."
48. John S. Levin, "Is the Management of Distance Education Transforming Instruction in Colleges?" *The Quarterly Review of Distance Education* 2, no. 2 (2001): 105–117.
49. Ibid.
50. Grubb, *Honored but Invisible: An Inside Look at Teaching in Community Colleges*, Roe, "Effects of Informational Technology on Community College Faculty."
51. Veronica Diaz and John J. Cheslock, "Distributed Learning Activity: Patterns of Faculty and Institutional Participation in Four-Year Colleges and Universities," (Unpublished manuscript, Tucson, AZ: The University of Arizona, 2004).
52. Ibid.
53. Ibid.
54. Wagoner, "The Contradictory Faculty: Part-Time Faculty at Community Colleges."
55. Ibid.
56. Levin, *Globalizing the Community College: Strategies for Change in the Twenty-First Century.*
57. Diaz, "The Digitization and Control of Intellectual Property: Institutional Patterns of Distributed Learning Behavior and the Organizational Policy Response," Slaughter and Rhoades, *Academic Capitalism and the New Economy: Markets, State, and Higher Education.*
58. Carnevale, "More Professors Teach by Using Other College's Online Courses."
59. Roe, "Effects of Informational Technology on Community College Faculty."

## 6 Part-Time Community College Faculty as New Economy Temporary Labor

1. This majority is calculated by using the number of employees classified as faculty. See Arthur Cohen and Florence Brawer, *The American Community College* (San Francisco: Jossey-Bass, 2003).

2. Stanley Aronowitz and William Di Fazio, *The Jobless Future: Sci-tech and the Dogma of Work* (Minneapolis: University of Minnesota Press, 1994), Vicki Smith, *Crossing the Great Divide: Worker Risk and Opportunity in the New Economy* (New York: Cornell University Press, 2001).
3. We use the term "part-time" or "part-timers" to refer to that class or group of faculty who are employed as official temporary labor. Other terms, such as "adjunct" or "sessional" are used as well in the literature.
4. Kent Phillippe and Madeline Patton, *National Profile of Community Colleges: Trends and Statistics*, 3rd ed. (Washington, DC: Community College Press, American Association of Community Colleges, 2000). We use the 1999 national figures although in the May 2005 update from the National Center for Educational Statistics, *2004 National Study of Postsecondary Faculty (NSOPF: 04): Report on Faculty and Instructional Staff in Fall 2003* (Washington, DC: U.S. Department of Education, 2005) the figure for part-time faculty has risen to 66.7%.
5. John Levin, "The Business Culture of the Community College: Students as Consumers; Students as Commodities," in *Arenas of Entrepreneurship: Where Nonprofit and For Profit Institutions Compete. New Directions for Higher Education*, ed. Brian Pusser (San Francisco: Jossey-Bass Publishers, 2005): 11–26, John Levin, "In Education and Work: The Globalized Community College," *The Canadian Journal of Higher Education* XXXII, no. 2 (2002): 47–78.
6. N. Carol Eliason, "Part-Time Faculty: A National Perspective," in *Using Part-Time Faculty Effectively*, ed. Michael H. Parsons, *New Directions for Community Colleges* no. 3 (San Francisco: Jossey-Bass, 1980), 1–12.
7. Judith M. Gappa and David W. Leslie, "Two Faculties or One?: The Conundrum of Part-Timers in a Bifurcated Work Force," *New Pathways: Faculty Careers and Employment for the 21st Century* 6 (1997): 1–26.
8. William Bridges, *Job Shift* (Reading, MA: Addison-Wesley Publishing Company, 1994), Martin Carnoy, *Sustaining the New Economy: Work, Family, and Community in the Information Age* (New York: Russell Sage Foundation, 2000), Jeremy Rifkin, *The End of Work: The Decline of the Global Labor Force and the Dawn of the Post-Market Era* (New York: G.P. Putnam's Sons, 1995), Smith, *Crossing the Great Divide: Worker Risk and Opportunity in the New Economy.*
9. Manuel Castells, *The Rise of the Network Society*, 2nd ed. (Malden, MA: Blackwell, 2000).
10. Carnoy, *Sustaining the New Economy: Work, Family, and Community in the Information Age.*
11. Smith, *Crossing the Great Divide: Worker Risk and Opportunity in the New Economy.*
12. Paul Osterman et al., *Working in America: A Blueprint for the New Labor Market* (Cambridge, MA: MIT Press, 2001).
13. Carnoy, *Sustaining the New Economy: Work, Family, and Community in the Information Age*, Castells, *The Rise of the Network Society*, Smith, *Crossing the Great Divide: Worker Risk and Opportunity in the New Economy.*
14. Frederic Jacobs, "Using Part-Time Faculty more Effectively," in *The Growing Use of Part-Time Faculty: Understanding Causes and Effects*, ed. David W. Leslie, *New Directions for Higher Education* (San Francisco: Jossey-Bass, 1998), 9–18.
15. Ernest Benjamin, "Variations in the Characteristics of Part-Time Faculty by General Fields of Instruction and Research," in *The Growing Use of Part-Time*

*Faculty: Understanding Causes and Effects*, ed. David W. Leslie, *New Directions for Higher Education* (San Francisco: Jossey-Bass, 1998), 45–60, George E. Biles and Howard P. Tuckman, *Part-Time Faculty Personnel Management Policies* (New York: American Council on Education/Macmillan, 1986), Eliason, "Part-Time Faculty: A National Perspective," Judith M. Gappa and David. W. Leslie, *The Invisible Faculty: Improving the Status of Part-Timers in Higher Education* (San Francisco: Jossey-Bass, 1993), John D. Haeger, "Part-Time Faculty, Quality Programs, and Economic Realities," in *The Growing Use of Part-Time Faculty: Understanding Causes and Effects*, ed. David W. Leslie, *New Directions for Higher Education* (San Francisco: Jossey-Bass, 1998), 81–88, Jacobs, "Using Part-Time Faculty More Effectively," Gary Rhoades, "Reorganizing the Faculty Workforce for Flexibility: Part-Time Professional Labor," *The Journal of Higher Education* 67, no. 6 (1996): 626–659, John Roueche, Suanne Roueche, and Mark Milliron, *Strangers in their Own Land: Part-Time Faculty in American Community Colleges* (Washington, DC: Community College Press, 1995), Barbara A. Wyles, "Adjunct Faculty in the Community College: Realities and Challenges," in *The Growing Use of Part-Time Faculty: Understanding Causes and Effects*, ed. David W. Leslie, *New Directions for Higher Education* (San Francisco: Jossey-Bass, 1998), 95–100.

16. Rosemary Deem, " 'New Managerialism' and Higher Education: The Management of Performances and Cultures in Universities in the United Kingdom," *International Studies in Sociology of Education* 8, no. 1 (1998): 47–70, Cynthia Hardy, *The Politics of Collegiality: Retrenchment Strategies in Canadian Universities* (Buffalo: McGill-Queen's University Press, 1996).
17. Smith, *Crossing the Great Divide: Worker Risk and Opportunity in the New Economy.*
18. Richard L. Wagoner, Amy Scott Metcalfe, and Israel Olaore, "Fiscal Reality and Academic Quality: Part-Time Faculty and the Challenge to Organizational Culture at Community Colleges," *Community College Journal of Research and Practice* 29 (2005): 1–20.
19. John Levin, *Globalizing the Community College: Strategies for Change in the Twenty-First Century* (New York: Palgrave, 2001), Gary Rhoades, *Managed Professionals: Unionized Faculty and Restructuring Academic Labor* (Albany: State University of New York Press, 1998).
20. Emily K. Abel, *Terminal Degrees: The Job Crisis in Higher Education* (New York: Praeger, 1984), Kathleen Barker, "Toiling for Piece Rates and Accumulating Deficits: Contingent Work in Higher Education," in *Contingent Work: American Employment Relations in Transition*, ed. Kathleen Barker and Kathleen Christensen (Ithaca, NY: Cornell University Press, 1998), 195–220.
21. Barker, "Toiling for Piece Rates and Accumulating Deficits: Contingent Work in Higher Education," p. 199.
22. Gappa and Leslie, *The Invisible Faculty: Improving the Status of Part-Timers in Higher Education*, Roueche, Roueche, and Milliron, *Strangers in Their Own Land: Part-Time Faculty in American Community Colleges.*
23. The Academic Senate for California Community Colleges, "Part-Time Faculty: A Principled Perspective" (Sacramento, CA: The Academic Senate for California Community Colleges, 2002).
24. Smith, *Crossing the Great Divide: Worker Risk and Opportunity in the New Economy.*

25. Carnoy, *Sustaining the New Economy: Work, Family, and Community in the Information Age*, Castells, *The Rise of the Network Society*, Smith, *Crossing the Great Divide: Worker Risk and Opportunity in the New Economy.*
26. We use fictitious names for actual colleges based on our agreements with institutional officials to maintain their colleges' anonymity. Thus we use Suburban Valley Community College, North Mountain College, and Cactus College in this chapter to refer to actual colleges, but we have changed their names.
27. Smith, *Crossing the Great Divide: Worker Risk and Opportunity in the New Economy.*
28. Richard Wagoner, "The Contradictory Faculty: Part-Time Faculty at Community Colleges," (Unpublished doctoral dissertation, Tucson, AZ: The University of Arizona, 2004).
29. Arthur Cohen and Florence Brawer, *The American Community College*, 3rd ed. (San Francisco: Jossey-Bass, 1996).
30. Gappa and Leslie, *The Invisible Faculty: Improving the Status of Part-Timers in Higher Education*, Roueche, Roueche, and Milliron, *Strangers in Their Own Land: Part-Time Faculty in American Community Colleges.*
31. Carnoy, *Sustaining the New Economy: Work, Family, and Community in the Information Age*, Castells, *The Rise of the Network Society*, Smith, *Crossing the Great Divide: Worker Risk and Opportunity in the New Economy.*
32. Benjamin, "Variations in the Characteristics of Part-Time Faculty by General Fields of Instruction and Research."
33. Michael Dubson, ed., *Ghosts in the Classroom: Stories of Adjunct Faculty—and the Price We all Pay* (Boston: Camel's Back Books, 2001), Zachary Karabell, *In What's College for? The Struggle to Define American Higher Education* (New York: Basic Books, 1998).
34. Osterman et al., *Working in America: A Blueprint for the New Labor Market.*
35. Carnoy, *Sustaining the New Economy: Work, Family, and Community in the Information Age*, Castells, *The Rise of the Network Society*, Osterman et al., *Working in America: A Blueprint for the New Labor Market.*
36. Osterman et al., *Working in America: A Blueprint for the New Labor Market.*
37. Aronowitz and Di Fazio, *The Jobless Future: Sci-tech and the Dogma of Work*, Carnoy, *Sustaining the New Economy: Work, Family, and Community in the Information Age*, Castells, *The Rise of the Network Society.*
38. Levin, *Globalizing the Community College: Strategies for Change in the Twenty-First Century.*
39. Marcia L. Bellas, "Disciplinary Differences in Faculty Salaries: Does Gender Bias Play a Role?" *The Journal of Higher Education* 68, no. 3 (1997): 299–321.
40. Gappa and Leslie, "Two Faculties or One?: The Conundrum of Part-Timers in a Bifurcated Work Force."
41. Gappa and Leslie, *The Invisible Faculty: Improving the Status of Part-Timers in Higher Education*, Howard P. Tuckman, "Who is Part-Time in Academe?" *AAUP Bulletin* 64 (1978): 305–315.
42. James R. Valadez and James S. Antony, "Job Satisfaction and Commitment of Two-year College Part-Time Faculty," *Community College Journal of Research and Practice* 25 (2001): 97–108.
43. Dubson, ed., *Ghosts in the Classroom: Stories of Adjunct Faculty—and the Price We all Pay*, Gappa and Leslie, *The Invisible Faculty: Improving the Status of Part-Timers*

*in Higher Education*, Karabell, *In What's College for? The Struggle to Define American Higher Education*, Gary Rhoades, "Reorganizing the Faculty Workplace for Flexibility: Part-Time Professional Labor," *The Journal of Higher Education* 67, no. 6 (1996): 626–659, Roueche, Roueche, and Milliron, *Strangers in Their Own Land: Part-Time Faculty in American Community Colleges.*

## 7 Corporatism and Neo-Liberal Ideology: The Values and Meanings of Faculty Work

1. Catherine Casey, *Work, Society and Self: After Industrialism* (New York: Routledge, 1995), Noam Chomsky, *Profit over People: Neoliberalism and Global Order* (New York: Seven Stories Press, 1999).
2. Gary Rhoades, *Managed Professionals: Unionized Faculty and Restructuring Academic Labor* (Albany: State University of New York Press, 1998).
3. Martin Carnoy, *Sustaining the New Economy: Work, Family, and Community in the Information Age* (Cambridge, MA: Harvard University Press, 2000), John Levin, *Globalizing the Community College: Strategies for Change in the Twenty-First Century* (New York: Palgrave, 2001).
4. Matthew Miles and A. Michael Huberman, *Qualitative Data Analysis* (Thousand Oaks, CA: Sage Publications, 1994).
5. Casey, *Work, Society and Self: After Industrialism*, Rosemary Deem, " 'New Managerialism' and Higher Education: The Management of Performances and Cultures in Universities in the United Kingdom," *International Studies in Sociology of Education* 8, no. 1 (1998): 47–70, Cynthia Hardy, *The Politics of Collegiality: Retrenchment Strategies in Canadian Universities* (Buffalo: McGill-Queen's University Press, 1996).
6. Derek Bok, *Universities in the Marketplace: The Commercialization of Higher Education* (Princeton: Princeton University Press, 2003), Anthony P. Carnavele and Donna M. Desrochers, "Community Colleges in the New Economy," *Community College Journal* 67, no. 5 (1997, April/May): 26–33, Eric Gould, *The University in a Corporate Culture* (New Haven: Yale University Press, 2003), Larry L. Leslie and Sheila A. Slaughter, "The Development and Current Status of Market Mechanisms in United States Postsecondary Education," *Higher Education Policy* 10 (1997, March/April): 238–252, Levin, *Globalizing the Community College: Strategies for Change in the Twenty-First Century*, Sheila Slaughter and Larry Leslie, *Academic Capitalism, Politics, Policies, and the Entrepreneurial University* (Baltimore: The Johns Hopkins University Press, 1997), Sheila Slaughter and Gary Rhoades, *Academic Capitalism and the New Economy: Markets, State, and Higher Education* (Baltimore: The Johns Hopkins University Press, 2004).
7. John Levin, "The Revised Institution: The Community College Mission at the End of the 20th Century," *Community College Review* 28, no. 2 (2000): 1–25, Mary Ann Roe, *Education and U.S. Competitiveness: The Community College Role* (Austin: IC2 Institute, University of Texas at Austin, 1989), Daniel Schugurensky and Kathy Higgins, "From Aid to Trade: New Trends in International Education in Canada," in *Dimensions of the Community College: International, Intercultural, and Multicultural*, ed. Rosalind Latiner Raby and Norma Tarrow (New York: Garland Publishing, 1996), 53–78, Lynn Taber, "Chapter and Verse: How We Came to be Where We Are," in *The Company We Keep: Collaboration in the*

*Community College*, ed. John Roueche, Lynn Taber, and Suanne Roueche (Washington, DC: American Association of Community Colleges, 1995), 25–37, Barbara Townsend and Susan Twombly, eds., *Community Colleges: Policy in the Future Context* (Westport, CT: Ablex, 2001).

8. Province of Alberta, *Encouraging Excellence and Rewarding Success in Alberta's Public Adult Learning System* (Edmonton, AB: Alberta Advanced Education and Career Development, 1996, December), Province of Alberta, *New Directions for Adult Learning in Alberta: Adult Learning Access through Innovation* (Edmonton, AB: Alberta Advanced Education and Career Development, 1994).
9. John Levin, "Organizational Paradigm Shift and the University Colleges of British Columbia," *Higher Education* 46, no. 4 (2003): 447–467.
10. Thomas R. Bailey and Vanessa Smith Morest, "The Organizational Efficiency of Multiple Missions for Community Colleges" (New York: Teachers College, Columbia University, 2004), Arthur Cohen and Florence Brawer, *The American Community College* (San Francisco: Jossey-Bass, 2003), John Dennison and Paul Gallagher, *Canada's Community Colleges* (Vancouver: University of British Columbia Press, 1986), Levin, *Globalizing the Community College: Strategies for Change in the Twenty-First Century*, James Ratcliff, "Seven Streams in the Historical Development of the Modern Community College," in *A Handbook on the Community College in America*, ed. G. Baker (Westport, CT: Greenwood Press, 1994), 3–16.
11. Bailey and Morest, "*The Organizational Efficiency of Multiple Missions for Community Colleges*," Darrel Clowes and Bernard Levin, "Community, Technical and Junior Colleges: Are They Leaving Higher Education?" *The Journal of Higher Education* 60, no. 3 (1989): 349–355, David F. Labaree, *How to Succeed in School Without Really Learning* (New Haven: Yale University Press, 1997), John Levin, "The Community College as a Baccalaureate-Granting Institution," *The Review of Higher Education* 28, no. 1 (2004): 1–22.
12. Chomsky, *Profit over People: Neoliberalism and Global Order*, Gordon Laxer, "Social Solidarity, Democracy and Global Capitalism," *The Canadian Review of Sociology and Anthropology* (1995, August): 287–312, Gary Teeple, *Globalization and the Rise of Social Reform* (New Jersey: Humanities Press, 1995).
13. Casey, *Work, Society and Self: After Industrialism.*
14. Scott Davies and Neil Guppy, "Globalization and Educational Reforms in Anglo-American Democracies," *Comparative Education Review* 41, no. 4 (1997): 435–459, Richard De Angelis, "Globalization and Recent Higher Education Reforms in Australia and France: Different Constraints; Differing Choices in Higher Education Structure, Politics and Policies" (Paper for 9th World Congress on Comparative Education. Sydney, July: 1997).
15. John Ralston Saul, *The Unconscious Civilization* (Concord, ON: House of Anansi Press, 1995).
16. Jane Kenway, "Fast Capitalism, Fast Feminism, and Some Fast Food for Thought" (Paper presented at the Annual Meeting of the American Educational Research Association, San Diego, April, 1998).
17. John Levin, "Public Policy, Community Colleges, and the Path to Globalization," *Higher Education* 42, no. 2 (2001): 237–262.
18. Stanley Deetz and Dennis Mumby, "Power, Discourse, and the Workplace: Reclaiming the Critical Tradition," in *Power and Politics in Organizations*, ed. Cynthia Hardy (Brookfield, VT: Dartmouth, 1995), 457–486.

19. Levin, *Globalizing the Community College: Strategies for Change in the Twenty-First Century.*
20. Cohen and Brawer, *The American Community College.*

## 8 In Their Own Words

1. Kent Phillippe and Madeline Patton, *National Profile of Community Colleges: Trends and Statistics*, 3rd ed. (Washington, DC: Community College Press, American Association of Community Colleges, 2000).
2. In our efforts to protect those who participated in our research, we use pseudonyms for colleges and individuals. We have slightly altered the text of interviews to hide the identity of institutions and people.
3. We approach the narratives of the three faculty in this chapter as text that reflects personal revelation as well as the creation of personal identity. See Carolyn Baker, "Ethnomethodological Analyses of Interview," in *Handbook of Interview Research: Context and Method*, ed. Jaber Gubrium and James Holstein (Thousand Oaks, CA: Sage Publications, 2002), 777–795, Catherine Riessman, "Analysis of Personal Narratives," in *Handbook of Interview Research: Context and Method*, ed. Jaber F. Gubrium and James A. Holstein (Thousand Oaks, CA: Sage Publications, 2002), 695–710.
4. W. Norton Grubb, *Honored but Invisible: An Inside Look at Teaching in Community Colleges* (New York: Routledge, 1999).

## 9 The Professional Identity of Community College Faculty

1. Thomas R. Bailey and Vanessa Smith Morest, "The Organizational Efficiency of Multiple Missions for Community Colleges" (New York: Teachers College, Columbia University, 2004).
2. John Levin, *Globalizing the Community College: Strategies for Change in the Twenty-First Century* (New York: Palgrave, 2001).
3. Aaron Wildavsky and Naomi Caiden, *The New Politics of the Budgetary Process*, 3rd ed. (New York: Longman, 1997).
4. Steven Brint, *In an Age of Experts: The Changing Role of Professionals in Politics and Public Life* (Princeton: Princeton University Press, 1994).
5. Roland W. Scholz and Olaf Tietje, *Embedded Case Study Methods: Integrating Quantitative and Qualitative Knowledge* (Thousand Oaks, CA: Sage Publications, 2002).
6. Bailey and Morest, "The Organizational Efficiency of Multiple Missions for Community Colleges," Kevin Dougherty, "The Evolving Role of the Community College: Policy Issues and Research Questions," in *Higher Education: Handbook of Theory and Research*, ed. John Smart and William Tierney (Dordrecht, Netherlands: Kluwer, 2002), 295–348, John Levin, "The Community College as a Baccalaureate-Granting Institution," *The Review of Higher Education* 28, no. 1 (2004): 1–22, Levin, *Globalizing the Community College: Strategies for Change in the Twenty-First Century*, John Levin, "In Education and Work: The Globalized Community College," *The Canadian Journal of Higher Education* XXXII, no. 2 (2002): 47–78.
7. Terry O'Banion and Associates, *Teaching and Learning in the Community College* (Washington, DC: Community College Press, 1995), John Tagg, *The Learning Paradigm College* (Bolton, MA: Anker Publishing Company, 2003).

8. W. Norton Grubb et al., *Workforce, Economic and Community Development: The Changing Landscape of the Entrepreneurial Community College* (Berkeley: National Center for Research in Vocational Education, The University of California, 1997).
9. Levin, *Globalizing the Community College: Strategies for Change in the Twenty-First Century.*
10. Rosemary Deem, " 'New Managerialism' and Higher Education: The Management of Performances and Cultures in Universities in the United Kingdom," *International Studies in Sociology of Education* 8, no. 1 (1998): 47–70.
11. Ibid., p. 50.
12. Alan Freeman, "Why not eat children?" *Guardian Weekly* (2004): 6.
13. Brint, *In an Age of Experts: The Changing Role of Professionals in Politics and Public Life.*
14. John Levin, "The Business Culture of the Community College: Students as Consumers; Students as Commodities," in *Arenas of Entrepreneurship: Where Nonprofit and For Profit Institutions Compete. New Directions for Higher Education*, ed. Brian Pusser (San Francisco: Jossey-Bass Publishers, 2005): 11–26, Levin, *Globalizing the Community College: Strategies for Change in the Twenty-First Century*, Levin, "In Education and Work: The Globalized Community College," Simon Marginson and Mark Considine, *The Enterprise University: Power, Governance and Reinvention in Australia* (New York: Cambridge University Press, 2000), Sheila Slaughter and Larry Leslie, *Academic Capitalism, Politics, Policies, and the Entrepreneurial University* (Baltimore: The Johns Hopkins University Press, 1997), Sheila Slaughter and Gary Rhoades, *Academic Capitalism and the New Economy: Markets, State, and Higher Education* (Baltimore: The Johns Hopkins University Press, 2004).
15. U.S. Department of Education. National Center for Education Statistics, "Table 206," in http://www.nces.ed.gov/program/digest/d02/table/dt206.asp (2004). It is estimated that there are as many as five million community college students who undertake noncredit coursework.
16. "College Enrollment by Racial and Ethnic Group, Selected Years," *The Chronicle of Higher Education*, August 27, 2004.
17. Arthur Cohen and Florence Brawer, *The American Community College* (San Francisco: Jossey-Bass, 2003), George Vaughan, "The Big Squeeze at Community Colleges," *The News & Observer*, March 24, 2002.
18. Susan Choy, "Nontraditional Undergraduates. The Condition of Education," (U.S. Department of Educational Research and Improvement. NCES 2002–05, 2002 pp. 25–38), Penelope E. Herideen, *Policy, Pedagogy and Social Inequality: Community College Student's Realities in Post-Industrial America* (Westport, CT: Bergin & Garvey, 1998), John S. Levin, *Non-Traditional Students and Community Colleges: The Conflict of Justice and Neo-Liberalism* (New York: Palgrave Macmillan, forthcoming).
19. Marginson and Considine, *The Enterprise University: Power, Governance and Reinvention in Australia*, Gary Rhoades, *Managed Professionals: Unionized Faculty and Restructuring Academic Labor* (Albany: State University of New York Press, 1998), Slaughter and Rhoades, *Academic Capitalism and the New Economy: Markets, State, and Higher Education.*
20. W. Norton Grubb, *Honored but Invisible: An Inside Look at Teaching in Community Colleges* (New York: Routledge, 1999).
21. W. Norton Grubb, Noreen Badway, and Denise Bell, "Community Colleges and the Equity Agenda: The Potential of Noncredit Education," *The Annals* (2003, March): 218–240, Penelope. E. Herideen, *Policy, Pedagogy, and Social*

*Inequality: Community College Student Realities in Post-Industrial America.* (Westport, CT: Bergin & Garvey., 1998), Jerry A. Jacobs and Sarah Winslow, "Welfare Reform and Enrollment in Postsecondary Education," *The Annals of the American Academy of Political and Social Sciences* (2003, March): 194–217, Christopher Mazzeo, Sara Rab, and Susan Eachus, "Work-First or Work-Study: Welfare Reform, State Policy and Access to Postsecondary Education," *The Annals* (2003, March): 144–171, Kathleen Shaw and Sara Rab, "Market Rhetoric versus Reality in Policy and Practice: The Workforce Investment Act and Access to Community College Education and Training," *The Annals* (2003, March): 172–193.

22. Brint, *In an Age of Experts: The Changing Role of Professionals in Politics and Public Life.*
23. John Corson, *Governance of Colleges and Universities* (New York: McGraw Hill, 1960), John Dennison, "The University-College Idea: A Critical Analysis," *The Canadian Journal of Higher Education* XXII, no. 1 (1992): 109–124, Kenneth Mortimer and Thomas Raymond McConnell, *Sharing Authority Effectively*, 1st ed. (San Francisco: Jossey Bass, 1978).
24. Burton Clark, *The Academic Life: Small Worlds, Different Worlds* (Princeton, NJ: The Carnegie Foundation for the Advancement of Teaching, 1987).
25. Gary Rhoades, "Reorganizing the Faculty Workforce for Flexibility: Part-Time Professional Labor," *The Journal of Higher Education* 67, no. 6 (1996): 626–659.
26. The Academic Senate for California Community Colleges, Part-Time Faculty: A Principled Perspective (2002). Available from http://www.academicsenate.cc.ca.us.
27. John Levin, "What's the Impediment? Structural and Legal Constraints to Shared Governance in the Community College," *The Canadian Journal of Higher Education* XXX, no. 2 (2000): 87–122.
28. Henry Mintzberg, *Power in and around Organizations* (Englewood Cliffs, NJ: Prentice Hall, Inc., 1983), Henry Mintzberg, "The Professional Bureaucracy," in *Organization and Governance in Higher Education*, ed. Marvin Peterson (Needham Heights, MA: Simon & Schuster, 1991).
29. Levin, "The Community College as a Baccalaureate Granting Institution."
30. Ibid.
31. Brint, *In an Age of Experts: The Changing Role of Professionals in Politics and Public Life.*

# References


Abel, Emily K. *Terminal Degrees: The Job Crisis in Higher Education.* New York: Praeger, 1984.

Alberta, Province of. *New Directions for Adult Learning in Alberta: Adult Learning Access Through Innovation.* Edmonton, AB: Alberta Advanced Education and Career Development, 1994.

———. *Encouraging Excellence and Rewarding Success in Alberta's Public Adult Learning System.* Edmonton, AB: Alberta Advanced Education and Career Development, 1996, December.

Alderman, Geoffrey. "The Globalization of Higher Education: Some Observations Regarding the Free Market and the National Interest." *Higher Education in Europe* 26, no. 1 (2001): 47–52.

Alfred, Richard, and Patricia Carter. "New Colleges for a New Century: Organizational Change and Development in Community Colleges." In *Higher Education: Handbook of Theory and Research*, edited by John C. Smart and William G. Tierney, 240–283. New York: Agathon Press, 1999.

Annunziato, Frank. "From Conflict to Accord: Collective Bargaining at the Academy." *New Directions for Higher Education* 92 (1995): 51–57.

Apple, Michael. "Comparing Neo-Liberal Projects and Inequality in Education." *Comparative Education* 37, no. 4 (2001): 409–423.

Arnold, Gordon B. *The Politics of Faculty Unionization: The Experience of Three New England Universities.* Westport, CT: Bergin & Garvey, 2000.

Aronowitz, Stanley, and William Di Fazio. *The Jobless Future: Sci-tech and the Dogma of Work.* Minneapolis: University of Minnesota Press, 1994.

Autor, David H., Lawrence F. Katz, and Alan B. Kreuger. "Computing Inequality: Have Computers Changed the Labor Market?" *Quarterly Journal of Economics* 113, no. 4 (1998): 1169–1213.

Ayers, D. Franklin. "Neoliberal Ideology in Community College Mission Statements: A Critical Discourse Analysis." *The Review of Higher Education*, 28, no. 4 (2005): 527–549

Bailey, Thomas R., and Irina E. Averianova. "Multiple Missions of Community Colleges: Conflicting or Complementary." Occasional paper, Community College Research Center, Teachers College, New York, 1998.

Bailey, Thomas R., and Vanessa Smith Morest. "The Organizational Efficiency of Multiple Missions for Community Colleges." New York: Teachers College, Columbia University, 2004.

Baker, Carolyn. "Ethnomethodological Analyses of Interview." In *Handbook of Interview Research: Context and Method*, edited by Jaber Gubrium and James Holstein, 777–795. Thousand Oaks, CA: Sage Publications, 2002.

Baker, George, and Associates. *Cultural Leadership: Inside America's Community Colleges.* Washington, DC: The Community College Press, 1992.

Baldridge, J. Victor, Frank R. Kemerer, Barbara Adams, Joyce Najita, Caesar Naples, Sue Schlesigner, and John A. Thompson. "Assessing the Impact of Faculty Collective Bargaining." Washington, DC: AAHE-ERIC/Higher Education Research Report No. 8/The George Washington University, 1981.

Baldwin, Beatrice. "Linking Instructional Productivity Measures and Fiscal Policy: Accountability in Higher Education." Paper presented at the Annual Meeting of the American Educational Research Association, Chicago, IL, March 24–28, 1997.

Barker, Kathleen. "Toiling for Piece Rates and Accumulating Deficits: Contingent Work in Higher Education." In *Contingent Work: American Employment Relations in Transition*, edited by Kathleen Barker and Kathleen Christensen, 195–220. Ithaca, NY: Cornell University Press, 1998.

Barnet, Richard, and John Cavanagh. *Global Dreams: Imperial Corporations and the New World Order*. New York: Simon & Schuster, 1994.

Barr, Robert, and John Tagg. "From Teaching to Learning: A New Paradigm for Undergraduate Education." *Change* (1995, November/December): 13–25.

Baumol, William. "Macroeconomics of Unbalanced Growth: The Anatomy of Urban Crisis." *American Economic Review* 57, no. 3 (1967): 415–426.

Baumol, William, and Sue Blackman. "How to Think About Rising Colleges Costs." *Planning for Higher Education* 23, no. 4 (1995): 1–7.

Bellas, Marcia L. "Disciplinary Differences in Faculty Salaries: Does Gender Bias Play a Role?" *The Journal of Higher Education* 68, no. 3 (1997): 299–321.

Benjamin, Ernest. "Variations in the Characteristics of Part-Time Faculty by General Fields of Instruction and Research." In *The Growing Use of Part-Time Faculty: Understanding Causes and Effects*, edited by David. W. Leslie, 45–60. San Francisco: Jossey-Bass, 1998.

Berger, Andrea, Rita Kirshstein, Yu Zhang, and Kevin Carter. "A Profile of Part-Time Faculty: Fall 1998." Washington, DC: National Center for Educational Statistics, 2002.

Biles, George E., and Howard P. Tuckman. *Part-Time Faculty Personnel Management Policies.* New York: American Council on Education/Macmillan, 1986.

Birnbaum, Robert. *How Colleges Work.* San Francisco: Jossey-Bass Publishers, 1988.

———. *Management Fads in Higher Education: Where They Come From, What They Do, Why They Fail.* San Francisco: Jossey-Bass, 2000.

Bok, Derek. *Universities in the Marketplace: The Commercialization of Higher Education.* Princeton: Princeton University Press, 2003.

Bowen, Blannie, and Rama B. Radhakrishna. "Job Satisfaction of Agricultural Education Faculty: A Constant Phenomena." *Journal of Agricultural Education* 32, no. 2 (1991): 16–22.

Bowen, William. *The Economics of Major Private Research Universities.* Berkeley, CA: Carnegie Commission on Higher Education, 1967.

Bragg, Debra D., and James D. Layton. "The Role of the Urban Community College in Educational Reform." *Education and Urban Society* 27, no. 3 (1995): 294–312.

Bridges, William. *Job Shift.* Reading, MA: Addison-Wesley Publishing Company, 1994.

Brint, Steven. *In an Age of Experts: The Changing Role of Professionals in Politics and Public Life.* Princeton: Princeton University Press, 1994.

———. "Few Remaining Dreams: Community Colleges Since 1985." *The Annals of the American Academy of Political and Social Sciences* (2003, March): 16–37.

Brint, Steven, and Jerome Karabel. *The Diverted Dream: Community Colleges and the Promise of Educational Opportunity in America, 1900–1985.* New York: Oxford University Press, 1989.

Bullock, Cheryl, and John Ory. "Evaluating Instructional Technology Implementation in a Higher Education Environment." *American Journal of Evaluation* 21, no. 3 (2000): 315–328.

Burgess, Robert. *In the Field: An Introduction to Field Research.* London: George Allen and Unwin, 1984.

Campbell, John, and Ove Pedersen. "Introduction: The Rise of Neoliberalism and Institutional Analysis." In *The Rise of Neoliberalism and Institutional Analysis,* edited by John Campbell and Ove Pedersen, 2–23. Princeton: Princeton University Press, 2001.

Carnevale, Anthony P. "Community Colleges and Career Qualifications." *New Expeditions Issue Paper Series* 11. Washington, DC: Community College Press, 2000.

Carnevale, Anthony P., and Donna M. Desrochers. "Community Colleges in the New Economy." *Community College Journal* 67, no. 5 (1997, April/May): 26–33.

Carnevale, Dan. "More Professors Teach by Using Other College's Online Courses." *Chronicle of Higher Education* (October 15, 2004), A28–A29.

Carnoy, Martin. *Sustaining the New Economy: Work, Family, and Community in the Information Age.* New York: Russell Sage Foundation, 2000.

Casey, Catherine. *Work, Society and Self: After Industrialism.* New York: Routledge, 1995.

Castells, Manuel. *The Rise of the Network Society.* 2nd ed. Malden, MA: Blackwell, 2000.

Chomsky, Noam. *Profit Over People: Neoliberalism and Global Order.* New York: Seven Stories Press, 1999.

Choy, Susan. "Nontraditional Undergraduates. The Condition of Education." U.S. Department of Educational Research and Improvement. NCES 2002–05, 2002, pp. 25–38.

Clark, Burton. "Small Worlds, Different Worlds: The Uniqueness and Troubles of American Academic Professions." *Daedalus* 126, no. 1 (1997, Fall): 21–42.

———. *The Academic Life: Small Worlds, Different Worlds.* Princeton, NJ: The Carnegie Foundation for the Advancement of Teaching, 1987.

Clowes, Darrel, and Bernard Levin. "Community, Technical and Junior Colleges: Are They Leaving Higher Education?" *The Journal of Higher Education* 60, no. 3 (1989): 349–355.

Cohen, Arthur. *Dateline '79: Heretical Concepts for the Community College.* Beverly Hills: Glencoe Press, 1969.

Cohen, Arthur, and Charles Outcalt. "A Profile of the Community College Professoriate." A Report Submitted to the Small Research Grant Program of the Spencer Foundation. Center for the study of community colleges, Los Angeles, CA, June, 2001.

Cohen, Arthur, and Florence Brawer. *The American Community College.* San Francisco: Jossey-Bass, 2003.

"College Enrollment by Racial and Ethnic Group, Selected Years." *The Chronicle of Higher Education,* August 27, 2004.

Colleges, The Academic Senate for California Community. "Part-time Faculty: A Principled Perspective." Sacramento, CA: The Academic Senate for California Community Colleges, 2002. Available from http://www.academicsenate.cc.ca.us.

Connole, Helen. "Cyborgs and Knowledge Workers? Gendered Constructions of Workers in Vocational Education and Training." *Studies in Continuing Education* 18, no. 2 (1996): 122–134.

Cooper, Harris M. "The Integrative Research Review: A Systematic Approach." In *Applied Social Research Methods Series*, 2, Beverly Hills, CA: Sage, 1984.

Cooper, James L., Pamela Robinson, and Molly McKinney. "Cooperative Learning in the Classroom." In *Changing College Classrooms*, edited by Diane Halpern and Associates, 74–92. San Francisco: Jossey-Bass, 1994.

Corson, John. *Governance of Colleges and Universities.* New York: McGraw Hill, 1960.

Cowan, John. "Effectiveness and Efficiency in Higher Education." *Higher Education* 14, no. 3 (1985): 235–239.

Cross, K. Patricia. "Community Colleges on the Plateau." *The Journal of Higher Education* 52, no. 2 (1981): 113–123.

———. "Determining Missions and Priorities for the Fifth Generation." In *Renewing the American Community College*, edited by William Deegan, Dale Tillery and Associates, 34–50. San Francisco: Jossey-Bass Publishers, 1985.

Currie, Jan, and Janice Newson, eds. *Universities and Globalization.* Thousand Oaks, CA: Sage Publications, 1998.

Davies, Scott, and Neil Guppy. "Globalization and Educational Reforms in Anglo-American Democracies." *Comparative Education Review* 41, no. 4 (1997): 435–459.

Davis, James. *Interdisciplinary Courses and Team Teaching: New Arrangements for Learning.* Phoenix: American Council on Education and Oryx Press, 1995.

De Angelis, Richard. "Globalization and Recent Higher Education Reforms in Australia and France: Different Constraints; Differing Choices in Higher Education Structure, Politics and Policies." Paper for 9th World Congress on Comparative Education. Sydney, July, 1997.

Deden, Ann, and Vicki K. Carter. "Using Technology to Enhance Students' Skills." In *Preparing Competent College Graduates: Setting New and Higher Expectations for Student Learning*, edited by Elizabeth A. Jones, 81–92. San Francisco: Jossey-Bass Publishers, 1996.

Deegan, William, Dale Tillery, and Associates, eds. *Renewing the American Community College.* San Francisco: Jossey-Bass, 1985.

Deem, Rosemary. " 'New Managerialism' and Higher Education: The Management of Performances and Cultures in Universities in the United Kingdom." *International Studies in Sociology of Education* 8, no. 1 (1998): 47–70.

Deetz, Stanley, and Dennis Mumby. "Power, Discourse, and the Workplace: Reclaiming the Critical Tradition." In *Power and Politics in Organizations*, edited by Cynthia Hardy, 457–486. Brookfield, VT: Dartmouth, 1995.

DeMartino, George. *Global Economy, Global Justice: Theoretical Objections and Policy Alternatives to Neoliberalism.* New York: Routledge, 2000.

Dennison, John. "The University-College Idea: A Critical Analysis." *The Canadian Journal of Higher Education* XXII, no. 1 (1992): 109–124.

———. "Community College Development in Canada Since 1985." In *Challenge and Opportunity*, edited by John Dennison, 13–104. Vancouver: The University of British Columbia Press, 1995.

———. "Characteristics of the University College in British Columbia: Governance and Administration." Paper for an international conference on new developments in higher education, Bermuda, October, 2000.

———. "Comment." Personal communication, Vancouver, British Columbia, February 14, 2004.

Dennison, John, and Paul Gallagher. *Canada's Community Colleges.* Vancouver: University of British Columbia Press, 1986.

DeNoia, Lynn A., and John L. Swearingen. "Linking Administrative and IT Productivity in Higher Education." *Cause/Effect* 15, no. 3 (1992): 34–41.

Denton, Jon J., Chiou-Yueh Tsai, and Connie Cloud. "Productivity of Faculty in Higher Education Institutions." *Journal of Teacher Education* 37, no. 5 (1986): 12–16.

Dever, John T., and Robert G. Templin, Jr. "Assuming Leadership: Community Colleges, Curriculum Reform, and Teaching." *Educational Record* 75, no. 1 (1994): 32–34.

Diaz, Veronica. "The Digitization and Control of Intellectual Property: Institutional Patterns of Distributed Learning Behavior and the Organizational Policy Response." Unpublished doctoral dissertation, Tucson, AZ: The University of Arizona, 2004.

Diaz, Veronica, and John J. Cheslock. "Distributed Learning Activity: Patterns of Faculty and Institutional Participation in Four-Year Colleges and Universities." Unpublished manuscript, Tucson, Arizona, The University of Arizona, 2004.

DiMaggio, Paul, and Walter Powell. "The Iron Cage Revisited: Institutional Isomorphism and Collective Rationality in Organizational Fields." *American Sociological Review* 48 (1983): 147–160.

Dixon, Helen. "The Effects of Policy on Practice: An Analysis of Teachers' Perceptions of School Based Assessment Practice." Palmerston, NZ, Massey University, 1999.

Dougherty, Kevin. *The Contradictory College.* Albany: State University of New York Press, 1994.

———. "State Policies and the Community College's Role in Workforce Preparation." In *Community Colleges: Policy in the Future Context*, edited by Barbara Townsend and Susan Twombly, 129–147. Westport, CT: Ablex, 2001.

———. "The Evolving Role of the Community College: Policy Issues and Research Questions." In *Higher Education: Handbook of Theory and Research*, edited by John Smart and William Tierney, 295–348. Dordrecht, Netherlands: Kluwer, 2002.

Dougherty, Kevin, and Marianne Bakia. "The New Economic Role of the Community College: Origins and Prospects." Occasional Paper, Community College Research Center, Teachers College, New York, June, 1998.

———. "Community Colleges and Contract Training: Content, Origins, and Impact." *Teachers College Record* 102, no. 1 (2000): 197–243.

Dubson, Michael, ed. *Ghosts in the Classroom: Stories of Adjunct Faculty—and the Price We All Pay.* Boston: Camel's Back Books, 2001.

Dundar, Halil, and Darrell R. Lewis. "Determinants of Research Productivity in Higher Education." *Research in Higher Education* 39, no. 6 (1998): 607–637.

Eisenhardt, Kathleen. "Building Theories From Case Study Research." *Academy of Management Review* 14, no. 4 (1989): 532–550.

Eliason, N. Carol. "Part-Time Faculty: A National Perspective." In *Using Part-Time Faculty Effectively*, edited by Michael H. Parsons, 1–12. San Francisco: Jossey-Bass, 1980.

Ely, Donald P. "Conditions that Facilitate the Implementation of Educational Technology Innovations." *Journal of Research on Computing in Education* 23, no. 2 (1990): 298–305.

Erickson, Frederick. "Qualitative Methods in Research on Teaching." In *Handbook of Research on Teaching*, edited by Marvin Wittrock, 119–161. New York: Macmillan Publishing Company, 1986.

Ferrara, F. Felicia. "Faculty Management: Maximizing Autonomy and Job Satisfaction under Economic, Administrative and Technological Changes." Paper presented at the Annual Meeting of the Popular Culture Association and the Annual Conference of the American Culture Association, Orlando, FL, April 8–11, 1998.

Ferris, James M. "Competition and Regulation in Higher Education: A Comparison of the Netherlands and the United States." *Higher Education* 22, no. 1 (1991): 93–108.

Finkelstein, Martin J., Robert K. Seal, and Jack K. Schuster. *The New Academic Generation*. Baltimore: The Johns Hopkins University Press, 1998.

———. "New Entrants to the Full-Time Faculty of Higher Education Institutions. 1993 National Study of Postsecondary Faculty (NSOPF-93). Statistical Analysis Report." Washington, DC: National Center for Education Statistics, 1998.

Fonte, Richard. "Community College Funding: Presidential Perceptions of State Plans." *Community/Junior College Quarterly of Research and Practice* 16, no. 2 (1992): 123–132.

Freeman, Alan. "Why not eat children?" *Guardian Weekly* (2004): 6.

Frye, John. "Educational Paradigms in the Professional Literature of the Community College." In *Higher Education: Handbook of Theory and Research*, edited by John Smart, 181–224. New York: Agathon Press, 1994.

Gappa, Judith M., and David W. Leslie. *The Invisible Faculty: Improving the Status of Part-Timers in Higher Education*. San Francisco: Jossey-Bass, 1993.

———. "Two Faculties or One?: The Conundrum of Part-Timers in a Bifurcated Work Force." *New Pathways: Faculty Careers and Employment for the 21st Century* 6 (1997): 1–26.

Gee, James Paul, Glynda Hull, and Colin Lankshear. *The New Work Order: Behind the Language of the New Capitalism*. Boulder, CO: Westview Press, 1996.

Gilbert, Steven. *Punished for Success*. Washington, DC: The TLT Group, American Association for Higher Education, 1998.

Gilmour, Joseph, Jr. "Participative Governance Bodies in Higher Education: Report of a National Study." *New Directions for Higher Education* 75 (1991): 27–39.

Giroux, Henry. "The War on the Young." In *Growing up Postmodern: Neoliberalism and the War on the Young*, edited by Ronald Strickland. Lanham, MD: Rowman & Littlefield, 2002.

Gladieux, Lawrence, and Watson Swail. *The Virtual University and Educational Issues of Equity and Access for the Next Generation*. Washington, DC: The College Board, 1999.

Gould, Eric. *The University in a Corporate Culture*. New Haven: Yale University Press, 2003.

Green, Kenneth C. "The Campus Computing Project." The 12th National Survey of Computing and Information Technology in Higher Education, 2001.

———. "2002 Campus Computing Report. The 2002 National Survey of Information Technology in U.S. Higher Education." Encino, CA: Campus Computing, 2002.

Green, Kenneth C., and Steven Gilbert. "Great Expectations: Content, Communications, Productivity, and the Role of Information Technology in Higher Education." *Change* 27, no. 2 (1995): 8–18.

Griffith, Melanie, and Ann Connor. *Democracy's Open Door: The Community College in America's Future*. Portsmouth, NH: Boynton/Cook Publishers, 1994.

Grubb, W. Norton. *Honored but Invisible: An Inside Look at Teaching in Community Colleges*. New York: Routledge, 1999.

Grubb, W. Norton, Noreen Badway, and Denise Bell. "Community Colleges and the Equity Agenda: The Potential of Noncredit Education." *The Annals* (2003, March): 218–240.

Grubb, W. Norton, Noreen Badway, Denise Bell, and Marisa Castellano. *Community Colleges and Welfare Reform: Emerging Practices, Enduring Problems*. California Welfare Information Clearinghouse, 2002 [cited October 30, 2003. Available from http://www.financeprojectinfo.org/cwic/calcommunitycollege.asp.

Grubb, W. Norton, Norena Badway, Denise Bell, Debra Bragg, and Maxine Russman. *Workforce, Economic and Community Development: The Changing Landscape of the Entrepreneurial Community College*. Berkeley: National Center for Research in Vocational Education, The University of California, 1997.

Guillén, Mauro. "Is Globalization Civilizing, Destructive, or Feeble? A Critique of Five Key Debates in the Social Science Literature." *Annual Review of Sociology* 27 (2001): 235–260.

Gumport, Patricia. "The Contested Terrain of Academic Program Reduction." *The Journal of Higher Education* 64, no. 3 (1993): 283–311.

Haeger, John D. "Part-Time Faculty, Quality Programs, and Economic Realities." In *The Growing Use of Part-Time Faculty: Understanding Causes and Effects*, edited by David W. Leslie, 81–88. San Francisco: Jossey-Bass, 1998.

Hardy, Cynthia. "Configuration and Strategy Making in Universities: Broadening the Scope." *The Journal of Higher Education* 62, no. 4 (1991): 363–393.

———. *The Politics of Collegiality: Retrenchment Strategies in Canadian Universities*. Buffalo: McGill-Queen's University Press, 1996.

Hebel, Sarah. "No Room in the Class: As Student Populations Explode in Some States, Public Colleges Struggle to Find Enough Places—Even for High Achievers." *Chronicle of Higher Education* (July 2, 2004), 19.

Held, David, Anthony McGrew, David Goldblatt, and Jonathan Perraton. *Global Transformations: Politics, Economics and Culture*. Stanford, CA: Stanford University Press, 1999.

Henkel, Jan W., and Norman J. Wood. "Legislative Power to Veto Collective Bargaining Agreements by Faculty Unions: An Overlooked Reality?" *Journal of Law and Education* 11, no. 1 (1982): 79–95.

Herideen, Penelope E. *Policy, Pedagogy and Social Inequality: Community College Student's Realities in Post-Industrial America*. Westport, CT: Bergin & Garvey, 1998.

Hines, Edward. "The Governance of Higher Education." In *Higher Education: Handbook of Theory and Research, XV*, edited by John Smart and William Tierney, 105–155. New York: Agathon Press, 2000.

Hoos, Ida R. "The Costs of Efficiency: Implications of Educational Technology." *The Journal of Higher Education* 46, no. 2 (1975): 141–160.

Hurd, Richard, Jennifer Bloom, and Beth Hillman Johnson. "Directory of Faculty Contracts and Bargaining Agents in Institutions of Higher Education." Baruch College, The City University of New York: The National Center for the Study of Collective Bargaining in Higher Education and the Professions, 1998.

Jacobs, Frederic. "Using Part-time Faculty More Effectively." In *The Growing Use of Part-time Faculty: Understanding Causes and Effects*, edited by David W. Leslie, 9–18. San Francisco: Jossey-Bass, 1998.

Jacobs, Jerry A., and Sarah Winslow. "Welfare Reform and Enrollment in Postsecondary Education." *The Annals of the American Academy of Political and Social Sciences* (2003, March): 194–217.

Jalongo, Mary Renck. "Faculty Productivity in Higher Education." *Educational Forum* 49, no. 2 (1985): 171–182.

Johnson, Larry, ed. *Common Ground: Exemplary Community College and Corporate Partnerships.* Mission Viejo, CA: League for Innovation in the Community College, 1996.

Kaplin, William, and Barbara Lee. *The Law of Higher Education: A Comprehensive Guide to Legal Implications of Administrative Decision-Making.* 3rd ed. San Francisco, CA: Jossey-Bass, 1995.

Karabell, Zachary. *In What's College for? The Struggle to Define American Higher Education.* New York: Basic Books, 1998.

Kater, Sue, and John Levin. "Shared Governance in Community Colleges in the Global Economy." *Community College Journal of Research and Practice* 29, no. 1 (2005): 1–24.

Kater, Susan. "Shared Governance in the Community College: The Rights, Roles, and Responsibilities of Unionized Community College Faculty." Unpublished doctoral dissertation, Tucson, AZ: The University of Arizona, 2003.

Katz, Henry C., and Thomas A. Kochan. *An Introduction to Collective Bargaining and Industrial Relations.* Boston: Irwin McGraw-Hill, 2000.

Kempner, Ken. "The Community College as a Marginalized Institution." Unpublished paper presented at Annual Meeting of Association of the Study of Higher Education, Boston, 1991.

———. "Understanding Cultural Conflict." In *Culture and Ideology in Higher Education*, edited by William. G. Tierney, 129–150. New York: Praeger, 1991.

Kenway, Jane. "Fast Capitalism, Fast Feminism, and Some Fast Food for Thought." Paper presented at the Annual Meeting of the American Educational Research Association. San Diego, April, 1998.

Kingfisher, Catherine. *Western Welfare in Decline: Globalization and Women's Poverty.* Philadelphia: University of Pennsylvania Press, 2002.

Kwiek, Marek. "Globalization and Higher Education." *Higher Education in Europe* 26, no. 1 (2001): 27–38.

Labaree, David F. *How to Succeed in School Without Really Learning.* New Haven: Yale University Press, 1997.

Laxer, Gordon. "Social Solidarity, Democracy and Global Capitalism." *The Canadian Review of Sociology and Anthropology* (1995, August): 287–312.

Leslie, Larry L., and Sheila A. Slaughter. "The Development and Current Status of Market Mechanisms in United States Postsecondary Education." *Higher Education Policy* 10 (1997, March/April): 238–252.

Levin, John "The Revised Institution: The Community College Mission at the End of the 20th Century." *Community College Review* 28, no. 2 (2000): 1–25.

———. "What's the Impediment? Structural and Legal Constraints to Shared Governance in the Community College." *The Canadian Journal of Higher Education* XXX, no. 2 (2000): 87–122.

———. *Globalizing the Community College: Strategies for Change in the Twenty-First Century.* New York: Palgrave, 2001.

———."The Higher Credential." Tucson, Arizona: The Canadian Embassy in Washington, DC, 2001.

———. "Is The Management of Distance Education Transforming Instruction in Colleges?" *The Quarterly Review of Distance Education* 2, no. 2 (2001): 105–117.

———. "Public Policy, Community Colleges, and the Path to Globalization." *Higher Education* 42, no. 2 (2001): 237–262.

———. "In Education and Work: The Globalized Community College." *The Canadian Journal of Higher Education* XXXII, no. 2 (2002): 47–78.

———. "Neo-Liberalism, Higher Education, and the Challenge for Faculty, Administrators, and Trustees." Paper presented at the Moore chair lecture, North Carolina State University, Raleigh, NC, November 19, 2003.

———. "Organizational Paradigm Shift and the University Colleges of British Columbia." *Higher Education* 46, no. 4 (2003): 447–467.

———. "Two British Columbia University Colleges and the Process of Economic Globalization." *The Canadian Journal of Higher Education* XXXIII, no. 1 (2003): 59–86.

———. "The Community College as a Baccalaureate-Granting Institution." *The Review of Higher Education* 28, no. 1 (2004): 1–22.

———. "The Business Culture of the Community College: Students as Consumers; Students as Commodities." In *Arenas of Entrepreneurship: Where Nonprofit and for Profit Institutions Compete. New Directions for Higher Education*, Number 129, edited by Brian Pusser. San Francisco: Jossey-Bass Publishers (2005): 11–26.

———. *Non-Traditional Students and Community Colleges: The Conflict of Justice and Neo-Liberalism.* New York: Palgrave Macmillan, forthcoming.

Levin, John, Sue Kater, Cristie Roe, and Rick Wagoner. "Not Professionals?: Community College Faculty in the New Economy." Symposium for the Annual Meeting of the American Educational Research Association, Chicago, April, 2003.

London, Howard. *The Culture of a Community College.* New York: Praeger Publishers, 1978.

Lorenzo, Albert L., and Nancy A. LeCroy. "A Framework for Fundamental Change in the Community College." *Community College Journal* 64, no. 4 (1994): 14–19.

Lovell, Cheryl, and C. Trought. "State Governance Patterns for Community Colleges." *New Directions for Community Colleges* 117 (2002): 91–100.

Lubienski, Chris. "The Relationship of Competition and Choice to Innovation in Education Markets: A Review of Research on Four Cases." Paper presented at the Annual Meeting of the American Educational Research Association, Seattle, WA, 2001.

Lucey, Carol. "Civic Engagement, Shared Governance, and Community Colleges." *Academe* 88, no. 4 (2002): 27–31.

March, James, and Michael Cohen. *Leadership and Ambiguity: The American College President.* New York: McGraw-Hill Book Company, 1974.

Marginson, Simon. "Response to Burton Clark." Paper presented at the Annual meeting of the Association for the Study of Higher Education, Kansas City, MO, November 3, 2004.

Marginson, Simon, and Mark Considine. *The Enterprise University: Power, Governance and Reinvention in Australia.* New York: Cambridge University Press, 2000.

Marris, Robin. "Higher Education and the Mixed Economy: The Concept of Competition." *Studies in Higher Education* 11, no. 2. (1986): 131–154.

Marshall, Catherine, and Gretchen Rossman. *Designing Qualitative Research.* 3rd ed. Thousand Oaks, CA: Sage Publications, 1999.

Martin, Joanne, and Debra Meyerson. "Organizational Cultures and the Denial, Channeling and Acknowledgment of Ambiguity." In *Managing Ambiguity and Change*, edited by Lewis R. Pondy, Richard J. Boland and Howard Thomas, 93–125. New York: John Wiley & Sons, 1988.

Mason, Edward S. "The Apologetics of Managerialism." *Journal of Business* 31, no. 6 (1958): 1–11.

Mason, Jennifer. *Qualitative Researching.* Thousand Oaks, CA: Sage Publications, 1996.

Massy, William F. "Improving Productivity in Higher Education Microform: Administration and Support Costs." U.S. Dept. of Education OERI, ERIC, 1991.

Massy, William F., and Andrea K. Wilger. "Technology's Contribution to Higher Education Productivity." *New Directions for Higher Education* 26, no. 3 (1998): 49–59.

Massy, William F., and Robert Zemsky. *Using Information Technology to Enhance Academic Productivity.* Washington, DC: Educom, 1995.

Mazzeo, Christopher, Sara Rab, and Susan Eachus. "Work-First or Work-Study: Welfare Reform, State Policy and Access to Postsecondary Education." *The Annals* (2003, March): 144–171.

Mazzeo, Christopher, Sara Y. Rab, and Julian L. Alssid. *Building Bridges to College and Careers: Contextualized Basic Skills Programs at Community Colleges.* Brooklyn, NY: Workforce Strategy Center, 2003.

Mazzoli, Andrew Joseph. "Faculty Perceptions of Influences on the Curriculum in Higher Education." In *ERIC Clearinghouse, No: HE034523*, 2000.

McBurnie, Grant. "Leveraging Globalization as a Policy Paradigm for Higher Education." *Higher Education in Europe* 26, no. 1 (2001): 11–26.

McCartan, Anne-Marie. "The Community College Mission: Present Challenges and Future Visions." *The Journal of Higher Education* 54, no. 6 (1983): 676–692.

McGill, Molly A., and Sally M. Johnstone. "Distance Education: An Opportunity for Cooperation and Resource Sharing." In *Distance Education Strategies and Tools*, edited by Barry Willis, 265–276. Englewood Cliffs, NJ: Educational Technology Publications, 1994.

McGrath, Dennis, and Martin Spear. *The Academic Crisis of the Community College.* Albany, NY: State University of New York Press, 1991.

Meier, Ken. "*The Community College Mission: History and Theory.*" Unpublished manuscript, Bakersfield, CA: 2004.

Meyer, Heinz-Dieter. "Universal, Entrepreneurial, and Soulless? The New University as a Contested Institution." *Comparative Education Review* 46, no. 3 (2002): 339–347.

Meyer, Katrina. "Quality in Distance Education: Focus on Online Learning." In *ASHE-ERIC Higher Education Reports*, Vol. 29, No. 4, pp. 1–150, 2002.

Miles, Matthew, and A. Michael Huberman. *Qualitative Data Analysis.* Thousand Oaks, CA: Sage Publications, 1994.

Mintzberg, Henry. *Power in and Around Organizations.* Englewood Cliffs, NJ: Prentice Hall, Inc., 1983.

———. "The Professional Bureaucracy." In *Organization and Governance in Higher Education*, edited by Marvin Peterson. Needham Heights, MA: Simon & Schuster, 1991.

Mitra, Ananda, Timothy Steffensmeier, and Stefne Lenzmeier. "Changes in Attitudes Toward Computers and Use of Computers by University Faculty." *Journal of Research on Computing in Education* 32, no. 1 (1999): 189–202.

Moore, Michael G. "Recent Contributions to the Theory of Distance Education." *Open Learning* 5, no. 3 (1990): 10–13.

Morgan, Gareth. *Images of Organization*. Thousand Oaks, CA: Sage Publications, 1997.

Morphew, Christopher. "Challenges Facing Shared Governance Within the College." *New Directions for Higher Education* 105 (1999): 71–79.

Mortimer, Kenneth, and Thomas Raymond McConnell. *Sharing Authority Effectively*. 1st ed. San Francisco: Jossey-Bass, 1978.

Moxley, Linda S. "Job Satisfaction of Faculty Teaching Higher Education. An Examination of Herzberg's Dual-Factor Theory and Porter's Need Satisfaction Research." In *Education ERIC Document No. ED. 139–349*, 1977.

Nadesan, Majia Holmer. "Fortune on Globalization and the New Economy: Manifest Destiny in a Technological Age." *Management Communication Quarterly* 14, no. 3 (2001): 498–506.

National Center for Education Statistics, U.S. Department of Education. "Table 206." In http://www.nces.ed.gov/program/digest/d02/table/dt206.asp, 2004.

Nickerson, Mark, and Sue Schaefer. "Autonomy and Anonymity: Characteristics of Branch Campus Faculty." *Metropolitan Universities: An International Forum* 12, no. 2 (2001): 49–59.

Nixon, John "Professional Identity and the Restructuring of Higher Education." *Studies in Higher Education* 21, no. 1 (1996): 5–16.

Nixon, John S., and Sara Lundquist. "The Partnership Paradigm: Collaboration and the Community College." *New Directions for Community Colleges* 103, (1998): 43–50.

Noble, David. *Digital Diploma Mills: The Automation of Higher Education* [Web site]. 1998 [cited. Available from http://www.firstmonday.dk/issues/issue3_1/noble/.

O'Banion, Terry. *The Learning College for the 21st Century*. Phoenix, AZ: American Council on Education and the Oryx Press, 1997.

O'Banion, Terry, and Associates. *Teaching and Learning in the Community College*. Washington, DC: Community College Press, 1995.

Olssen, Mark. *The Neo-Liberal Appropriation of Tertiary Education Policy: Accountability, Research and Academic Freedom* 2000 [cited May 2004]. Available from http://www.surrey.ac.uk/Education/profiles/olssen/neo-2000.htm.

Osterman, Paul, Thomas A. Kochan, Richard M. Locke, and Michael J. Piore. *Working in America: A Blueprint for the New Labor Market*. Cambridge, MA: MIT Press, 2001.

Outcalt, Charles. *A Profile of the Community College Professoriate, 1975–2000*. New York: Routledge Falmer, 2002.

Owen, Polly S., and Ada Demb. "Change Dynamics and Leadership in Technology Implementation." *The Journal of Higher Education* 75, no. 6 (2004): 636–666.

Palmer, James C. "Funding the Multipurpose Community College in an Era of Consolidation." In *A Struggle to Survive: Funding Higher Education in the Next Century. 17th Annual Yearbook of the American Educational Finance Association*, edited by Kathleen C. Westbrook. Thousand Oaks, CA: Corwin, 1996.

Palmer, James, and L. Zimbler. "Instructional Faculty and Staff in Public 2-year Colleges." Washington, DC: U.S. Department of Education, Office of Educational Research and Improvement, 2000.

Patton, Michael. *Qualitative Evaluation Methods.* Newbury Park, CA: Sage Publications, 1990.

Paulson, Karen. "Reconfiguring Faculty Roles for Virtual Settings." *The Journal of Higher Education* 73, no. 1 (2002): 123–140.

Peng, Chao-Ying Joanne, Tak-Shing Harry So, Frances Stage, and Edward St. John. "The Use and Interpretation of Logistic Regression in Higher Education Journals: 1988–1999." *Research In Higher Education* 43, no. 4 (1999): 259–293.

Pfeffer, Jeffrey, and Gerald Salancik. *The External Control of Organizations: A Resource Dependence Perspective.* New York: Harper and Row, 1978.

Phillippe, Kent, and Madeline Patton. *National Profile of Community Colleges: Trends and Statistics.* 3rd ed. Washington, DC: Community College Press, American Association of Community Colleges, 2000.

Pincus, Fred. "Contradictory Effects of Customized Contract Training in Community Colleges." *Critical Sociology* 16, no. 1 (1989): 77–93.

Plascak-Craig, Faye D., and John P. Bean. "Education Faculty Job Satisfaction in Major Research Universities." Paper presented at the Annual Meeting of the Association for the Study of Higher Education, Atlanta, GA, November 2–5, 1989.

Pollicino, Elizabeth A. "Faculty Satisfaction with Institutional Support as a Complex Concept: Collegiality, Workload, Autonomy." Paper presented at the Annual Meeting of the American Educational Research Association, New York, NY, April 8–13, 1996.

PsychSim 4.0: *Interactive Graphic Simulations for Psychology.* Worth, New York.

Puiggrós, Adriana. *Neoliberalism and Education in the Americas.* Boulder, CO: Westview Press, 1999.

Quick, Don, and Timothy Gray Davies. "Community College Faculty Development: Bringing Technology into Instruction." *Community College Journal of Research and Practice* 23, no. 7 (1999): 641–653.

Ratcliff, James. "Seven Streams in the Historical Development of the Modern Community College." In *A Handbook on the Community College in America*, edited by George Baker, 3–16. Westport, CT: Greenwood Press, 1994.

Readings, Bill. *The University in Ruins.* Cambridge, MA: Harvard University Press, 1997.

Rhoades, Gary. "The Production Politics of Teaching and Technology: Deskilling, Enskilling, and Managerial Extension." Unpublished Manuscript, 1996.

———. "Reorganizing the Faculty Workplace for Flexibility: Part-Time Professional Labor." *The Journal of Higher Education* 67, no. 6 (1996): 626–659.

———. *Managed Professionals: Unionized Faculty and Restructuring Academic Labor.* Albany: State University of New York Press, 1998.

Rhoads, Robert, and James Valadez. *Democracy, Multiculturalism, and the Community College.* New York: Garland Publishing, 1996.

Richardson Jr., Richard. C., Clyde E. Blocker, and Louis W. Bender. *Governance for the Two-Year College.* Englewood Cliffs, NJ: Prentice-Hall, 1972.

Richardson, Richard, and Louis Bender. *Fostering Minority Access and Achievement in Higher Education.* San Francisco: Jossey-Bass Publishers, 1987.

Richardson, Richard, Elizabeth Fisk, and Morris Okun. *Literacy in the Open-Access College.* San Francisco: Jossey-Bass Publishers, 1983.

Riessman, Catherine. "Analysis of Personal Narratives." In *Handbook of Interview Research: Context and Method*, edited by Jaber F. Gubrium and James A. Holstein, 695–710. Thousand Oaks, CA: Sage Publications, 2002.

Rifkin, Jeremy. *The End of Work: The Decline of the Global Labor Force and the Dawn of the Post-Market Era.* New York: G.P. Putnam's Sons, 1995.

Rifkin, Tronie. "Differences Between the Professional Attitudes of Full-and Part-Time Community College Faculty." Paper presented at the American Association of Community Colleges, Miami, April 1998.

Riley, Gary. L., and Victor J. Baldridge, eds. *Governing Academic Organizations: New Problems New Perspectives.* Berkeley, CA: McCutchan Publishing, 1977.

Ritzer, George. *The McDonaldization Thesis: Explorations and Extensions.* Thousand Oaks, CA: Sage Publications, 1998.

Robertson, Roland. *Globalization: Social Theory and Global Culture.* London: Sage Publications, 1992.

Robst, John. "Cost Efficiency in Public Higher Education Institutions." *The Journal of Higher Education* 72, no. 6 (2001): 730–750.

Roche, Michael M., and Lawrence D. Berg. "Market Metaphors, Neo-liberalism and the Construction of Academic Landscapes in Aotearora/New Zealand." *The Journal of Geography in Higher Education* 21, no. 2 (1997): 147–161.

Roe, Cristie E. "Effects of Informational Technology on Community College Faculty." Unpublished doctoral dissertation, Tucson, AZ: The University of Arizona, 2002.

———. "Effects of Information Technology on Community College Faculty." Paper Presentation, American Education Research Association, Chicago, April, 2003.

Roe, Mary Ann. *Education and U.S. Competitiveness: The Community College Role.* Austin: IC2 Institute, University of Texas at Austin, 1989.

Rogers, Everett. *Diffusion of Innovations.* 3rd ed. New York: The Free Press, 1983.

Rogers, William H. "Regression Standard Errors in Clustered Samples." *State Technical Bulletin* 13 (1993): 19–23.

Roueche, John, and George A. Baker, III. *Access and Excellence.* Washington, DC: The Community College Press, 1987.

Roueche, John, and Suanne Roueche. *Between a Rock and a Hard Place.* Washington, DC: Community College Press, 1993.

Roueche, John, Suanne Roueche, and Mark Milliron. *Strangers in Their Own Land: Part-Time Faculty in American Community Colleges.* Washington, DC: Community College Press, 1995.

Rups, P. "Training Instructors in New Technologies." *T.H.E. Journal* 26, no. 8 (1999): 66–69.

Saul, John Ralston. *The Unconscious Civilization.* Concord, ON: House of Anansi Press, 1995.

Scholz, Roland W., and Olaf Tietje. *Embedded Case Study Methods: Integrating Quantitative and Qualitative Knowledge.* Thousand Oaks, CA.: Sage Publications, 2002.

Schugurensky, Daniel, and Kathy Higgins. "From Aid to Trade: New Trends in International Education in Canada." In *Dimensions of the Community College: International, Intercultural, and Multicultural*, edited by Rosalind Latiner Raby and Norma Tarrow, 53–78. New York: Garland Publishing, 1996.

Scott, Peter. "The Death of Mass Higher Education and the Birth of Lifelong Learning." In *Lifelong Learning. Education Across the Lifespan*, edited by Mal Geicester, 29–42. London: Routledge Falmer, 2000.

Scott, W. Richard. *Institutions and Organizations.* Thousand Oaks, CA: Sage Publications, 1995.

Seidman, Earl. *In the Words of the Faculty.* San Francisco: Jossey-Bass Publishers, 1985.

Sennett, Richard. *The Corrosion of Character: The Personal Consequences of Work in the New Capitalism.* New York: W.W. Norton & Company, 1998.

———. "A Flawed Philosophy." *Guardian Weekly* June 20–26 (2002): 15.

Shaw, Kathleen. "Defining the Self: Construction of Identity in Community College Students." In *Community Colleges as Cultural Texts,* edited by Kathleen Shaw, James Valadez and Robert Rhoads, 153–171. Buffalo: State University of New York Press, 1999.

Shaw, Kathleen, and Sara Rab. "Market Rhetoric versus Reality in Policy and Practice: The Workforce Investment Act and Access to Community College Education and Training." *The Annals* (2003, March): 172–193.

Shaw, Kathleen, Robert Rhoads, and James Valadez, eds. *Community Colleges as Cultural Texts.* Albany: State University of New York Press, 1999.

———. "Community Colleges as Cultural Texts: A Conceptual overview." In *Community Colleges as Cultural Texts,* edited by Kathleen Shaw, James Valadez and Robert Rhoads. Albany: State University of New York Press, 1999.

Shupe, David A. "Productivity, Quality, and Accountability in Higher Education." *Journal of Continuing Higher Education* 47, no. 1 (1999): 2–13.

Simkins, Tim. "Education Reform and Managerialism: Comparing the Experience of Schools and Colleges." *Journal of Education Policy* 15, no. 3 (2000): 317–332.

Sink, David W., Jr., and Karen Luke Jackson. "Successful Community College Campus-based Partnerships." *Community College Journal of Research and Practice* 26, no. 1 (2002): 35–46.

Sites, William. *Remaking New York: Primitive Globalization and the Politics of Urban Community.* Minneapolis, MN: University of Minnesota Press, 2003.

Skolnik, Michael. "The Virtual University and the Professoriate." In *The University in Transformation: Global Perspective on the Futures of the University,* edited by Sohail Inayatullah and Jennifer Gidley, 55–67. Westport, CT: Bergin & Garvey, 2000.

Slaughter, Sheila. "Federal Policy and Supply-side Institutional Resource Allocation at Public Research Universities." *The Review of Higher Education* 21, no. 3 (1998): 209–244.

Slaughter, Sheila, and Gary Rhoades. "The Neo-Liberal University." *New Labor Forum* (2000, Spring/Summer): 73–79.

———. *Academic Capitalism and the New Economy: Markets, State, and Higher Education.* Baltimore, MD: The Johns Hopkins University Press, 2004.

Slaughter, Sheila, and Larry Leslie. *Academic Capitalism, Politics, Policies, and the Entrepreneurial University.* Baltimore: The Johns Hopkins University Press, 1997.

Smircich, Linda. "Concepts of Culture and Organizational Analysis." *Administrative Science Quarterly* 28 (1983): 339–358.

Smith, Joshua L., and Fayyaz A. Vellani. "Urban America and the Community College Imperative: The Importance of Open Access and Opportunity." *New Directions for Community Colleges* 27, no. 3 (1999): 5–13.

Smith, Vicki. *Crossing the Great Divide: Worker Risk and Opportunity in the New Economy.* New York: Cornell University Press, 2001.

Smith, Victoria. "Teamwork vs. Tempwork: Managers and the Dualisms of Workplace Restructuring." In *Working in Restructured Workplaces: New Directions for the*

*Sociology of Work.*, edited by Holly McCammon, 7–28. Thousand Oaks, CA: Sage, 2001.

Strauss, Linda C. "Addressing the Discourse on the Future of Post-Secondary Education: The Relationship between Mission and Funding in Community Colleges." In *Eric Clearinghouse for Community Colleges*, Los Angeles: CA, 2001.

Stromquist, Nelly P. *Education in a Globalized World: The Connectivity of Economic Power, Technology, and Knowledge.* Lanham, MD: Rowman & Littlefield, 2002.

Sturgeon, Julie. "Coping with the Crunch." *College Planning and Management* 3, no. 3 (2000): 22–24.

Taber, Lynn. "Chapter and Verse: How We Came to Be Where We Are." In *The Company We Keep: Collaboration in the Community College*, edited by John Roueche, Lynn Taber and Suanne Roueche, 25–37. Washington, DC: American Association of Community Colleges, 1995.

Tagg, John. *The Learning Paradigm College.* Bolton, MA: Anker Publishing Company, 2003.

Tapscott, Don. *The Digital Economy: Promise and Peril in the Age of Networked Intelligence.* New York: McGraw Hill, 1996.

Teeple, Gary. *Globalization and the Rise of Social Reform.* New Jersey: Humanities Press, 1995.

The League for Innovation in the Community College. Website 2005 [cited March 2005]. Available from http://www.league.org.

Tierney, William. "Organizational Culture in Higher Education: Defining the Essentials." In *Organization and Governance in Higher Education*, edited by Marvin Peterson, 126–139. Needham Heights, MA: Simon & Schuster, 1991.

——, ed. *Competing Conceptions of Academic Governance: Negotiating the Perfect Storm.* Baltimore, MD: The Johns Hopkins University Press, 2004.

Toma, Douglas. Personal communication. April 2001.

Torres, Carlos A., and Daniel Schugurensky. "The Political Economy of Higher Education in the Era of Neoliberal Globalization: Latin America in Comparative Perspective." *Higher Education* 43 (2002): 429–455.

Townsend, Barbara, and Susan Twombly, eds. *Community Colleges: Policy in the Future Context.* Westport, CT: Ablex, 2001.

Tuckman, Howard P. "Who is Part-Time in Academe?" *AAUP Bulletin* 64 (1978): 305–315.

Tuller, Charlie, and Diana Oblinger. "Information Technology as a Transformation Agent." *Cause and Effect* 20, no. 4 (1998): 33–45.

Twombly, Susan, and Barbara Townsend. "Conclusion: The Future of Community Policy in the 21st Century." In *Community Colleges: Policy in the Future Context*, edited by Barbara Townsend and Susan Twombly, 283–298. Wesport, CT: Ablex, 2001.

U.S. Department of Education. Office of Educational Research and Improvement. National Center for Educational Statistics. *Background Characteristics, Work Activities, and Compensation of Faculty and Instructional Staff in Postsecondary Institutions: Fall 1998.* Washington, DC: National Center for Educational Statistics, 2001.

Valadez, James. "Cultural Capital and its Impact on the Aspirations of Nontraditional Community College Students." *Community College Review* 21, no. 3 (1996): 30–44.

Valadez, James R., and James S. Antony. "Job Satisfaction and Commitment of Two-Year College Part-Time Faculty." *Community College Journal of Research and Practice* 25 (2001): 97–108.

Vallas, Steven Peter. *Power in the Workplace: The Politics of Production at AT&T.* Albany, NY: State University of New York, 1993.

Vaughan, George. "The Big Squeeze at Community Colleges." *The News & Observer*, March 24, 2002, 29a.

Wagoner, Richard. "Community College Faculty Satisfaction Across Missions and Over Time: A Quantitative Analysis." Paper presented at the Annual Meeting of the Association for the Study of Higher Education, Portland, November, 2003.

———. "The Contradictory Faculty: Part-Time Faculty at Community Colleges." Unpublished doctoral dissertation, Tucson, AZ: The University of Arizona, 2004.

Wagoner, Richard L. Amy Scott Metcalfe, and Israel Olaore. "Fiscal Reality and Academic Quality: Part-Time Faculty and the Challenge to Organizational Culture at Community Colleges." *Community College Journal of Research and Practice* 29 (2005): 1–20.

Waters, Malcolm. *Globalization.* New York: Routledge, 1996.

Weis, Lois. *Between two Worlds: Black Students in an Urban Community College.* Boston: Routledge and Keegan Paul, 1985.

Welch, Anthony P. "Globalisation, Post-Modernity and the State: Comparative Education Facing the Third Millennium." *Comparative Education* 37, no. 4 (2000): 475–492.

White, Kenneth. "Shared governance in California." *New Directions for Community Colleges* 102 (1998): 19–29.

Wildavsky, Aaron, and Naomi Caiden. *The New Politics of the Budgetary Process.* 3rd ed. New York: Longman, 1997.

Williams, Gwen B, and Perry A. Zirkel. "Academic Penetration into Faculty Collective Bargaining Contracts in Higher Education." *Research in Higher Education* 28, no. 1 (1988): 76–95.

Winner, Langdon. *The Whale and the Reactor: Searching for Limits in an Age of High Technology.* Chicago: University of Chicago Press, 1986.

Woodworth, Warner, and Christopher Meek. *Creating Labor-Management Partnerships.* Reading, MA: Addison-Wesley, 1995.

Wyles, Barbara A. "Adjunct Faculty in the Community College: Realities and Challenges." In *The Growing Use of Part-Time Faculty: Understanding Causes and Effects*, edited by David W. Leslie, 95–100. San Francisco: Jossey-Bass, 1998.

Yin, Robert. *Case Study Research: Design and Methods.* Thousand Oaks, CA: Sage Publications, 1994.

# Index